Will Your Way Back

"This is a great book. It's extremely readable, carries you forward with no slow parts, and is amazingly full of important insights."

—Mrs. Joseph Carlton Petrone, widow of Colonel and Ambassador Joseph Carlton Petrone

"For anyone with a challenge, whether health-wise or professional or marital, this book has brilliant advice and equally brilliant inspiration. You owe it to yourself to read it."

—Mrs. Frank Perdue (Mitzi), author of *Tough Man, Tender Chicken* and *I Didn't Bargain For This*

"In his book *Will Your Way Back*, James Osborne teaches a master class in humanity and grace. If you're feeling great, read this book and learn compassion. If you're enduring more than you think you can bear, this book will give you hope."

—Joan Broughton, author and *Resist Ageism* blogger

"This is a great story of hope, determination, persistence, and a positive mental attitude. I highly recommend this book to anyone for a superb example of courage and bravery."

—Carl G. Schneider, Major General, USAF (retired)

"After a tragic accident that could have left him paralyzed for life, Jamie unabashedly shares, in great detail, his discouragements, determination, love, and sheer will that helped him cross an unbridgeable chasm to overcome great odds."

—John J. Nicholas, Author, former US Navy Officer

"Jamie's book is one of the most exquisitely observed, genuine, and inspiring memoirs I've had the pleasure of reading. He reveals with heartfelt rawness, the painful moments and beautiful blessings he has navigated along his unexpected journey. Jamie's book is completely captivating, drawing you in as if you're sitting in Jamie's home listening to him tell his story directly to you. It is beautifully written and truly inspiring."

—Stephanie Percy, owner, Omni Creative

"With tireless determination, unstoppable will, and the ability to tell a story of triumph from the heart, *Will Your Way Back* shows the reader that nothing is impossible and, against all odds, life can be beautiful even after the darkest of days."

—Adriana Brown, personal trainer, Seattle Athletic Club

"Jamie's story is an emotional rollercoaster where he masterfully shows that the difference between the light and the dark, where happy and sad are blurred when something traumatic happens. In his raw approach to his post injury world, he illustrates that the darkest places of our being, can in fact help us in finding the most wonderful experiences due to the hidden and the unseen powers that drive us as humans."

—Barry Long, owner, Talk and Roll Enterprises

"Inspirational. Relatable. Raw. Visual. Educational. Hopeful. Exemplary read! *Will Your Way Back* is almost impossible to stop reading—it is so good! You can see, feel, and relate to Jamie's story as though you were there with him, through the entire ride to current day, willing your way back with him, every step of the way."

—Ivy Meadors, CEO, speaker, author, High Tech High Touch Solutions, Inc.

"From the first page, Jamie's story pulled me in with raw emotion, detailed facts, and inspiration. First, I felt sadness and sympathy. But that quickly turned to amazement and admiration. What followed were feelings of hope, self-reflection, and a rush of motivation to never give up no matter what cards you are dealt!! Do yourself a favor and read *Will Your Way Back*."

—Dereck Soo, technology manager, Copacino + Fujikado

"The story of Jamie's injury and his remarkable recovery is something for the ages. But beyond the story of personal challenge and his will to live are life lessons that any of us can learn from as we cope with personal or business speed bumps that seem in the light of day to pale against Jamie's struggle. This is not just a primer for those that are facing the new challenges of spinal cord injury, but a must read for anyone on how to cope with the ups and downs of life."

—Conrad M Bessemer, president, Novatec Inc.; executive chairman,
Prophecy Sensorlytics, LLC

"Whether fighting back from an injury or simply dealing with age-related limitations, you will benefit from Jamie's personal story as he describes his journey back from a near fatal bicycle accident. *Will Your Way Back* is a very personal story of physical and emotional recovery driven by the authors courage, tenacity, and hope."

—Dennis Madsen, community nonprofit leader and former retail executive

"Our school's motto is *Aspirando et Perseverando*. In 'defining his terms, taking a stand, and choosing to win' in the face of an ultimate form of adversity, Jamie has captured the essence of this motto in *Will Your Way Back* better than any individual I have ever known. His inspiring journey provides a powerful example—indeed a road map—for all of us of how to confront, navigate through, and overcome the most daunting challenges in our lives."

—Peter Evans, dean, Avon Old Farms School, Avon, Connecticut

"To anyone who has suffered a devastating physical injury, *Will Your Way Back* is the inspirational and heart-wrenching true story of the commitment, desire, and courage to never give up and to never give in. You will close the book believing there is no problem you cannot solve, no mountain you cannot climb, no obstacle you cannot overcome to lead the life you desire to live."

—Robert Dugoni, *Wall Street Journal* and *New York Times*
best-selling author of *My Sister's Grave*

"James Osborne's personal story is nothing short of amazing. He is completely candid about the struggles he faces, both physical and psychological, throughout his journey forward from his tragic accident. His is a lesson of personal focus, growth, determination, and the sequence of thousands of minuscule successes required to achieve such goals. His is also a message in humility, as he quietly chooses to continue each and every day."

—Dave Stockwell, technology leader and entrepreneur

"*Will Your Way Back* is about Jamie Osborne's tenacious recovery from a severe spinal cord injury incurred in an unimaginable cycling accident. This superbly written book is intended to empower others who are adjusting to life with a disability. In telling his story, Jamie vividly describes the impact of his injury and recovery on his identity, spirituality, and relationships. Jamie openly unveils his doubts, fears, losses, and setbacks and joyfully celebrates his remarkable victories."

—Eric N. Newberg, professor of theological and historical studies, Oral Roberts University

"The true devastation of spinal cord injury and paralysis on patients and their families remains truly underappreciated by the general public and—outside of the affected specialties—most of the medical establishment. *Will Your Way Back* by James Osborne vividly describes the amazing power of the human mind to bounce back from an overwhelming injury. It also shows medical professionals how much more there is to learn and do to overcome paralysis, from which over three million US citizens suffer."

—Jens R. Chapman, MD, Swedish Neuroscience Institute, Seattle, Washington

JAMES H. OSBORNE

WILL
YOUR
WAY
BACK

How One Man Overcame Tragedy
with a WINNING MINDSET

RIVER GROVE
BOOKS

This book is intended as a reference volume only. It is sold with the understanding that the publisher and author are not engaged in rendering any professional services. The information given here is designed to help you make informed decisions. If you suspect that you have a problem that might require professional treatment or advice, you should seek competent help.

Published by River Grove Books
Austin, TX
www.rivergrovebooks.com

Distributed by River Grove Books

Design and composition by Greenleaf Book Group
Cover design by Greenleaf Book Group
Cover image © Calin Tatu, 2017. Used under license from Shutterstock.com

Cataloging-in-Publication data is available.

Print ISBN: 978-1-63299-112-6

eBook ISBN: 978-1-63299-113-3

First Edition

To Diane, my wife of thirty-six years.

After my accident and permanent impairments, you had every reason to say "This is not the life I signed up for" and leave. Many spouses, in this situation, do. You did not. You have been by my side—attentive, caring, and loving—even in the most difficult times. To you, my dear, I make this dedication. Your love has brought me back.

THE PRICE I PAY

It may not seem obvious
When I do things each way
Stand, walk, step, or sit
There is always a price to pay.

Resistance is formidable
Strong headwinds on display
Given the choice, I'd rather not
There is always a price to pay.

It comes in many forms
Fear of tripping and falling away
Chronic pain all over my body
It's part of the price I pay.

I fight it with mindfulness
Tuned carefully as I look each way
It always helps protect me
from the price I pay.

I fight with medications
Six in total, three times a day;
It helps calm the muscle seizing
That's part of the price I pay.

Love is a great analgesic
Like a hug from Alana Ray
It helps to calm my system
From the price I pay.

Exercise produces endorphins
When I'm at the gym to play
It provides me sanctuary
From the price I pay.

It takes enormous will
To get my body to obey
Every action and movement
It's part of the price I pay.

It's been hard to trust myself
When my faculties betray
Watching my extremities spasm
It's part of the price I pay.

I don't look forward to bedtime
It's not the time I go hurray
Getting up eight times a night
It's part of the price I pay.

So what does get me through it?
What is there to take away
From the challenges I face?
That's part of the price I pay.

Define my terms and take a stand
It's the place I start and say
Choosing to win and getting better
Overcomes the price I pay.

Contents

Part Three: All Is Not as It Seems   123

Part Four: In Pursuit of a New Normal   175

Preface

Sports have always been my sanctuary. They have been a safe place I could go to feel alive, excited, and good about myself. My introduction to sports—aerobic, heart-pumping sports—began in college, late freshman year, when a friend introduced me to crew; after that, I went full speed ahead in running, skiing, tennis, squash, golf, and cycling. Playing sports became a refuge where I could manage emotional pain. It allowed me to work out the things I struggled with and gain new perspectives. I could accomplish goals. I could excel. I could be confident. I could be part of a community.

In June 2007, my sanctuary was taken away from me. I never saw it coming. In a flash I was different. One moment my heart was pumping at its anaerobic maximum, the next I was fighting for my life. I am now impaired. I am living a new life, one filled with countless adjustments. There are things I can no longer do. There are places I can no longer go. There are people who have dropped out of my life. I have feelings I have never felt before. There is work I am unable to do. My injury has touched every aspect of my life—personal, emotional, marital, familial, professional, and recreational. Next to a brain injury, this is as difficult an injury to recover from as there can be. It is cruel and relentless.

We all have our story. All of us are dealing with some kind of struggle, challenge, adversity, setback, or life-changing event, or we know someone who is. Perhaps it is a physical infirmity, disease, addiction, broken relationship, professional setback, or despondence. You are not alone. My life was turned upside down as a consequence of my spinal cord injury—in the words of my doctor, an "unimaginable injury." I wrote *Will Your Way Back* to share the "what" and the "how"—what I've faced in all aspects of my life and how I approached it through an unwavering commitment to aspire, persevere, and prevail.

I am not a victim. I don't feel sorry for myself. I have hope. While I endured much loss, and I don't intend to downplay it, there is much for which I am grateful. Come take a journey with me through a process of recovery that has been filled with ups and downs, triumphs and tragedies, and losses and victories. I'll share stories, reflections, and insights. I'll reveal the wanton cruelty of this injury. I'll talk about gaining new perspectives. I'll tell you about personal change. You'll see all of me. Nothing is filtered. Some of this is deeply personal and leaves me vulnerable. It is authentic and real. Perhaps you'll see a little of yourself. Maybe my writing will cause you to pause, reflect, or even change in some small way. It is my story, my gift to you, and I thank you for the opportunity to share it.

In 2008, after presenting at a meeting for patients dealing with or having dealt with a myriad of afflictions, I wrote the following passage. It encapsulates my mantra for life post injury.

. . .

Any parent with children will tell you that the hardest part of parenting is watching their child suffer. They would do anything to take that suffering away and assume it themselves. It's a strange juxtaposition in my family to find that situation reversed. My children often lament how much they dislike seeing their dad suffer and would do anything to take it away.

All of us, especially those who have experienced or are dealing with disease, illness, or a major injury, suffer. People suffer for any number of reasons: addiction, marital challenges, or loss of a loved one. Even those indirectly associated with the person who is suffering will also suffer in some way. I am afflicted with a serious injury following a road cycling accident and know about suffering. I experience it every day. Often it is chronic pain, loss of control, or feeling trapped. My ever-present struggle is trying to rediscover my identity and what will bring fulfillment and joy into my life.

How do I combat suffering? Call it stubborn, dogged determination, but I decided early on to take a stand. One thing I didn't lose was my mind and ability to make choices. I chose to win. For me, winning doesn't mean that I'll necessarily be whole again, without pain, or free of residual deficits. Winning is not succumbing to the daily suffering, discomfort, and limited movements. Winning is getting up every day and choosing to make the most of what I can do.

Yes, I got dealt a crummy hand. That doesn't mean there aren't many more good hands to play. There are. At night, it's going to bed and thanking myself for doing the day.

Define your terms. Take a stand. Choose to win.

We all have challenges—physical, emotional, relational, professional, or situational. Defining your terms means being guided by your instincts, goals, dreams, and aspirations. Often we find ourselves living out the advice or guidance of others. Instead, follow the vector or beacon that stirs within you. Taking a stand is committing to your terms. You will move forward and live your life, sturdy and resolute in the decision. You will not waver, bend, or fall off course. Your direction is clear.

You will encounter road bumps, but know that you can push through and persevere. Keep your eyes on the prize and stay focused. Choosing to win is about making a choice to prevail, regardless of the headwinds, and it will overcome any obstacle. Winning doesn't necessarily mean you cross the finish line first (although you may!). It's not about winning in the absolute sense or that doing so means there is someone who doesn't. It is winning on your terms. You choose. Make the choice to accomplish your goals, realize your dreams, and win!

Acknowledgments

There are many people who have encouraged me to tell my story—frank, real, unabashed, and without filter. Tell it like it was and is. My family—Diane, Kevin, and Alana—have been nudging me down this road for years. Write it, read it, and tell it. John, a longtime Seattle friend, has been encouraging me in this direction since the days he spent in the hospital with me.

My mental health therapist, Dr. Diane, has been gently encouraging me to write for several years. We've talked about rethinking an approach to my next life's work. She has helped me down a path of careful reflection, introspection, confidence, and building self-esteem after I was injured and, subsequently, separated from my last job.

My very good Seattle friends Rick, Peter, and Doug have been by my side since day one of the accident, have observed all the trials and tribulations of my injury, and also felt that my story was one of hope and inspiration from which others might find benefit. Whenever I am with them, I'm always laughing—something I need to do more often.

My friend Karen has been gently nudging me to tune into the energy of the universe and pay attention to its message. I would often try to strong-arm my way through each day just trying to survive without listening and understanding what the universe was telling me. Karen helped me grasp the importance of doing this.

My business colleague and personal friend, Ivy, and I have had numerous discussions about public speaking and book writing. Ivy has been a mentor to me, and even to members of my family. She is an entrepreneur, self-made millionaire, owner of her own successful business, and world-renowned public speaker. I respect Ivy as an extraordinarily gifted person who has unselfishly shared her expertise and knowledge with so many.

I have known Bob for over thirty-five years, ever since my wife and I moved to Seattle. Bob and I have talked about this subject for years as well, and he has urged me to share my story and touch the lives of others. Bob, too, has been by my side throughout this entire journey, from the time he came to my hospital bed and I could see the emotion in his face, and it touched me.

My relatives, throughout the generations, especially on my mother's side of the family, have authored books, so in a sense I have a genetic predisposition to undertake something so daunting. This includes my grandfather Ernest, aunts Mitzi and Augusta, and uncles Ernest and Barclay. My mother, Victoria, is an author and gifted writer in her own right. On my father's side of the family, his father, Thomas Mott Osborne I, wrote about prison reform. He wrote books because he had ideas that could help others in their journey through life.

My siblings Molly, Tom, Rob, and Allyson have been there every step of the way to lift me up when I was down, loving me unconditionally. It is very special to grow up in a family whose connections are as strong today, living all over the country, as they were when we were all together in our suburban Boston home.

I have known Bob, Jason, Don, and John for over forty years, since our days together at Avon Old Farms School 1971–1975. They have been there to support and love me through this difficult time in my life. We live in different parts of the country (except Don who is less than two miles away) but have always stayed in contact. We enjoy annual reunions together when I am able to travel to Nantucket Island, Massachusetts, in October for the start of scalloping season. These bonds are forever.

Orthopedic physician Dr. Jens Chapman and physiatrist Dr. Barry Goldstein were my primary practitioners specializing in spinal cord injury. After participating together in a medical conference in 2008, both doctors indicated that I had a way with words and encouraged me to share my experience with others. Many other friends and family members have asked me to do the same thing, feeling that my story deserved to be told and could positively impact the lives of others.

I wish to thank all the members, trainers, and employees of the Seattle Athletic Club (SAC) in downtown Seattle, both those I know and those I don't. You all inspire me.

I wish to thank the entire team at Greenleaf Book Group and River Grove Books. You have all been professional and responsive in guiding me through the entire process of bringing this book to life. I would like to especially recognize my developmental editor, Tess Mallory, who worked patiently with me through every detail of this book. Tess asked a lot of great questions, helped me expound in areas I might not otherwise have gone, rearranged content to improve flow, and offered suggestions in the overall book construction. She provided a safe place to work, and I am fortunate to have had the opportunity to work with her.

I actually had done a lot of writing since 2007, thinking a book might be possible, writing at different times with varying levels of interest and motivation. I kept journals as soon as I was discharged from the hospital, only for purposes of finger dexterity and trying to teach myself how to write and keyboard again. Holding and moving a pen seems trivial, except when your nerve impulses are impeded and need to be retrained.

After my last job of eighteen years abruptly concluded in December 2012, I was faced with the difficult decision of what to do as my next life's work. I had been meandering for several years, lost, drifting, and discouraged, until I met Tim, one of Peter's friends. In November 2014, while I was living in Arizona, Tim, Peter, and I met for dinner. Tim, a veteran, was inspired by my story and thought I should meet with Carl, one of his friends in the Phoenix area who was also a two-star general and aviator in both the Korean and Vietnam Wars. Carl is well connected and very active in numerous veteran support activities in the greater Phoenix area.

Carl, Tim, and I did meet, and that's also when I met John, a friend of Carl's. John is a former US Navy officer, author/publisher, and very active—like Tim and Carl—in supporting our veterans returning home from service. John was intrigued by my story and extended a hand in helping to bring form to my diffused and scattered content and make it into a book. He thought my story had a strong message for people—especially our veterans—dealing with serious afflictions, trauma, catastrophic injury, PTSD, and other life setbacks. Although I am not a military person and have never served, I can still feel connected.

After John produced an initial draft, I left Arizona and moved back to Washington in May 2015. Work on *Will Your Way Back* languished until October 2015 when I met Stephanie, a local publicist. It was a chance meeting at the SAC where we both worked out, and I quickly learned that Stephanie could help restart my interest in sharing this story through public-speaking events. She found my story inspiring and felt very strongly that it needed to be shared in a book. I told her I had been fence-sitting on this effort for many years. There were so many messages the universe had been sending to prod me along. Write it, read it, and tell it. I'm not especially spiritual, but I believe meeting Stephanie was the final nudge to get it completed.

I am grateful to have the opportunity to tell my story. I am most grateful for the people acknowledged here and so many others that have encouraged me to "come out" with my story and, in the process, hopefully touch the lives of others in a meaningful way.

Introduction

It's not lost on me that I've made a remarkable recovery. It's not lost on me that this injury could have been much worse. It's not lost on me that this road cycling accident would not have happened had the product been properly made. The product failed; I was seriously injured and am permanently paralyzed because of it.

I've struggled for nine years, trying to find a meaningful way forward. I have made an enormous commitment to physical and mental recovery. At a minimum, it has been equivalent to a part-time job, committing to at least twenty hours a week and often more. It has been incredibly hard work, filled with setbacks and victories, milestones and trials.

The good news, despite the roller-coaster ride, is that my overall recovery trajectory continues upward. The continuing rehab improvements I am making are gratifying and motivate me to keep pushing forward with hard work. People I have met, who have commented on my work ethic, progress, and how I have inspired them, have in turn inspired me. I continue to set new recovery goals and give everything I have to achieving them.

In spite of this, I still feel restless inside, as though there is something bigger I should be doing. While I continue to work on my recovery, and have spent a considerable amount of time dealing with family and other personal matters, my gut still churns with uncertainty. There is a part of me that still feels a deep void inside, along with a sense of being purposeless, even useless. I don't want to just exist. Sometimes I feel lost, trapped in circular thinking, orbiting around familiar feelings of inadequacy, but not doing anything about it.

I'm approaching my sixtieth birthday. Perhaps that reality is heightening my sense of urgency to do something even more impactful and far reaching; to find a new, more meaningful path than the one I am on now. I want to contribute, be useful, make a difference, and matter. To do that means harnessing more of my capabilities, taking some risk, getting out of my comfort zone, and stepping through fear.

In the past, my sense of value came from my job. I was a dedicated professional, worked hard, accomplished some very cool things, and by all accounts was good at what I did. It gave me back something—a sense of belonging, value, importance, respect, and confidence. In December 2012, I was abruptly separated from my company. I submitted approximately three hundred applications over the next couple of years and, until just recently, came up completely empty-handed.

During this time, I struggled with feelings of worthlessness, unimportance, and feeling unwanted, which touched on some long-ago feelings I'd had as a child. It was discouraging, even a bit humiliating, given my work history, experience, and history of accomplishments and recognitions. After almost three years, I began to wonder if the traditional work world had passed me by.

As I continued that process—applying, writing cover letters, filling out online job applications, trying to put my best foot forward with positivity and enthusiasm—it was hard not to feel defeated; I could understand why so many millions had stopped looking for work during this national economic recovery. I had to fight those feelings, but they were a substantial headwind against finding new purpose and filling that empty restlessness inside of me.

Thankfully, in late January 2016, I was offered and accepted a position at Bellevue College in Bellevue, Washington as an IT manager. This is a more junior position compared to posts I have held in the past, but I decided to accept it for a couple of reasons.

The most important reason is the college's commitment to diversity and inclusion, which matters a lot to me. The second reason is that both my children attended the college when it was still a two-year community college (it now offers four-year degrees). Both Kevin and Alana benefited from their experience at the college, each receiving an associate's degree before going on to receive a four-year degree. Third, it is a form of giving back to the community and the college that did so much for my children. It's a mission and culture I believe in.

But strangely, there is an oppositional force at work in my life right now. As much as I want to fill that void and do something more meaningful with my life, there is a part of me that wants to retreat, step back, and just settle in for the long term with my exercise routine and remain home for the rest of the time. This would be the path of least resistance. It would be easier.

It would probably involve less suffering and discomfort. I wouldn't have to move around as much and could return to spending my days largely as I did before, exercising, writing, reading, napping, spending social time with friends, calling friends, chasing down desk chores at home, managing our budget, and ensuring all our home office activities (bills, finances, estate plans, directives, family issues, taxes, filing, planning) are up to date. This alternate path would be reclusive, which in some ways has an appeal to it. I'd only have to deal with myself for the most part.

What do I want more? To make an impact on people's lives, or to live a life of peaceful seclusion? As much as I'd like to take the easy road and sit back, the calling that keeps churning in my head is to get out there and do it. I think people need to hear my story. My inner voice is imploring, "Write it. Read it. Tell it."

The universe has been nudging me in this direction for nine years, and I have been struggling with this decision the whole time. At times, I've tried to ignore it, but the pings from the universe keep coming. Countless people keep telling me the same thing: "Jamie, you need to tell your story. People need to hear what you've been through, how you have dealt with it, what you've learned." "Jamie, how many people who know your story have come up to you and said how inspired they are by you?" "People who are feeling hopeless will draw hope and possibility from your story." "Jamie, your story is unique and compelling." These are incredibly kind words to hear. They lift me up and encourage me.

I have pondered writing a book for years, in part, out of my own interest and also as a consequence of encouragement from others. The book idea has been through fits and starts. I've struggled with how to make the book unique, personable, real, revealing, and meaningful.

At times I've wondered how my story is going to be any different from the plethora of other amazing, inspirational stories out there. I don't want my story to be just another recovery story about a devastating injury or disease. My fervent wish is that it will touch people in ways other stories haven't and be differentiated in some unique way.

When sharing my thoughts about this with my publicist, Stephanie, whom I met at the SAC, she had some very helpful advice. "Jamie, don't worry about everyone else," she said. "You have an important and compelling story to tell, and people need to hear it. Just be you. It's your story, no one else's, and the rest will take care of itself."

This quote from H. Stanley Judd captures the essence of my internal deliberation. It reads, "In the end, we do battle only with ourselves. Once we understand this, and focus our energy on what we can do to control our lives, we begin to gain important insights into how life works."[1]

There are about a quarter of a million spinal cord injury patients in the United States. Approximately ten to twelve thousand spinal cord injuries occur every year. There are many resources out there to assist people in dealing with this injury—associations, community groups, social media, video vignettes, and websites. In addition to writing this book and giving talks, I have a vision to build out a website, which will be named www.JamesHOsborne.com. In addition, I plan to leverage other social media venues to reach people. Organizing a foundation to raise money for spinal cord injury (SCI) research is another goal. It will be the James H. Osborne Foundation and will have a governance structure in place to

....

1   H. Stanley Judd, Alvin I. Haimson, and Frederick D. Smith, *Think Rich* (Delacorte Press, 1978), 167.

manage appropriations. The vision I have is to provide resources—informative, inspirational, and financial—to the SCI community and more broadly to any people facing significant life adversity.

There is no doubt that as the effort progresses, this vision will evolve to best meet the needs of our SCI community and to reach communities of others who are dealing with infirmities of one kind or another.

Mahatma Gandhi said it best: "The best way to find yourself is to lose yourself in the service of others."[2]

My decision is made. I've chosen to move forward with writing and telling my story. *Will Your Way Back* is the result of that decision. There is no turning back. I realize this calling is not accidental; it is what I am supposed to do. I have a story to tell, and lives are waiting to be reached.

....

2   Attributed to Gandhi in Joshua David Stone, *The Full Spectrum Synthesis Bible* (iUniverse, 2001).

PART

ONE

THE

INJURY

CHAPTER 1

Just Keep Breathing

My life was shattered in an instant.

The day was clear and sunny, with deep blue skies behind Mount Rainier, visible in all its glory. The sun was right overhead, casting a small shadow in front of me. I had just descended a steep hill on my road bicycle and rounded the corner to start heading north on Frager Road, adjacent to the Green River. I was utterly spent, exhausted from the preceding ten miles of up and down climbs at race pace, most of the time breathless, gasping for air, and fighting for oxygen.

My lungs were screaming. My legs were on fire from the exertion. All the rapid breaths I was taking did little to quell the intense suffering I felt. The fast descent provided little respite for recovery, and when I turned the corner, I could see a small cadre of my cycling comrades trying to pull away from me. Every fiber in my body said, "Accelerate, Jamie, close that gap and catch up to them!" The gap was about one hundred yards. We were racing, and I was determined not to get "dropped."

I implored the engine room in my gut to give me the energy I needed to pedal faster. At the same time, I had to make my breathing more rhythmic. I gripped the handlebars a little tighter and moved my hands down into the "drops," the lowest level of the handlebars that mostly flattens your back parallel to the ground to reduce air friction and helps the rider go a little faster.

As I rode, my mind flashed back to six hours earlier, when I had commuted twenty-five miles to work on my bicycle. It was a gorgeous ride, most of it along the southern portion of Lake Washington, and the remainder through the Kent Valley. I remember seeing Mount Rainier being illuminated by a rising sun, the sky painted in hues of blue and pink, and I cheered out loud at that moment, wishing I could freeze myself in time, feeling incredibly happy and thankful. The crisp spring air had caressed my face with the aromas of the surrounding landscape, trees in bloom, and flowers of different colors accented against the morning mist.

My brief mental diversion was short-lived, and I was back in the moment, having closed the gap by half. I was making progress but could sense there was very little gas left in my physical tank. I glanced at the Garmin 305 GPS device attached to my handlebars. It displayed several data points, including time and speed. It showed a time of about 12:30 p.m. and a speed of twenty-five miles per hour.

The thought crossed my mind that perhaps I shouldn't have commuted into work that morning on my bike and tried to follow up that excursion with a competitive lunch ride. Perhaps I wasn't in the top physical condition I thought I was, or maybe I hadn't eaten enough breakfast earlier to refuel my system. I displaced those thoughts by igniting the last few matches I had inside—and finally closed the gap.

I got on the wheel of the last cyclist in the pace line group, my front tire just a few inches directly behind his back tire, allowing me to draft, which is a common road cycling tactic. The cyclist in front has to work harder because he is facing directly into the wind, unobstructed, which creates resistance and consequently requires more effort to go the same speed as those following right behind. The people following the lead cyclist in a group or pace line don't have to work as hard, about thirty percent less than the person in front, to go the same speed. The lead rider is "pulling"—essentially towing the riders immediately behind him.

Now that I had gotten on the wheel of the rider in front of me, I was able to ride in this small, trailing air pocket of less resistance. This enabled me to recover faster and get my breathing and leg pain under control so I could surge again as we finished the final eight miles of our road cycling race.

Before I could entertain another thought, I heard the sound of cracking, crunching, and metal on metal. I felt for a moment like I was falling, being dropped straight down as if there were nothing underneath to support me. It was like the proverbial rug being pulled out from under me, except in this case I was lying facedown on it, four feet off the ground, moving forward at twenty-five miles per hour.

BOOM! The right side of my head slammed into the pavement. Thank *God* I had my helmet on. My neck snapped back to my shoulder, and my forward speed caused my body to roll forward, contorting my neck toward my back in the process. At some level I was aware of what was happening, but I don't have a visual memory of it. It happened so quickly, in the space of nanoseconds.

And then all at once, everything was very still.

Where was I? I couldn't see anything. It was pitch black. Or maybe I had just closed my eyes? I don't know. What I did know was that I was in pain, unimaginable pain.

I was aware of being in this tangled mess, feeling something wirelike lying across my face. It was a nightmare. This couldn't be real. I would open my eyes in a moment and find myself in my bed, waking up and looking forward to cycling into work. But the pain said otherwise.

I was incapacitated, shocked, stunned, dazed—with pain spiking through my upper body like lightning bolts repeatedly striking me. Strangely enough, I couldn't feel anything in any other part of my body. It was as if part of my body was asleep. I felt like I was having an out-of-body experience, like I was separated from myself; floating above, and looking down at this terrifying scene.

Someone had crashed. Who? It was all so surreal. I could feel these sensations but was in a state of disbelief. Suddenly I was aware of someone cradling my head between his hands. I could hear a man's calm voice telling someone not to move me.

Fuck, I thought, *it's me. I'm the one who's down.*

"Does anyone have a cell phone?" the man keeping me still said. "Call 911. *Now!*"

Soon there were the sounds of sirens moving in our direction, growing progressively louder, and then, someone was speaking to me.

"Can you hear me?"

An EMT? I wasn't sure. "Yes," I whispered. There was a lot of commotion, other indistinguishable voices; more sirens. I was looking straight up; I couldn't make out faces, just partial views of a man standing over me. I wanted to move my head to try to look around him, but my head was being held stationary between two strong hands. It was frightening, and I closed my eyes.

"What about your arms?"

My arms?

"Can you move them?"

I remember feeling like my right arm lifted up, but I wasn't sure whether I was doing it or someone was lifting it for me.

"Slight movement in elbows," the EMT reported.

"No other response in arms or hands," someone else said.

The EMT asked if I could move my legs. I blinked up at him. "Legs unresponsive," he said.

The same questions were asked as I watched two men—more medics I supposed—poke me again and again all over the lower two-thirds of my body. *Can you feel this? Can you move that?* I couldn't feel anything. I couldn't move.

"You're going to be all right," the person still cradling my head said.

"I'm scared," I whispered. "I'm really scared."

It was like I had been cut in half. My upper torso hurt terribly, especially my upper back, shoulders, and neck; but below the chest I couldn't feel my stomach, waist, legs, or feet. They were numb. *What had happened?*

"You're going to be okay," he said again, in a soothing, calm voice.

I later learned that it was my friend, Pat, holding me, trying to keep me calm. He had been right behind me when I crashed and had T-boned into me when I was on the pavement. He was the lucky one, somersaulting after hitting me while still attached to his bike. He rotated 360 degrees in midair and landed on his buttocks. After he landed on the pavement, he noticed that he was still wearing his bike shoes, which were still clipped in to the foot pedals of his bike. He was a few yards away from me.

Dazed, but not unconscious, he saw I wasn't moving and was the first one to reach me.

"Keep breathing, keep breathing, don't stop breathing," I said to myself.

My eyes opened again, or at least I thought they were open. They had to be open, because I was looking up at the overhanging branches above me, the sun filtering through them, causing me to squint. There were more voices, lots of voices, a blur of voices.

"I can't get a BP reading," one voice remarked, sounding frantic.

"Try the other arm!" another ordered.

"It's 60 over 38!"

"That can't be right, try the other arm again and see what you get!"

"Same thing," came the response.

"Keep breathing. Don't stop breathing." I had to keep breathing. If I stopped breathing it was going to be lights out. Over. Dead.

I didn't want to die.

The EMTs strapped me onto a transport board to keep my body immobile and loaded me into the ambulance. They immediately began debating where they should take me. Federal Way? Valley General? Saint Joseph's in Tacoma?

"No," I managed to say. "We're going to Harborview!"

Harborview Medical Center (HMC) is the number-one regional trauma center in Seattle, perhaps even west of Chicago. Within minutes, the doors to the ambulance closed, and we were on our way to HMC.

As the sirens wailed above me, the pain in the upper third of my body became even more excruciating, off the charts. I was completely incapacitated. The medic explained he couldn't give me any painkillers because my condition hadn't yet been diagnosed. Finally one of the EMTs gave me an injection. It didn't help my agony, but my terror seemed to recede a bit. I was awake, but in a daze. Shocked and stunned, my mind and vision were blurred with pain and fear as the surreal ride continued. Being fastened, bolted really, to the rock-hard transport board was driving me crazy. I get claustrophobic easily.

My mind began to drift, and the thumping sensation of the ambulance, navigating the roads up to Interstate 5, receded. I remember flashing back to a small, after-work business party I had attended in the Denny Regrade area of downtown Seattle. It took place in winter 1992 and was held at the condo of a work colleague. We all had some beer, wine, and cheese as appetizers before making the short walk up to the Seattle Center Coliseum (now known as KeyArena) for an evening sporting event. My wife, Diane, and son, Kevin, had joined me. The condo was on the fourth floor of the building.

When it came time to leave, most of us went to the elevator for the short ride down to the first floor. After I walked into the elevator with my family, at least ten more people shoved inside, not paying attention to whether they were overloading the elevator. The elevator door began to shut, when someone stopped the door from closing and, shockingly, about five more people shoehorned their way in, pinning me and my family against the elevator wall. The elevator door shut, and the car lurched downward. After a few moments, it abruptly stopped.

Everyone was talking, laughing, immersed in a happy-hour buzz, oblivious to what had just happened. The thought went through my mind to tell someone to find the phone at the front of the elevator and make a call. The person closest to it called, but there was no answer.

I knew our situation was very dire. There had to be about eighteen people crammed into this elevator, chest to chest, unable to move. I knew that it would be hours before anyone would find us, not counting the time it would take to get us out. I was claustrophobic and nearing panic. The laughing chatter died down as people slowly began to realize we were in trouble. I was unable to move, and neither could anyone else.

How on earth were we going to be able to manage staying here, crammed together, for at best four hours but probably longer? A few soft moans of fear began to fill the air. I looked up at the elevator ceiling and noticed it was recessed with four plastic grates hanging down. There was a hand railing around the inside of the elevator about waist high.

Wedged into the corner, I asked the people around me to try to lift me up, so I could put my feet on the railing. I hoped to reach the recessed ceiling and push aside the suspended ceiling grates to see if there might be an escape hatch above. I was quickly lifted up into position.

After pushing aside a grate, I noticed there was indeed an escape hatch, but I had no idea whether it was open, locked, or even usable for an escape. I pushed my hand against it and felt it move slightly. Elated, I asked the people just below me to help stabilize my position on the handrails, gave the escape hatch a stronger push, and was able to fully open it.

The opening wasn't very large, but it was big enough for me to slither through. With help from the people below, I was able to climb up and out on top of the elevator car. There I could see the cage was wedged on hydraulic runners that presumably had been activated to stop the elevator due to overweight. Looking up, I could see the fourth-floor landing about three feet above me. I managed to climb up to the ledge and find the door opening mechanism to the landing. It opened, and I could see the party revelers who had remained behind.

Now that I knew we had an escape route, I went back to the top of the elevator and helped pull all seventeen people up through the ceiling opening in the elevator, and then up to the fourth-floor landing. This time, we all walked down the stairs.

· · ·

Hearing the ambulance sirens abruptly stop blaring snapped me out of my daydream and back to the nightmare of reality.

The doors of the vehicle opened, and I was hustled out by the EMTs, one on each side, the legs of the gurney lowering to the pavement with a thump. As I was wheeled into the emergency room at HMC, I suddenly realized my wife Diane was by my side. I remember her face, red, eyes swollen, tears pouring down her face. I don't remember conversing, just the look of horror on her face. I must have looked terrible, bloodied, with deep contusions, and wrapped tightly to a transport board.

I later learned that when she reached the ER she was contacted by a social worker, cautioning her that she would need to be counseled before seeing me. This only happens if the injury is very serious. With her health-care background, Diane knew my situation was dire. I must have looked like hell when she saw me. The right side of my face was completely bloodied. I was moving in and out of consciousness, anxiously waiting for test results.

A neurosurgeon leaned over the rails of the gurney and gave me his name, but I couldn't hold on to it. He explained I had broken my neck and injured my spinal cord and would likely require extensive spinal fusion, involving as many as four cervical vertebrae.

The look in the doctor's eyes frightened me. He seemed determined, intent on doing surgery. It was like he had already decided what was going to be done and I would have nothing to say about it. I had worked in the medical field for over a decade and have a pretty good understanding of medical protocol and lexicon. I also know my body and have a discerning mind. I wanted to know more, but before I could get any words out, he was already gone.

Surgery has always been a choice of last resort for me. I remember one surgery I had to repair an anal fissure. The surgeon I consulted with was the best in the field. I had at least three consults with him before deciding to proceed. I was so cautious in making that decision. I'll never forget the final consult appointment when the surgeon banged his fist on the table and said, "Look, Jamie, are we going to proceed or not?" I did have surgery then, and it was successful.

I had experienced neck problems in the past and was aware I had spinal stenosis in the cervical region. I also had herniated two discs in the same area a decade prior but, fortunately, resolved that situation without surgery after intensive physical therapy. I've always been dialed into my body; the thought of being rushed into the operating room without discussion didn't sit well with me. I didn't trust the man.

I begged Diane to find my orthopedic doctor, Dr. Jens. I didn't want any surgical decision made until he had been consulted. Dr. Jens and I had met years before. We lived in the same town and both had daughters of similar ages; we had both participated in a father-daughter program for several years.

I knew his profession, specialty, and reputation. An incredibly busy man, it was sheer luck that Diane was able to reach him at his clinic across the street from HMC. When I was admitted to the ICU, my wife told me he was there, but I don't have any memory of actually seeing him until I was in acute care two days later.

I lay on the gurney for what seemed like a very long time and began to feel nauseated. I somehow moved my neck slightly to the left and a little dribble of liquid rolled across my cheek. Nobody noticed. Diane was still with me but on the phone coordinating with Dr. Jens.

Suddenly, another wave of nausea hit me, and vomit spewed out—straight up and right back down into my face—filling my mouth, eyes, nose, everything. I was gagging for breath. I couldn't move my head to expel the disgusting fluid. Finally, I heard a nurse yell something, and then someone rushed to my aid. I don't know how I kept from suffocating.

The nausea was due to a high-powered steroid injection I had been given, called methylprednisilone. It is critical to controlling the inflammation response in the spinal cord, especially secondary damage and ultimately how much damage I would sustain. As it turns out, the first eight hours after injury are most critical in terms of the timing of getting that shot. Later, I learned that I had received this injection about two hours after the crash, which was fortuitous.

The crash happened around 12:30 p.m., and I was admitted to HMC ER around 1:30 p.m. The shot was ordered soon after, when it was determined that I had little or no feeling or movement in the lower two-thirds of my body. I am convinced today that receiving that shot so quickly had a positive impact on mitigating the amount of secondary damage in the spinal cord that typically can occur after a traumatic injury. Gaining control of the inflammation response in the central cord is critical in those initial hours.

One of my close work colleagues, Carol, came to the ER almost immediately after hearing about the accident. She asked if I needed to pass on any information. Strangely enough, I went into this very detailed list of actions and follow-ups that would need to be handled in my absence.

My ability to do this surprised even me. I realized at that moment that my brain seemed to be okay, even though I couldn't move any other part of my body. Carol later said she was stunned at the clarity of my thinking, given the severity of my injury.

I vaguely remember having a multitude of X-rays taken and, later, coming out of the MRI tunnel. Dr. Jens stayed and talked with Diane and Carol while all of these exams were going on. The idea of a cervical fusion had been considered because at the time of the trauma I had no ligament support on the right side of my neck for my cervical spine.

Ultimately, Dr. Jens decided to keep me in a neck brace for three months, do a follow-up CT myelogram at six months post injury, and then make a decision on surgery at that time. My cervical spine had recoiled back into a quasi-straight position, despite a number of spinous fractures, and he thought that all the frayed ligamentous damage on the right side of my neck might heal on its own, if properly supported with a neck brace for several months.

I spent the next eight hours sliding in and out of consciousness, periodically asking for more morphine, and settling back into a blind stupor. My surroundings were obscured. I remember seeing what looked like telemetry equipment by the bed, wires and tubes and a curtain hanging from the ceiling. Pain was everywhere, utterly intense, and diffuse. I couldn't move. I knew I was in bad shape, but I was too drugged to even care.

Electrical "spikes" shot down the length of my entire body, starting in my head and reaching my feet, mostly on my left side. These impulses came and went. There was no pattern. I didn't know what to make of it—was it a good thing or a bad thing?

The nighttime hours seemed to crawl by. I was in an overflow area due to the high volume of patients in the ICU. The magnitude of my injuries hadn't really hit me. I was in a haze. All I knew was that I had sustained a spinal cord injury and that my prognosis was unclear. The next seventy-two hours would be crucial to the rest of my life.

CHAPTER 2

Growing Up Jamie

I was born James Henderson Osborne in Waltham, Massachusetts, on January 1, 1957 to Victoria Henderson and Thomas Mott Osborne II. I am the fourth of five children, and along with my brothers and sisters—Molly, Tom, Rob, and Allyson—I grew up in a small suburban town just west of Boston called Weston. I attended Weston public schools through junior high and then was enrolled in an all-boys boarding school in Avon, Connecticut, for high school.

Called Avon Old Farms School, it was a small school of three hundred–plus resident and day student boys in an idyllic setting. My father was an alum, and my older brother Rob also attended, two years ahead of me. After high school, I attended Ithaca College in upstate New York, in the Finger Lakes region at the southern end of Lake Cayuga.

In my teenage years, one of the harder things I struggled with in my life was the feeling of not being "good enough" for those around me, especially my brother, Rob. He was two years older and a junior at Avon Old Farms School when I came in as a freshman. Rob was well known at Avon, highly respected, and an exceptional athlete.

My brother was captain of the football, wrestling, and lacrosse teams; tops in academic honors; a resident monitor; and very active in other social activities, including student government. Senior year he was the class president at Avon, known as the "Warden."

Rob was my hero when I was growing up. I wanted so desperately to be like him—known, respected, athletic, and smart. For the two years we overlapped at Avon, I navigated in his shadow, his little brother, but with none of his physical, social, or leadership characteristics. I decided the only way I could try to emulate him was through my studies, and that's where I focused most of my time. I yearned to have people respect me the way I saw faculty and students respecting my brother. It never happened.

One night during my sophomore year at Avon, my English professor, Sid Clark, had me over to his on-campus home for a quiet dinner. It was an easy conversation until he asked me a very pointed question.

"Jamie," he said, "why do you compare yourself so much to your brother? It seems like you are trying to emulate him in everything you do. I can see that you've chosen the academic route, because you think that is how you can be most like him. Have you ever thought about just being yourself? Being your own you?"

"Yes, I have," I answered, "but I don't care for that person. I want to be admired and respected like Rob!" My eyes started to water, and I fought back tears, not wanting to break down in front of my professor. His tender eyes caught mine, and then he said something very poignant.

"Jamie, you have many gifts. We all have many gifts. Your gifts are different from Rob's. Make your own path; find joy on your own terms. Don't move through life with the boat's anchor around your ankle, trying to be like someone else."

I knew he was right. I was chasing something at the time, trying to be like someone else. The answer I was seeking was actually right in front of me, which was simply being myself.

"Being good enough," Mr. Clark explained, "is simply being you. Being good enough means making your best effort, doing what you are capable of doing, and not using others as your measuring stick.

"Go forward in life, Jamie," he said, "and be the best you you can be. Every day."

Rob went on to attend Williams College in Williamstown, Massachusetts, a highly selective New England college. Being accepted into its hallowed halls was incredibly hard. I applied there, and to Bowdoin College, and received rejection letters from both. Once again I didn't measure up; I fell short. I was eventually accepted by and attended Ithaca College.

My self-esteem continued to be low during this time. I was not proud of myself. Then, one day, late in my freshman year, a friend introduced me to the sport of rowing. The crew tryouts were on the other side of town, using the indoor facilities at Cornell. I had tagged along with my friend Jason to hang out and watch while he was trying out for the team.

As it turned out, there was an empty seat in one of the shells, and to my surprise, Coach Ward approached me and said, "You look like you have a good build for the lightweight boat, how about giving it a go?"

I said, "Okay, let's give it a go."

After being seated in one of the rowing shells, I received some brief instruction. I was told how to move on the slide, catch the oar blade in the "water," drive my legs down, and finish with the proper hand movement to bring the oar out of the water. Repeat. It wasn't long into the session before I had worked up a good sweat and was getting the hang of the motion, although there was a lot to think about.

There was a large mirror in front of the shell so I could get a good frontal visual of my form. With the cadence quickening, my face beaded with sweat; my legs, back, and hands began to hurt from the effort. I worked harder, trying to listen to the coach's prompts for proper technique. Coach Ward commented on my "backsplash," an indicator of being able to set the oar blade correctly in the water before initiating leg drive.

My legs were now burning. Sweat stung my eyes. I could feel this swell of anger, and I wanted to drive it right out of my body through the oar blade, through the water, and through the finish. The anger I felt in my gut gave me the strength to move the oar blade. After twenty minutes, I was dripping with sweat, but I wanted to go longer and feel more pain.

Why? Why did I feel this need to push myself to the limit, even though it was painful? Why was I so angry? I wouldn't know the answer to that question for many years.

All the same, as I wrapped my fingers around the oar blades, these feelings came bubbling to the surface, like magma; but instead of explod-ing into the air, my anger and pain were channeled into the resistance of the water as I pulled the oar blade with all my might. I was totally immersed, in the "zone," oblivious to everything around me except the task of pulling the oar blade. It felt wonderful.

The more I pulled, the harder I wanted to do it. Soon I was out of breath and had to slow down. I loved the feeling of exertion, sweat dripping down my forehead, and being with seven other newbies trying to do the same thing, even as uncoordinated as I'm sure we all looked. I was hooked.

After a while, the coach woke me up out of my intense focus and said that was good for a first go. He encouraged me to continue with tryouts. I got up out of the shell, walked over to my friend, and told him I wanted to try out for crew.

I didn't know it then, but I had discovered something that allowed me to be good enough for me. I made the team and joined in fall 1976, which was my sophomore year. I became a committed oarsman and rowed crew for my final three years of college.

After that, sports became my way of being the best that I could be. It became the antidote for the self-destructive, punishing behaviors that had begun to churn inside of me. When I discovered exercise, I realized there was a way to lift myself up, make the effort, and channel my energy productively to improve my emotions and attitude, and to strengthen my body.

Over the next three decades, sports became a kind of addiction, as I transitioned from rowing crew, to running, to squash, and to road cycling. I enjoyed other sports like skiing and golf that provided a similar rush, but nothing compared to the elation of a hard aerobic workout. Toss in some friendly competition, and the high I experienced became a craving. When I went without it for more than a few days, my mood would change. I needed my fix. Consistently.

Along with rowing crew, I began training to be a runner in the off-season. After graduating from Ithaca, I continued running. I achieved one of my first running goals by completing my one and only marathon, the Maine Coast Marathon. It was set along the Southern Maine Coast region, in and around the area of Kennebunkport.

I graduated from college in 1979 with a bachelor of science degree in healthcare administration and extended studies in financial management. I had two jobs in the New Jersey area where I met my future wife Diane. At the time, I was living in Mahwah, New Jersey, finishing my second college internship.

One weekend, I went home to Shrewsbury, Massachusetts, to visit my dad and wonderful stepmother, Jean. Dad and Jean had married in 1974 and had thirteen terrific years together. While visiting, Jean had two of her good friends, Muriel and Alan Bessemer, over for a dinner visit, and they mentioned that their daughter Diane was living in Manhattan and working for Blue Cross Blue Shield of Greater New York.

Coincidentally, Diane had graduated from Penn State University with the same degree I had. Realizing Diane and I had similar degrees and lived in the same general area, I decided that perhaps we should have a "professional" visit. Little did I know at the time that Muriel and Alan went directly to Manhattan to see Diane, and told her that they had found the man they wanted her to marry.

Innocently, I did reach out to Diane, and we talked by phone for several weeks before agreeing to visit at a beach location on Long Island. We were married a little over a year later on October 11, 1980.

Eight months after that, we packed our bags, pulled up stakes, and moved to Seattle in June 1981. We loved it and have never looked back. We were blessed with two amazing children: Kevin (1988) and Alana (1994). Kevin is married to a lovely Chinese woman named Viki (Ma Guang). They are now living on Mercer Island, one-half mile from us.

After receiving his associate's degree from Bellevue Community College (now Bellevue College) Kevin transferred to Seattle University, where he received his bachelor's degree in environmental science, with a minor in Mandarin. He graduated with top academic honors and notable awards, including the Global Business Club Leadership Award given by the Seattle University Business School.

Kevin moved to China where he worked and lived for five years, his final two spent building organic, sustainable, aquaponic food-growing systems in Shanghai. That's where he met and married Viki. Earlier in 2016 Kevin and Viki returned to the States and are working together to start their own business, importing high-quality porcelain china adorned with incredible custom artistry.

Alana graduated from an accelerated honors program from the Walter Cronkite School of Mass Communications and Journalism at Arizona State University. She graduated with both an undergraduate and master's degree at the age of twenty. She is working now in digital media. We couldn't be more proud of all of them.

When we first moved to Seattle, I worked for a large medical center for nine years doing IT systems analysis and management. I left the non-profit sector at that time and joined a real estate investment company for three years as an IT officer, followed by six months at an Internet start-up from 1993–1994, leading the Software Product Development team. In 1994, I took an IT management position for a national retailer, where I continued to work for the next eighteen years.

The last company was one I had wanted to work at for several years before I actually joined them. They are a well-known local company with a national presence. They sell outdoor sporting goods, which I have a strong affinity for, especially products associated with skiing, cycling, climbing, camping, and water sports. People I knew spoke very highly of this company's culture and employee engagement.

After some informational networking with the IT VP at the company, a few years later a position opened up. I was overqualified for the job but wanted to work for them. The interview process worked out, and I joined them in May 1994.

From my rowing crew days in college through my thirty-plus-year professional career, exercise had become an integral part of my life, as important as eating, sleeping, and going to work. I couldn't survive without it. In Seattle, I continued running, mostly 10K races. I also took up racquetball and quickly transitioned to squash, which I played until 1995.

I continued running, although in fewer races, but did high-intensity training with steep hills and descents.

In 1998, after being encouraged by some friends, I transitioned to cycling. I bought a road bicycle that sat in its delivery box for a year before I finally opened it and had it assembled. It was an Italian-made steel bike. I knew nothing about cycling, especially when it came to cycling in a group. I quickly learned the proper etiquette and techniques, and it became my passion for the next eight years. I bought a couple of higher-end road bicycles as my fitness improved.

Road cycling brought me years of enjoyment through organized rides in the greater Seattle area and long climbs in the Cascade Range in addition to some of the most storied rides and mountain climbs in the French Alps. During all these years, I continued to ski and golf, two of my other favorite sports.

I had a great job, a wonderful family, and enjoyed my life. Until one day I woke up . . . to a new reality.

CHAPTER 3

The Cruel Reality

My crash occurred on Thursday, June 14, 2007. I woke up the next morning and found I was quite lucid, a consequence of the steroid injection I had received the day before. I asked my ICU nurse Carrie to tell me more about what had happened. She explained that I had damaged my spinal cord but that it was too early to say how seriously. She said I had a very deep contusion on the right side of my neck. I asked her how bad it was, and she hesitated, which made me even more anxious to know.

At first she wanted to defer the question to my doctor, but then she acquiesced and told me about vertebral arteries. It wasn't something I had heard of up to that point. She explained that I had dissected the vertebral artery between C2 and T1 on the right side of my neck and that it would need to be monitored for the next several days.

I didn't know what "monitored" meant, but she explained that this vertebral artery is a source of blood supply to the brain. She said that there is another vertebral artery on the left side of my neck and that it was compensating for the loss of the one on the right. She didn't elaborate any further, and I didn't ask any more questions.

A few days later Dr. Jens explained that the vertebral arteries run through the vertebrae on both sides of the body, service the spinal cord, and merge together at the base of the brain, feeding it with blood. Fortunately, there is redundancy at the points where I had demolished mine. If there hadn't been, my accident would have been fatal. I was so focused on my inability to move, the paralysis, pain, life adjustments, uncertainty, and fear that the gravity of losing a vertebral artery didn't register with me until several weeks later.

Quite a few visitors came by that day, including Diane and Kevin and Alana. It was great to see them. I was unusually hyped that day, and very chatty, due to the large dose of steroids I'd been given. Poor Kevin had to take an exam before he came and somehow keep his focus and concentration, knowing his dad was in the hospital.

I could see the understandable worry in their faces as they gazed down at me. I tried to cheer them up and promised I would be better soon, although I had no idea what might lie ahead. I could see they didn't buy it, but I wanted to encourage them. We all cried a lot, and I touched my children's faces with hands that had no feeling as I expressed how proud I was of them. I said they were destined to make huge impacts on the world.

I wanted my family, especially my children, to know how deeply I loved them, how important they were to me; no matter what the outcome, I wanted to express my unwavering belief in them. Mostly, I wanted them to focus on their futures and the tremendous possibilities that lay ahead for each of them.

They stayed by my side until the nurse said ICU visiting hours were over, and then Diane and the kids, the last ones remaining, gave me gentle kisses on the forehead and said their good-byes. They left my bedside, and I quietly soaked my pillowcase with tears. After a while I stopped and began to reflect on my current state. I was still energized by the steroid and had a few moments to just contemplate my situation.

My condition wasn't yet stable, but I was pretty sure I was going to survive. However, I didn't know what my prognosis would be and neither did the doctors. Later I learned a great deal about my condition and about the spine in general.

We all have a spine, composed of hard and soft tissue that runs from the base of our head to our buttocks. The hard tissues, which compose the spinal column, are the bony structures, or vertebrae. The spinal column includes thirty-three vertebrae. The top section is the cervical spine, which includes seven vertebrae that support the neck. The middle section is the thoracic spine, which includes twelve vertebrae that support the middle of the back and shoulders. The lower section is the lumbar spine, which includes five vertebrae that support the lower back. Below the lumbar are the sacrum and coccyx, which make up the final nine vertebrae.

Our vertebrae are the anchors that allow us to be upright, flex, move, and function. They are like oversized wing nuts that have a hole in the middle and smaller holes in each wing. Very important components of our body are threaded through those holes. The most important is the spinal cord, or central cord, which travels the length of the spine. It is the "pipe" or conduit through which billions of nerve signals travel every second between the brain and every other part of our body, from our internal organs to our extremities.

The spinal cord is the nerve center "superhighway." All nerve signals pass through this main highway. Numerous nerve roots—akin to "off-ramps"—are strategically placed along our spinal cord, through which nerve signals travel out to our extremities to tell our fingers, for example, what to do when we want to hold a utensil, or to tell our feet how to put one foot in front of the other, or to tell our muscles how to keep our body upright when we close our eyes.

There are other soft tissues involved with the spine. Each vertebra is separated by a spongy cushion, or disc, that allows the spine to flex and prevents the bony structures from rubbing against each other. In addition, there are arteries that run through holes on both sides of the "wing nut," eventually merging at the base of the skull and providing a blood supply source to the brain. These are called vertebral arteries.

There are basically two types of central cord injury—complete and incomplete. A *complete* injury is when the central cord is completely occluded or blocked with damage, which means no nerve signal traffic can get through. It is akin to an eight-lane highway with all lanes blocked and no vehicles getting through. All function below the level of injury is impacted. For example, the late actor Christopher Reeve suffered a complete injury. His level of injury was C2 and thus he had no function below that level. That is why he had difficulty talking, breathing without assistive devices, and why he was completely paralyzed from the top of his neck down.

An *incomplete* injury is when the central cord is damaged but not completely occluded with damage. Using the highway analogy, I have the rough equivalent of six lanes blocked and two lanes still open, which means there was an opportunity to rebuild new routes around the damaged area through the two open lanes remaining as well as expand or widen them. This is what rehabilitation is focused on—rebuilding new routes or circuits to tell internal organs and extremities what to do. Said differently, I have about seventy-five percent diminution of sensation and function below my level of injury. That's six of eight lanes.

The big challenge was building new routes and circuits around the blockage, recognizing that only so much traffic can get through the two remaining open lanes at any one time. Science doesn't have an answer yet as to why the six damaged lanes can't repair themselves like most other cells in the body. Nerve cells in the central cord don't behave that way. Unlike other cells in our body, they are not programmed to repair themselves. In fact, when damaged, they are programmed to do just the opposite. They are programmed to self-destruct when damaged or, at a minimum, wall off or resist attempts at repair.

There is a scale used to label the severity of spinal cord injury. It is called the American Spinal Injury Association (ASIA) scale. There are five levels—from A (most severe, with little or no opportunity for functional recovery) to E (least severe, with the best opportunity for functional recovery).

My injury was what they called "incomplete central cord damage." I had spinous fractures to several vertebrae, but my paralysis was caused by damage to the central spinal cord. I was admitted as an ASIA C incomplete, which meant some recovery prospects were possible, but not probable, and consequently, it was impossible to predict what function if any I would regain.

I didn't know at the time just how serious that arterial dissection was and how critical the first four days would be. Each morning, during those first four days, a technician came into the room to measure pulses from my vertebral arteries, both sides, to see if there were any abnormal pulses signaling small emboli (foreign matter like blood clots or gas bubbles) spewing into the base of my brain.

A device called a transcranial Doppler (TCD) was used, which was kind of like a mini-ultrasound scanner placed just below my ear. It would generate a pulsing sensation, similar to the sound a fetus in a mother's womb might make—*pshhh, pshhh, pshhh*. I practically held my breath in nervous anxiety for the thirty-minute session, fifteen minutes on each side. I'd watch the technician for any body language indicating a problem. Thank the Divine that all the tests remained negative, but what the future would hold for me was, at that point, anyone's guess.

I was immensely curious at this time as to whether or not I could move my legs. I knew I could move my arms, slightly, but I couldn't move my hands or fingers. The ICU nurse asked me to try to lift my foot, and although I had no sensation of lifting it, she said I had raised it nearly a foot. It was very weird, lifting my foot but having no feeling.

I was able to move my left leg only slightly. Another nurse gave me a breathing device to measure my lung output. I had to use it regularly to prevent fluid buildup and potential pneumonia. It was calibrated from 0 to 5,000. The ICU nurse Carrie said she didn't think I could break 3,000.

Fine, I thought, *give me a carrot, and I'll gladly take the challenge.* The first time I used it, I hit 4,200. She was amazed. So was I. Already I was discovering how important small victories could be. In the days that followed, I used the device regularly.

To my surprise, I felt no loss of competitive spirit, even when I was only competing against myself. Eventually, I learned this was the name of the new game I was only beginning to understand. Later that night, I was moved to an upright position in bed for some X-rays to be taken of my neck. The next morning, Saturday, June 16, 2007, I was taken to the acute care unit on the fifth floor, because my condition had stabilized.

My steroid high had begun to wear off. I was beginning to emotionally crash, both with the growing reality of my injury and my lack of movement and pain. Everything had to be done for me. I was also wearing a neck brace called a Miami J cervical collar, which would become, reluctantly, my tolerated friend for the next three months. I had to wear it all the time.

Realization was beginning to set in.

. . .

That Saturday marked the arrival of more family, including my older brother Rob and older sister Molly and my brother-in-law Jim. I felt happy and anxious to see them. It felt strange that I had just seen them the week before, a rare occurrence because we are lucky to be together as a family once a year, let alone twice in two weeks.

I was anxious, even feeling somewhat guilty, that I had imposed on their busy schedules to come see me following this traumatic accident, especially after they had made room in their schedules to spend the prior week in Utah celebrating my birthday. I knew I would do the same for any of them but oddly felt ashamed that it was "about me" again.

Jim brought some oversized pictures of our recent trip to Zion and Bryce Canyon National Parks, which we had visited to honor my fiftieth birthday. My mother and all my siblings—Molly, Tom, Rob, and Allyson—had gotten together to celebrate my birthday there, leasing a beautiful home for about a week. These ten-year birthday events had become a bit of a tradition with my brothers and sisters and me. The photos Jim showed me definitely brought some joy to my face, and then I would remember—everything in my life had changed.

We had had a great time in the national parks, hiking up Angels Landing in Zion and weaving around the scenic trails and famed hoodoos of Bryce Canyon. And now here I was, less than a week after returning from that trip, partially paralyzed. It would be many years before I would be able to hike any kind of trail again, even if only for a few hundred feet.

After they left, later that same day, a new kind of pain hit me. I was intensely constipated. The nurse tried an enema, laxative, and excessive water to try to get things moving. Nothing happened. I was suffering from something referred to now as opiate-induced constipation (OIC). Between my body being totally dormant and the narcotics that were flooding through my nervous system, my digestive system was severely backed up.

Around midafternoon, Dr. Recis came to evaluate my neurological condition. A ninety-minute process of poking, prodding, touching, and recording ensued, to provide a neurological baseline for future annual evaluations. The evaluation was also used to qualify me for the inpatient rehab unit.

At the time, my stomach was rolling in pain from all the bowel stimulation, so I finally implored Dr. Recis to suspend his evaluation and come back the next day. I was given a bedpan and, five hours later, was still backed up and in extreme abdominal agony. I called my nurse back in and asked if there was some kind of reclining type commode he could find that at least would get me up in some quasi-vertical position to have the assist of gravity. He found one.

He was a big man and used his strength to lift me off the bed and place me on the commode. I had been horizontal for almost four days. I became extremely dizzy and sweaty from being upright, and my blood pressure plummeted. I felt so awful I wanted to climb out of my body, but I wasn't going to be denied a bowel movement. After thirty minutes of groaning in pain, there was success and I returned to bed.

· · ·

The fourth day of my stay in the hospital was Father's Day, Sunday, June 17. Diane, Kevin, Alana, Jim, Molly, and Rob joined me in my room for dinner. Molly placed what looked like a get-well card on the hospital bed table, which was positioned over me as I lay slightly upright in bed. The card was in a sealed envelope. Molly loves to give cards to all her family and friends for various occasions; it's her way of sharing love and concern.

Diane, Kevin, and Alana prepared their Father's Day letters and each read them to me. These letters of love had become a tradition in our home, something we all cherished in lieu of material gifts. They were happy to be with me, but I could see in their eyes how hard it was and how afraid they were, seeing me so badly hurt and wondering what the future would hold.

I tried to lift them up with encouraging words, not knowing myself where things were headed. I was grateful they came to honor me on Father's Day, but it was a strange juxtaposition; strange to be honored, when all my days prior to the accident I was the engaged, happy, and helpful father, and now I was helpless.

With no finger strength or movement, I was initially unable to pick Molly's card off the table. I couldn't even touch my thumb to forefinger, let alone apply any pressure. I used my right forearm to slide the card off the table and onto my bed. From there I was able to wedge the card between my wrists and carefully lift it off the bed and back onto the table, holding the card upright.

At this point, the others took note of the difficulties I was having and offered to help out. Rob and Jim specifically offered but I declined. I was determined to find a way to open that envelope on my own. It was doable, even if I had no hand function. I was going to figure out a way.

The key to opening the card was sliding my right forefinger in between the envelope cover where the front fastens to the back. I had movement in my arm but couldn't move my forefinger up or down. I visualized my forefinger like it was a letter opener, rigid; if I could only wedge it underneath the flap seal. Little by little, I was able to get a corner of the sealed area to separate and eventually was able to wedge my entire finger underneath and begin to tear it open.

Once I was done "cutting" the top of the envelope open with my finger, I had the challenge of trying to get the card out. I realized the only way to do that was to repeat the same "cutting" motion down both sides of the envelope. At that point, I awkwardly cradled the envelope between my functionless hands, turned it upside down, and the card fell out on the bed table. Voila!

It took forty-five minutes to finally get the card out of the envelope. It had been a tedious and frustrating process, but I was elated I had been able to do it. I didn't know it at the time, but this was going to be one of the templates for my recovery, a foreshadowing of what was to come in inpatient rehab.

After my family left, I began to think about my situation. My entire body was impaired, and nothing was going to happen quickly. Regaining function, whatever I was going to be able to get back, was going to take an enormous amount of time and effort. I felt both challenged and uncertain—challenged, because that is my nature, to find the obstacle and find a way to overcome it; uncertain, because I knew that the prognosis for recovery in an incomplete central cord injury is impossible to predict. The spectrum of recovery from an incomplete central cord injury is very broad. I had pestered my doctors to tell me what function I would get back. Unfortunately, with an incomplete SCI, it wasn't possible for them to provide a definitive answer.

Dr. Jens had visited earlier that weekend, and he made one life-directing statement: "Jamie, get independent." This approach quickly became one of the most important principles I would apply to my recovery.

To me, independence was about not being enabled by anyone else. Everyone wanted to offer to help do things for me, but I always tried to do everything I could on my own. Take the wrapper off a straw. Open a carton of milk. Hold a utensil. Feed myself. Clip my nails. Floss my teeth. Open a water bottle. Keyboard. Write. Dress.

I tried for weeks to do all of these (and much more), and by the time I left the inpatient rehab unit, I was finally able to do many of these things, but certainly not all. It became a progressive thing, small, tiny, pedestrian victories leading to bigger victories.

Later that day, Dr. Recis came back to continue his assessment to create a baseline of my neurological state, and he ended up making a recommendation for me to be accepted into the inpatient rehab unit on the fourth floor.

. . .

I remained in the acute care unit for four nights. I had a few roommates, separated by a curtain. The first one suffered from broken bones received in a car crash. I had two other roommates after him, both gunshot victims from the central district. I could overhear their phone conversations, and those of their visitors. Being in HMC had exposed me to a different world, a world I wanted no part of. I was quiet, isolated, and afraid.

After being admitted to acute care, the nurses began trying to get me to sit up on the side of the bed and stand briefly, placing a walker in front of me for support. When I finally pushed up and stood, bent over, unstable, and sweating, I realized my feet didn't feel like my feet at all. They were simply stumps, with no sensation, no feeling. After just a few seconds, I felt like I was about to pass out and was quickly returned to a supine position in bed.

I lay on the bed, sweat soaked from the rapid drop in blood pressure, heart thumping in my chest from trying to reoxygenate. I was dizzy, with my head spinning briefly. After the nurses left, I started to cry. I cried like I've never cried before, convulsively, chest heaving, trying to catch my breath. The tears wouldn't stop. I felt defeated. Here was my moment to see if I could support myself standing, and it hadn't gone well.

Thoughts of being bound to a wheelchair went through my head. I tried to imagine life where I had no lower-half body movement. *How would I live? How was I going to manage? How would I take care of myself? Who would take care of me?* It was overwhelming to contemplate, and I sobbed more, a lot more.

At that moment, I came face to face with the first of the many, many obstacles to come; at that moment, I faced the fact that I might never walk again.

On Wednesday, June 20, 2007, I was transferred to the inpatient rehab unit at HMC. My journey to independence was about to begin.

PART

TWO

ANATOMY

OF A

RECOVERY

CHAPTER 4

Define Your Terms—
Take a Stand—Choose to Win

My time in the inpatient rehab unit at HMC was no picnic, although it is arguably one of the top inpatient rehab units in the country, primarily for patients with neurologic and orthopedic trauma. A patient is not automatically admitted to inpatient rehab. I had to be qualified by a medical practitioner who assessed my condition, my prognosis for improvement, and my motivation to improve. That was what Dr. Recis did in his assessment. I was very excited to be accepted to the unit and anxious to get started on making improvements. I thought it was going to be a huge turning point, with full recovery.

I was never told that I would attain full recovery, but the first few weeks of rehab would be telling in terms of the trajectory. I was told that a strong (steep) recovery trajectory begets a stronger recovery. In other words, if I was able to gain a lot of recovery in the first few weeks, the chances of regaining even more function later would be greater.

It wasn't as if someone said, "Jamie, if you can walk by week three, you'll likely be able to run in three months." The feedback wasn't that precise. It was more to the effect of work hard, listen to the practitioners, do all the exercises, and give yourself the best opportunity to regain function.

It became clear that the first few weeks and months, post injury, would be my best opportunity for recovery, and I wasn't going to squander it with excuses. I'd only have this opportunity once. In retrospect, it is true that my body was most malleable to change in the first six to twelve months following spinal cord trauma. Everything neurologically was scrambled, and my body was desperately trying to regain its equilibrium.

All the inputs my body received in rehab would be crucial in laying the foundation for my future physical and mental function. So in a sense, this *was* an important turning point, although my understanding that the first year was the best and only time for recovery was misplaced, as time would subsequently prove.

I did, however, look at those first six months as the time when the "clay" was slowly drying; a time when I would be able to move and shape it in such a way as to form the kind of "figure" I wanted—in my case, one that was functionally independent.

Little did I know, as my bed was wheeled from acute care to inpatient rehab, what I was in for—the excruciating rigor of double therapy sessions every day. To be able to do these sessions meant I had to be able to sit up and not pass out. It was harder than anything I had ever done before.

Each day in inpatient rehab started with the arduous process of first doing wound care, putting on compression socks, wrapping the rest of my legs in Ace bandages, and then finally placing a corset around my abdomen. This was done to try to keep my blood pressure up and to keep me from passing out due to lack of blood flow to my head. Low blood pressure has not typically been a problem for me; in fact, I've usually had the opposite issue.

I have high blood pressure, thanks to genetics, something called essential hypertension. I just have it—nothing related to smoking, diabetes, or being overweight. Low blood pressure is, however, a common consequence in the early years of SCI. Since I had to deal with that problem, I was taken off my pre-injury medication for high blood pressure. (As my recovery improved, my high blood pressure returned, and I was eventually placed back on the same medication.)

My room was semiprivate. I didn't have a roommate that first night and had the room to myself. I was relieved not to have a roommate.

Sleeping is difficult enough with all the activity, noises, and patients coughing, screaming, or moaning in adjacent rooms. Plus I wasn't interested in talking with anyone. My mind and body were already overwhelmed, dealing with the gravity of my injury, and I felt miserable.

At first, I was really struggling. I was in the hospital, so of course I assumed it was the staff's responsibility to direct my care. I soon found out that wasn't the case. The first day, one of my nurses in the rehab unit was asking what I wanted to do about my bowel problems.

"Well, what do you suggest?" I said. She gave me several options.

I asked again what I should do. She leaned close to me and politely said, "Mr. Osborne, you are in the inpatient rehab unit now. It is up to you to direct your care." In retrospect, it was the hardest and yet some of the best advice I've ever received.

However, at the time, I found her words incredibly frustrating. I wasn't ready to hear that. I was in no mood to think for myself. I wanted someone to tell me what to do, what to take, what to eat, where to go, when to get up, go to sleep, etc. I didn't feel I had the capacity to take on anything else. My plate was already overflowing. I was feeling very vulnerable at the time, overwhelmed, scared, and uncomfortable.

I was also confused. Wasn't I in the hospital because I needed others to take care of me? I didn't realize that moving to inpatient rehab would be a transitional period when I would be expected to take more control of my life and, ultimately, become completely independent. This change was abrupt and unexpected, and I was not prepared for it.

While I did want to be independent in my abilities, I didn't understand why I was supposed to make all the decisions about how my health care should be implemented. I was not a doctor. I was injured. I wanted to be cared for, and I wanted someone else to make all the appropriate decisions. It wasn't like I didn't know how to lead, but it was strange to be given this responsibility in a health-care setting.

The next night was Thursday, June 21. It was the longest night of my life.

. . .

Any enthusiasm I'd had about being moved into the inpatient rehab unit had worn off and had been replaced with the fear of being unable to meet the daily requirement of three hours of therapy. Up to this point, I had barely been able to sit up for fifteen seconds on the side of the bed without feeling like I was going to pass out.

That night, I thought back and contrasted this situation with cycling up one of the most famous climbs in France—Le Mont Ventoux. On that ride, I knew when I started the climb that I could do it. I had prepared for it with rigorous training. I had experience, ability, and strength on my side. Now, unbelievably, the prospect of sitting on the side of a hospital bed, dizzy, sweating, and hypotensive, seemed insurmountable. I had no idea what I was going to be able to do in the days ahead. Things felt extremely bleak.

The night crawled by. I'd open my eyes, thinking an hour had gone by, only to look at the clock again and see just a few minutes had passed. It was agonizing. I couldn't move on my own. I felt very alone, despondent, and depressed. It was as if I had been transferred to another time and place, a place I didn't belong. I was an athlete, not a patient. I was incredibly active, riding one hundred to two hundred miles a week. I was strong, conditioned, and fit. But now I wasn't. Not anymore.

Now I was at HMC, impaired, motionless, dependent, and in debilitating pain. Isolated. I felt disconnected from the reality I had been living, just a few days before. Now I couldn't do anything. I couldn't even move on my own, and I didn't know for sure if I would ever recover.

It wasn't like I broke my hip and needed a hip operation. In that case, I would have a good idea of the treatment plan and prognosis, with a high likelihood that after surgery and rehabilitation, I'd be able to walk normally again. For me, in that desperate moment, there was no certainty or high probability about anything. It was all up in the air—uncertain, vague, opaque.

Lying on that bed, unable to move, I felt trapped in my body, like I had chains wrapped around my arms and legs, each fastened to a corner of the bed. There was no slack in the chains, and I felt claustrophobic, stuck, almost like I couldn't breathe. It reminded me of a time when I was a teenager, living back on the East Coast.

My family and I had traveled up to the White Mountains in upstate New Hampshire to ski at a small resort called Black Mountain near North Conway. While taking a run down a narrow side trail, I caught my ski on its edge and fell awkwardly into a ditch. I was conscious and thought I could easily pull myself out and resume skiing, until I looked down at my left leg. I almost passed out.

Below my left knee, my leg was coiled 360 degrees, completely twisted around in a circle. I flailed violently and somehow got myself out of the ditch. My leg immediately recoiled, and the shock of what I had seen was replaced with intolerable pain.

I was taken by ambulance to Memorial Hospital and stayed there overnight to let the spiral fractures of my tibia and fibula have a chance to adjust to the full-length cast that the doctor had encased around my left leg. All the patient rooms were full, so I was placed on a gurney in the hallway. I spent a sleepless night there, dazed from the medications and intermittently aware of my surroundings.

I remember having an urge to urinate and trying to get off the gurney to find a bathroom. A nurse spotted me and immediately stopped me, got a urine bottle for me to use, and helped me back up on the gurney. I told her I was scared, and she responded, "Jamie, the doctor said he reset both broken bones successfully, and within a few months, your leg will heal and soon after will be as good as new."

How I yearned to hear those same words "as good as new" now, while lying in my bed at HMC. "As good as new" at that moment felt more like "as good as never." Nothing definitive had been communicated to me, other than the fact that I had a very serious injury and needed to apply myself as best I could in rehab. No clear prognosis, no certainty existed.

I had to page the nurses often that night for pain medication, or to be moved so as not to expose my skin to bedsores, or to ask for water because I was so thirsty. I had a catheter so peeing wasn't a problem, but my bowels were still plugged up, primarily from the oxycodone painkiller and other narcotics I had to take.

Every minute seemed to crawl by. The clock on the wall of my room stared at me, testing me to see if I could make it. I wanted to close my eyes and never wake up. It was dark; filtered light came in my door from the hallway, along with a constant cadence of nursing unit noises that made sleep impossible. I was scared, frightened, and uncertain.

My mind was churning, grinding on the dire consequences of the catastrophic injury I had sustained seven days before. I was alone in a semi-private room. I was unable to move anything from my mid-abdomen down to my toes. I was lying on my back, which I hate doing, unable to even roll onto my side without assistance. I could move my arms, but not my hands or fingers.

Things were grim. The pain was debilitating, and the oxycodone I was given every few hours for pain was like eating candy, of no use, and I couldn't have anything stronger. Sweat from my body drenched the sheets, despite the room temperature of sixty-nine degrees.

I didn't have the energy to call the nurse again, so I just remained idle, suffering, in a despondent haze of mixed-up feelings and foreign sensations. My body felt broken, nothing seemed to fit together, and I was powerless to do anything other than just lie on that bed, in agony.

I don't pray often, but that night I did. I don't remember what I prayed, other than to ask for the Divine's healing hands to hold me, lift me up, and heal me. I don't recall hearing anything like an answer, feeling any different, or having some kind of epiphany. I don't remember the Divine responding to me. But my mind began to slowly drift.

A ticker tape of visuals began rolling through my mind, of all the physical adventures I had experienced; all the times when I had pushed myself really hard in a sport. I had been fortunate to do this in so many different sports over the years—figure skating, rowing, snow skiing, hockey, tennis, soccer, baseball, running, golfing, hiking, camping, climbing, canoeing, water skiing, cycling, squash, badminton, pickle ball, and even feeble attempts at basketball and football.

Once, during my college years, I was home in Shrewsbury, Massachusetts on a holiday vacation during the winter. I went out for a 3.5-mile hilly run with my stepbrother Peter. Peter is an amazing athlete, extremely fit, an avid skier, cyclist, and skilled photographer. The weather was typical for midwinter in New England—snow-covered roads, biting cold, and windy.

Peter and I decided to go for a run that day. It was in the twenties, light snow falling, and the sidewalks were snow covered and slick. I dressed in several top layers, but only my running shorts, socks, and sneakers covered my legs and feet. I had put socks on my hands to try to keep them warm, and I wore a wool hat.

Peter and I were both competitive and enjoyed pushing each other. We started out at a brisk pace, in part to try to stay warm. About halfway into the run, a circular route, we started our return home and were still side by side. We started up a hill, and I decided to surge and see if I could separate myself from Peter.

Slowly a gap formed between us, and my feet were fighting for traction on the snow-covered road, making the effort that much more difficult. I had set my goal to try to accelerate up the hill, to put an insurmountable distance between the two of us before we reached the last mile of flats to the house. Pretty soon I was gasping for breath, deep into anaerobic maximum, and on the edge of giving up and slowing down—but I didn't.

I wouldn't allow it. I had decided before the run just how I wanted to run it, and I was doing it. I wasn't going to back off, even though my body was screaming at me to let up. Suddenly, I felt like I was having an out-of-body experience. I was looking down at myself from above, separated from the pain and agony, but still mindful of where I was and the distance remaining. My body had entered the "zone," my endorphins were active, and I was feeling euphoric. This was a hard-won sense of well-being—my body warmed up, motion was fluid, and I was feeling stronger. It was a "good" suffering; my investment of effort was paying off in feeling my body fight itself less and flow more freely.

After cresting the hill and hitting the flats, the wind was blowing hard in my face, and small ice particles kicked up from the road, stinging my exposed skin. Still, I pushed on, unwilling to give in. I had made my choice, and there was no alternative in my mind other than to push on and finish what I had started.

Slowly, my breathing became more aerobic, running a sustainable pace at a high level of effort. As I rounded the corner for the last half-mile to the house, I looked back and could see Peter a fair distance behind. I finished, and Peter arrived soon after.

After we got inside our home, my stepmother Jean asked how the run had gone. Peter shook his head and remarked, "Just another killer run with Jamie."

As I lay in my hospital bed that night and thought about this, I felt the energy that had come just from deciding, resolving, and determining how I would run that day, and what the outcome would be. Then the pain kicked in again, and my mind drifted to other memories.

I used to love to cycle around my hometown of Mercer Island, Washington. It's a beautiful location, in the middle of Lake Washington, just a few miles from Seattle, and central to just about everything in the greater Seattle area. There is a beautiful cycling route, about thirteen miles long, that goes around the perimeter of the island with water and mountain views everywhere.

Often I would begin and end my weekend doing training rides around the island. I rode the route so many times that I knew every turn, undulation, crack, pothole, rise, and descent. Most of the time, I would ride by myself, always on the lookout for a cyclist ahead of me, or even better, someone trying to pass me. I loved to compete.

If there was a cyclist in front of me I would ride as hard as I could to catch that person and pass them. If someone passed me, it was game on!

I took it as a challenge and would amp up my pace to catch up with the rider, and perhaps even sail past.

If there was no one in sight, I would compete with myself, tracking my speed and time, trying to improve on my personal bests, sometimes referred to as personal record (PR). Once a group of four cyclists passed me going along at a pretty good clip, around twenty-six miles per hour. I amped up my pace and got on the wheel of the last cyclist. I stayed with them until we approached the final climb. I could feel the group accelerate as we approached the hill and knew there was a competition on for KOM (King of the Mountain).

Everyone got out of the saddle and raced up the hill. "Out of the saddle" is a change in cycling position while riding. Rather than pedaling while seated, the cyclist stands up on the pedals and continues to ride. This can provide the cyclist with more power for brief periods, usually when climbing a hill or wanting to quickly accelerate on flat terrain.

I passed three of the four quickly but had difficulty shaking off the strongest rider. About two-thirds of the way up the hill, I urged myself to dig deeper. I was completely anaerobic, gasping for breath, the two of us side by side, looking at each other to see who would crack first. It wasn't going to be me.

There was a strong headwind that day, which made the climb even harder. I harnessed all the emotion and strength inside my gut and told myself—*You are going to prevail.* I surged ahead the last hundred yards, with the final cyclist falling behind as we approached the stop sign at the top of the hill.

Mission accomplished.

It took a few minutes to recover and get my lungs back, but I did, and then I soft-pedaled by myself for the rest of the ride, pleased with my effort and ability to overcome the competition.

While I enjoy the aspect of winning, I got the most reward from the competition and pushing myself to see how deep I could dig and to test the depths of my capability. When I was side by side with the last cyclist, trying to shake him off, I wanted to see what extra reserve I had and if I could harness it. That was what mattered most to me. How hard could I push myself? The competition was really with myself. The other cyclists were the triggers or "antagonists."

The memory faded, and once again I was back in my hospital bed. As the minutes passed, I continued to think about that ride. It recaptured something I desperately needed to remember—the power of choice, intention, resilience, and results.

There was so much uncertainty, anxiety, and fear going through my body and mind. I knew I was at a fork in the road—a crossroads, where it would be so easy to take the path of least resistance. Every cell in my body was screaming for me to give in.

Don't do it. It's too hard. The mountain is too high. The winds are too strong. The pain is too much. It's just not worth it. Just let someone hold your hand and fill you with painkillers. Let everyone else take care of you.

Or . . . I could fight the good fight.

I could put my head down and take it one day at a time, one hour at a time. Give it everything I had. Find a way to stay positive. Leverage all my physical training experience.

I could decide to not give up.

In a sense, the choice was easy. I've never been a quitter. And if the goal required such intense effort that I had to dig deep, climb hard, and call on every bit of strength inside of me, then I just had to remember that I had been there before—and I had prevailed. I would harness my competitive spirit and fight this new adversary, this injured body I now occupied.

I would listen and learn from my therapists; I would find out why I was doing certain exercises and what they were intended to accomplish. I would stay positive, give it my all, never surrender.

And I would start by defining my terms.

What does this mean, defining my terms? In my mind, terms should be aspirational, something to strive for—the goals and desires completely my own, not someone else's set for me. As I lay there that night, I knew my terms for going forward would include: getting independent, learning to walk, working again, riding a bike or taking a ski run, traveling with my family, and approaching every physical therapy (PT) and occupational therapy (OT) session like I was doing hill repeats on my bicycle at Flaming Geyser Park on its 1.5 mile, eight percent–grade climb.

I knew already there were going to be headwinds during my recovery, just as I knew there would always be the prescient force field of my limitations that I would have to push through to get my body to do the work. There were going to be setbacks and regressions, all part of the mysterious neurological progression in my body, as well as voices of doubt trying to creep in and sabotage my efforts. Chronic pain would invariably try to sap my strength and my commitment to getting better.

Unless I took a stand.

I decided that night to stand firm and push forward, no matter what forces were trying to push me back. I'd done it many times before, defeating other physical and emotional challenges, simply by harnessing an unwavering resolve. I was going to trust the same process I used then, to help push me through now. Every day, every hour, every minute was going to count. Not a moment was going to be wasted feeling sorry for myself. I wasn't going to be a poor sport, or be victimized, because I wanted to win.

I decided to win.

Winning doesn't mean winning in an absolute sense, as in crossing the finish line first. It means overcoming. It means pushing though barriers. It means succeeding in the face of adversity. For me it is "doing the day" and going to bed at night thanking myself for making it. It is finding victories in the most pedestrian of activities like holding a utensil, touching my thumb to each finger, or dressing myself.

Winning is seeing those little victories build and multiply and become bigger victories, like moving from a wheelchair to a walker, walking around my own neighborhood, getting relicensed to drive again, or taking a shower without any assistance.

Winning is making a steady, consistent effort to build a strong constitution, both physical and emotional. It is like building a beautiful sandcastle on the beach, set on a rock-solid foundation that can't be eroded by incoming waves.

I'll never forget that night in inpatient rehab. It was the longest night of my life, the night I decided to fight my way through whatever headwinds I encountered, whatever lay ahead.

I would define my terms, take a stand, and choose to win.

CHAPTER 5

To See and Be Seen

I never did fall asleep that night. The next morning Diane came in and brought me breakfast. Oatmeal. Despite my newfound resolve, I was still very down and had no appetite. It was one of the lowest points during my stay in the hospital. The mountain ahead was scary, enormous, and fraught with uncertainty. I didn't want to eat. I didn't want to do anything. Diane, undeterred, force-fed me for the next ninety minutes.

Diane was on overdrive during my time in the hospital. When she came to visit me, frequently I would notice she had facial skin rashes. She was placed on a couple of prednisone prophylaxes, but neither did much to quell the response. The rashes were caused by severe stress. Although she tried to deny it, time has clearly shown the skin issues to be stress induced. Understandably so. I can't imagine taking a call and learning that a loved one has been seriously injured and is on the way to HMC.

The next five weeks after my accident were frenetic for her. Cooking and bringing meals to me by 7:30 a.m.; maintaining a household; fielding hundreds of calls from family and friends; supporting the children; paying me visits at odd hours; coordinating renovations to the house; dealing with the prospects of a disabled husband, an uncertain future, and dashed dreams—it was a lot to take.

Kevin came to see me when I was in the ICU and acute care units but visited rarely when I was in the rehab unit. I understood why. Seven years earlier, when he was twelve, Kevin had suffered a neck injury that eventually led to an obscure medical condition called reflex neurovascular dystrophy (RND). It is a malfunctioning pain response of the sympathetic nervous system. Essentially, areas around his neck, shoulders, and upper back were constantly painful and intensely sensitive to touch of any kind. It was brought on by a close succession of three traumatic events, none life threatening, that somehow tripped his sympathetic nervous system. The fight or flight syndrome that we all have was stuck in fight mode. His body stress was "armed" in those areas and wouldn't let go.

Many people with this condition deal with a lifetime of pain management. Fortunately, Children's Hospital in Seattle had a treatment program for RND that had an eighty percent success rate. For six months, Kevin underwent excruciating physical therapy on both an in- and out-patient basis. It was gruesome and seemingly barbaric.

Essentially, Kevin's body was forced to do what it didn't want—be touched, stimulated, and exercised in the affected areas. He resented the time he had to do this treatment and hated the therapists, doctors, and us. He hated the treatment room. The good news is that after six months, Kevin had made a complete recovery.

The first time he saw me in the rehab unit it brought back all the misery of his treatment at Children's. He didn't need any more reminders and never came back to the hospital to visit, so mostly we talked on the phone. I missed seeing him but understood where he was coming from.

Alana visited a little more often, in between her summer basketball camps. She didn't seem as bothered by the medical setting, but I found out later how much my situation had truly affected her.

I also had a visit from my mother, Victoria, and my sister, Allyson, in those first days after the accident. Mother is in her eighties but still quite mobile and active. She is an independent person, gifted in many ways, and ahead of her time. Unfortunately, my mother and I have had a largely distant relationship throughout my adult years.

My relationship with my father was very different. Dad introduced all of us to sports—skiing, golf, tennis, sailing, and baseball. I felt very close to my father, especially when I reached my high school years. We often traveled together to our summer retreat in Dublin, New Hampshire, a short ninety-minute drive. We spent a lot of time sailing around Dublin Lake, climbing Mount Monadnock, and playing tennis and golf.

Some of my favorite memories were the times we spent talking on the drives back and forth to Dublin. Dad was a teacher for most of his life, earning a PhD in sociology and working as a professor at Wheaton College in Norton, Massachusetts. Tragically, he passed away in 1987, in his mid-sixties, just after he retired. I miss him dearly and especially regret that he never had a chance to meet Kevin or Alana. He and Kevin are very similar—gentle, kind spirits, committed to serving others.

I wish my relationship with my mother could have been as close. As a child, I had many allergies, especially to dairy and wheat products, and sadly to my mother's breast milk. I also had terrible skin problems in the form of eczema. Mother treated me the best that she knew how, with sometimes painful results. Often I would scratch at my skin so severely I would make it bleed. Portions of my arms wherever I could scratch would ooze for days, and my mother and babysitters wrapped me in gauze like a mummy to absorb the drainage. Sometimes the ooze would dry and stick to my skin. Removing the gauze would tear the scabs and new skin off my body, exposing new wounds. I would often scream in agony.

As much as my mother wanted to comfort and cuddle me, the pain got in the way. This went on for three years before I eventually grew out of it. I suffered in these early years. These were supposed to be the years of feeling warm, safe, comforted, and loved. They weren't. They were painful, very, very painful. I was tattooed with emotional scars that have shaped my life and that still affect me today.

As I got older, my internal pain morphed into a strange, twisted way of punishing myself. Like I was supposed to do it. Throughout most of my life, this is what I felt I deserved—to be in pain and suffer.

Growing up as a young adult, I had my share of dental problems—plenty of cavities, root canals, dentures, even a couple of oral surgeries. When I would visit the dentist to have cavities filled, my dentist would ask if I wanted novocaine. I would always say no. I wanted to prove I could suck it up and deal with the pain.

I remember gripping the armrests of the chair as the dental drill that was cleaning out the cavity would reach and aggravate the underlying nerve. It hurt like hell. The dentist could see my body contorting with pain and would stop and ask if he could relieve my pain with novocaine. I declined and said I could deal with it.

Sports rescued me. I had suffered a lot of pain as a child, along with more unproductive pain that I subjected myself to as a kind of punishment. Physical activity often produced pain, especially the harder I worked out, but this pain was productive pain. This new kind of positive pain improved my physical fitness, allowed me to eat as much as I wanted, and most importantly released endorphins. Endorphins produce incredible feelings of well-being, in addition to being the best natural analgesic the body can produce.

In recent conversations with my mother, she shared that when she was pregnant with me, she and my father had traveled to India. She believes the food she ingested there had a lot to do with my eczema. She also told me that she had wanted a girl and was disappointed when she had a boy. I was already aware of her disappointment, which had been made clear when she published her autobiography, *The Making of a Mystic,* prior to my injury. In her book, she describes this, stating she had these feelings of wanting a girl while I was in utero and that I must have sensed this.

By the time I was born, she says, the damage had already been done. She says I most likely rejected her breast milk as a consequence, suggesting that since she rejected me, I responded in kind. She goes on in her book to say that this was most likely the cause of the rift that has characterized our relationship.

I was thrilled to see my sister when she and Mother visited me. Allyson is my kindred sister. She is the youngest of five, and I am the second youngest. We have been through a lot together, especially in our young teen years after my mother got involved in some offbeat religious organizations. Allyson was kind to chauffeur Mother around when they came to visit me in rehab.

They both had a chance to observe me in inpatient rehab sessions, often talking with the therapists to better understand what the particular therapies were doing to help me. Mother asked a lot of very good questions, curious to understand the "why" behind what they were having me do. Hearing the therapists' explanations was helpful for me to hear too. I also appreciated the chance to demonstrate the progress I was making. Despite our difficulties over the years, it was good to have Mother there.

About a year after the accident, Allyson flew out from Colorado to stay with me, giving Diane an opportunity to get away for a few weeks to recharge. Allyson was terrific. It had been many years since we had spent any concentrated time together, and we talked about everything—our childhood, families, professions, my injury and symptoms, and my current living conditions.

Allyson is a genius when it comes to organizing a household, and she put a lot of work into helping make our home more efficient. She is also an outstanding cook and treated me to three wonderful meals a day, helping fatten me up a little, which I desperately needed. She also bought a pair of gloves made from a special material that, when coated with skin cream, could be used to provide a wonderful body massage. She was very kind to give me a massage every day, and I was extremely grateful.

I also had amazing phone conversations with my brother, Tom, while I was in HMC. He has a unique ability to get right to the heart of a subject and can instantly relate to people. He has a wonderful way of reaching out to others. I had several "release" moments while talking to him, sharing my deepest feelings, fears, frustrations, and uncertainty.

He has an ability to listen and say the right words. I cried convulsively every time we talked; I had so much emotion inside, and I felt safe releasing it with him. Tom has amazing intuition and an uncanny ability to know what you're feeling or thinking, even before you express it. He is such a gift.

. . .

During my stay at HMC, Carol (my company colleague who came to the ER originally) set up a nightly dinner-on-wheels program. Each night, someone would sign up to bring and have dinner with me. This was a treat, because it always meant a great meal and gave me the opportunity to have a quality visit with someone. The dinner program happened on most nights. Usually, only one person showed up to eat with me. On a couple of occasions a small group came.

Although I was always spent at the end of the day, dinnertime and visiting with a friend was a welcome distraction. Many were company colleagues—some from IT, others from the lunch ride, and many others outside of the company. Having this kind of support system and social interaction was very important in my recovery. It was motivational to feel their energy, encouragement, and stories. It helped keep my spirits up and determination going. It was good to know that this kind of caring and support was there for me.

Folks who came in to visit me in person often would bring cards, printed emails, and other words of encouragement from people who couldn't get on the dinner schedule. I thought it was a great idea. Although these visits were instrumental in helping my attitude, Dr. Jens had advised me early on to be judicious about the number of visitors and to focus as much energy as possible on therapy, rest, and getting better.

Dr. Jens also coached me to eat as much as possible, especially after a traumatic event when my body was screaming for calories. He said it didn't matter what I ate, just to get calories in my system. The dinner program seemed to be a good compromise.

Having a dinnertime-visiting schedule didn't stop additional visitors from showing up at other times besides dinner, however. Some would show up at lunch, or while I was doing therapy to watch, or just after my morning preparation program prior to 10:30 a.m. I always appreciated seeing people, but I can say the unannounced ones required an extra push of energy that took its toll.

During the day, I often had little time between my last morning session and my first one in the afternoon. My goal was to eat lunch quickly, at least as quickly as I could, which wasn't very fast at all, then try to briefly recline without interruption before my next appointment. Occasionally a visitor would come. Other times a practitioner would show up to introduce a new resident MD, or a new therapist to teach me about voice recognition, or someone from the mental health or vocational teams to teach me about their services.

As hard and draining as it was, staying engaged, social, hopeful, and encouraged can't be understated. Seeing people, though energy taxing, was vitally important in my recovery.

Atsuko was one of the first nonfamily visitors who came that day after the crash. She is a former employee of the company I was working for. Atsuko and I had worked very closely together when we, along with a team, opened a store and distribution center in Tokyo, Japan, in 2000. Atsuko is a special person and has an uncanny ability to make me laugh. Captain Linear, she would often call me, due to my not-so-surprisingly linear thought process. Of course, she made me laugh again.

Ben also came by that day to visit me in the ICU. He was a good friend, cyclist, and coworker at the same company. We had quite a long visit. I was very talkative, spending three hours with him, taking him through a parade of stories. I was very chatty due to the strength of the steroid injection I had been given.

I shared a lot of special moments with other friends when I was in rehab. One time was with my friend, John, someone I had known for a number of years through our old church. We were friends at church and had visited occasionally outside of church. We shared a few meals at HMC and some deep conversations. There were times we cried together.

Another friend, also named John, had worked closely with me for most of the previous thirteen years. John was great while I was in the hospital, bringing in hot, homemade meals. We talked about his three young daughters and how much he has appreciated watching them grow up. He's had the opportunity to see them more because he had been telecommuting several days a week for the past several years. He has such a huge heart. We shared some tender moments talking about our children, and stories of the amazing work we did together over the prior thirteen years.

My good friend Peter came to visit me on Sunday evenings and also brought in home-cooked dinners. I met Peter in the 1980s during the time I was an active squash player at the SAC. He also introduced me to one of his work colleagues at the company I eventually went to work for in 1994.

I don't know anyone who can tell a story, joke, or spontaneously offer a funny quip better than Peter. His sense of humor can't be duplicated and was often on display when he visited for dinner. He made me laugh countless times, which was good for my soul and important to help release stress and divert my focus from the impairments. After I was discharged, Peter was a regular visitor to my home.

There are many, many others who were by my side while I was in rehab. My dear friends Carol and Carol, who I had the privilege of knowing during my years at the company, came to visit many times while I was hospitalized. We shared many visits and conversations, and even a few tears. They were my main conduits to others at the company who were following my progress. Their smiles and energy always boosted me up, especially during some of my very difficult times when I was trying to come to grips with this life-changing event.

Another work colleague I'll call Abby came to visit multiple times in the early morning hours before therapy. Abby drove up from the south Seattle area, near the airport through terrible morning traffic to bring a hot breakfast with fruit and juice. I'll never forget those meals and the conversations we had. I was touched by the sacrifice she made to make the meal, fight traffic, spend time with me, and then return to the company's campus for her workday. I still consider her a very dear friend. I wish we still stayed in touch.

My good friends Lisa and Rick visited. Several of my IT colleagues came by to visit including Jim, Lisa, and Lorrie. Many other cycling comrades—Kevin, Brian, Pat, Mike, Dan, Bill Z.—visited. Several of my neighbors stopped by including Lory, Linda, Matt, Amy, Don, Jane, Scott, and Dan. Several other company officers came in to visit, including Sally and Brad J., and many others wrote notes, emails, and cards, made phone calls, and gave small gifts. I'm sure there were many others.

So much of my identity at the time was wrapped up in road cycling and the cycling community. I had spent countless hours cycling with these guys; they were a second family and people that I respected and admired. Many had mentored me in cycling and taught me techniques and etiquette of the sport. They were fierce competitors too, like me, and we had a lot of great memories of friendly competitions on the road.

CHAPTER 6

The Ride I Nearly Died

Over the next few nights, I received calls and emails from people, shedding more light on the events at the time of my injury. Road cycling during lunch hour was a tradition at the company where I worked. The tradition was ongoing, long before I took up the sport in 1998. The rides took place in the Kent Valley, in Kent, Washington, near the company's corporate headquarters.

The lunch ride became the big midday event. It was a fifteen- to twenty-mile ride in under an hour. Each day of the week had a different focus. Mondays and Wednesdays were typically tempo days—steady, sometimes hard—but not a designated "race" day with "attacks" or other racing strategies. The attack days were saved for Tuesday and Thursday.

The Tuesday ride was a "crit" or criterium-type ride: flat course; about eighteen miles; fast and filled with lots of attacks, counterattacks, bridging, and sprints. It was all out and almost entirely anaerobic—meaning it would push the riders to the max.

An attack is when a rider in the group accelerates off the front, creating a gap. The longer the rider can sustain the attack, the more the gap distance opens up. This forces the group, often referred to as the peloton, to contemplate how to respond. If a single rider is the attacker, it is more difficult for the gap to be sustained without the group bridging up and catching that person.

If the attack is coordinated among several riders, the peloton has a decision to make—whether to let the attack group go until they burn themselves out, or to coordinate their own effort to close it down (i.e., bridging the gap). These are some of the cycling strategies that go into a race for riders to gain position, drop other cyclists off the back, and push on to ultimately win the day.

The Thursday ride was hill day and included a couple of climbs and some miles on the flats before ending with an all-out sprint to a finish line. For me, it was the hardest ride of the week, again, frequently anaerobic, with short periods of recovery. Recovery is a time increment when your anaerobic effort, which is briefly sustainable, returns to an aerobic effort that is more sustainable.

Friday was known as "friendly Friday," a welcoming ride for anyone who wanted to enjoy a conversational pace and social time. Often on Friday there was plenty of talking in the peloton. Sometimes business was even conducted during those rides. This was the easy recovery ride before the weekend, when many of us would do long training or organized century rides (rides of one hundred miles or more).

The Thursday course had recently been extended in difficulty with the addition of a second climb up Veterans Drive back to Military Road, which came after the first climb up Route 516 to Military Road. The climbing portions were never gentle; instead, they were anaerobic and filled with attacks, counterattacks, and hard bridging. On these rides of about twenty miles, there was little recovery time.

These days we were often "on the rivet," a cycling expression used to indicate how close to the edge of effort you were before "blowing up" or hitting a point of diminishing return. The second climb was followed by a very fast descent down the "wall" (also known as 35th Avenue South with a steep gradient between fifteen and twenty percent). Some riders exceeded fifty miles per hour (not me) back into the Kent Valley. We then rode some flat terrain heading north along the Green River, a couple of loops up the "cemetery berg"—which was a short steep, eleven percent grade, just enough to sap your remaining reserves—before the last all-out mile to the finish.

The ride on that Thursday, June 14, 2007, abruptly ended for me after the descent down the "wall" where others may have exceeded fifty miles per hour. We were heading north on the flats along the west side of the Green River. It turned out that the peloton had broken into multiple groups on the second climb before descending the wall back into the Kent Valley.

I remember feeling I was at anaerobic maximum and thinking to myself how much I was hurting. Anaerobic exercise is a high intensity, short duration effort—usually less than two minutes—where the cyclist's breathing becomes labored and his lungs don't receive enough oxygen. This is not a sustainable condition. Anaerobic maximum happens when a person has reached the peak of that effort, and any further anaerobic effort will produce a diminishing return. An athlete's performance decreases and, as a result, his body will need to taper back to an aerobic level to get enough oxygen to sustain the effort.

In any physical effort, the body produces a waste product called lactic acid. In aerobic exercise, athletes can process enough lactic acid to allow them to continue performing at that level of activity, mainly because enough oxygen is being inhaled. However, in anaerobic effort, the body can't process lactic acid fast enough due to progressive oxygen debt. The concentration of lactic acid rises, and muscles become increasingly fatigued as a consequence.

As I raced down the hill that day, I was hurting badly because the lactic acid buildup had exhausted the strength in my muscles, mainly my quadriceps, hamstrings, and gluteus. I needed to recover by throttling back to a sustainable level of aerobic effort; however, the only way that was going to happen—while letting me remain competitive in the race— was for me to catch up with the group. Get on that wheel in front of me and find the pocket of least air resistance—that was my focus.

I was pushing hard when, all at once, I was falling.

Apparently, the main triangle frame, the supposed strongest part of the bike, had collapsed. As I began putting the information together that I had been given, going over it analytically, it was as if I could see the accident happening, as if I was back there, standing outside my body, a witness to the moment that had changed my life.

The bike had collapsed underneath me, and I went straight down. I was body-slammed into the pavement headfirst. Fortunately I didn't take a frontal face impact because, had that occurred, I would have likely been killed. My body, which was already leaning heavily forward, because I was in a racing position, holding the handlebars, began to rotate clockwise as I moved headfirst toward the ground. After I hit the ground, I was already partially turned. The right side of my helmet struck first, then my neck, right shoulder, right hip, and right leg.

Most of the impact force was on the right side of my neck, pushing my head backward and toward my left shoulder blade. My neck hyperflexed (i.e., contorted into a ninety-degree bent position), which is what must have jammed my cervical vertebrae into the central cord, causing damage and subsequent paralysis. The medical description was hyperflexion of the cervical spine, and the level of injury was C5–C7.

After hitting the pavement, I did a forward roll onto my back, where my neck most likely recoiled into a semistraight position. As a result of the impact force on my neck, the right vertebral artery was severed and all the ligamentous support on the right side of my neck was eviscerated. The medics told me I must have slid for a bit on my back before coming to a stop. The back of my racing jacket was shredded, but they still had to cut it off.

I had sustained a number of spinous fractures, a broken rib, and a deep contusion on the right side of my neck with more scrapes, bruises, and road rash all the way down the right side of my body. The right side of my face, ears, hands, shoulder, hips, and legs were all bloodied. My vertebral artery on the right side of my neck between C2 and T1 was dissected. And yet, somehow, I had lived.

In many respects, I've been fortunate.

It's never been lost on me that this injury could have been much worse. I could have taken a frontal assault on the pavement, which would have likely proven fatal. I could have had a stroke or series of strokes from rogue emboli coming out of the severed vertebral artery. I could have hemorrhaged blood into the base of my brain.

I could have been significantly disfigured, especially if my face had sustained frontal impact. Instead of ending up an "incomplete" quadriplegic, I could have been completely paralyzed with no hope of regaining function.

There could also have been unknown consequences if I hadn't been riding with other people, or hadn't been attended by the top medics of Medic One, or hadn't been treated at the best level-one trauma center in the Pacific Northwest. Even worse trauma could have resulted if I hadn't received the steroid injection so quickly, which likely controlled additional inflammation and secondary damage. And of course I was incredibly fortunate to be treated by the best of the best in orthopedic spinal cord trauma, Dr. Jens Chapman, and spinal cord injury rehabilitation, physiatrist Dr. Barry Goldstein.

In other respects, my accident was quite *un*fortunate, and it has never been lost on me that this accident never should have happened. Sometimes bad stuff happens in life—wrong place, wrong time—through no fault of your own. I was doing an activity I had done for years, safely, properly, consistent with what the bike should have been designed to do. I followed all the rules of cycling, avoided risky behaviors, maintained the bicycle properly, and was always cognizant of hazards that any cyclist faces when riding.

Sometimes there is no explanation for why bad things happen to good people. In someone else's case, it might be because a drunk driver ran a red light, or a father jumped off a dock to save his drowning daughter—with either scenario ending in an accident rendering the victim quadriplegic. In my case, it was due to a defective bike.

While acknowledging that my accident was, indeed, unfortunate, I choose to focus on the positive. I am lucky to still be here, residual deficits and all, and I intend with what remaining time I have to make the most of each day, to work hard, and hopefully to leave some lasting impact on the world in ways I couldn't have dreamed of before my life changed forever.

CHAPTER 7

Game On

There was a whiteboard in my rehab hospital room where a daily schedule was noted. Each day involved morning and afternoon sessions of both physical therapy (PT) and occupational therapy (OT). Once fed, bathed, wound-cared, and prepped for morning PT and OT sessions, I waited patiently in bed until 10:30 a.m., when my therapy practitioner would arrive in my room.

I never looked forward to it, because I knew how bad it was going to make me feel. Every cell in my body begged me: *No! Don't do it. It's too hard. It's not worth it!*

I didn't listen to what my body was saying. While it's not usually a good idea to ignore internal messages from your body, in this case I had to make an exception. I had come to understand from Dr. Barry that the first six months of recovery are the most important, because this is when the bulk of functional gains to be made are going to happen.

Dr. Barry Goldstein is a board-certified specialist in physical medicine and rehabilitation with a primary focus on patients with spinal cord injury. As a physiatrist, his focus was working with SCI patients on an outpatient basis, pursuing nonsurgical interventions such as medication management; vocational, mental health, physical, and occupational therapies; and durable medical equipment such as wheelchairs, walkers, and other assistive devices.

I was fortunate to be under his care for over six years until he shifted his full-time focus to the VA hospital in Seattle. He is a brilliant man and cares deeply about the well-being of his patients. His counsel to me was always helpful both in the good and the difficult times.

Dr. Barry had told me that this was the time when my body was considered to be the most malleable and most capable of making functional gains. This didn't mean that recovery stops after six months; it just meant the trajectory of recovery starts to gradually flatten out between six months and one to two years. It is generally accepted in medical circles and in population studies that after one to two years, physical recovery hits a plateau and little, if any, additional functional gains can be made.

While in inpatient rehab at HMC, I had to will myself to do everything. I don't know what to attribute those "headwinds" to, but they were real and pressing against me, trying to push me back from any progress I had made. While dealing with this invisible force field, I countered it with a determination to make the most of every situation I was in. I asked a lot of questions, learned the "why" behind the exercises I was doing, and gave it my all. Every day when the therapist came into my room at 10:30 a.m., I would say, "Let's get to work."

This was my way of trying to convince myself that I really wanted to do the work, when I did not. I didn't want to do anything. It's possible the drugs were partly to blame, but I don't think so. My neurological system, scrambled and in shock, with all kinds of foreign sensations, was screaming at me to just be idle. I didn't recognize my body. My body didn't recognize me. And yet, I fully understood that this time period was when my body would be best able to absorb the benefits of rehab.

In the early sessions, I had very little success with my fine motor skills. I couldn't push my index finger close enough to my thumb to hold a straw, let alone peel off the wrapper. OT focused on building those fine motor skills through hand and finger strengthening, dexterity exercises, and a lot of repetition of very menial tasks. I practiced picking up cards from the table, pinching clothesline pins, turning over coins in my hands, holding marbles, placing small pegs in pegboards, doing wrist rotations, arm curls, lateral muscle curls, and on and on.

Each session was forty-five minutes long. I always felt dreadful during these times, having to suppress the nausea in my stomach and dizziness from low blood pressure. Cold sweats, rapid breathing, and general malaise were common.

My nurse, Roland, was summoned multiple times to the exercise room to put tighter compression socks on my feet, to rewrap my legs with Ace bandages, or to wrap a larger waist belt around my abdomen to keep my blood pressure from dropping when I was upright.

My body was saying no, but I overrode the objections with a determined mental approach. I resolved to make the most of being in rehab, hold nothing back, and pretend I was looking forward to every session, even when I wasn't. I told myself to treat each session as if I were on my road bicycle doing a training ride, working at it like one of the vigorous workouts I had done in the past.

The morning bowel program was a priority for me. My bowels were plugged up from the narcotics like oxycodone. It was still uncomfortable despite the amount of Metamucil, prunes, and vegetable juice I was consuming. The first two weeks in rehab required a lot of nursing assistance in being able to move my bowels. A few times, poor Roland would have to extract stool using digital stimulation, sticking his gloved finger up my rectum.

It hurt so much initially, which in a weird way was a good sign. I had feeling there, and this might potentially mean that I would be able to control my bowels without long-term dependence on suppositories, diapers, etc. I did have to use suppositories almost every day in the hospital and for about a month after being discharged.

Roland showed me how to do the suppository process on my own, putting on a protective glove, using lubrication, and handling the small, slippery insert. Because my hand function was so poor, I dropped things constantly, which he then calmly picked up and gave back to me or assisted me where needed. The objective was to teach me how to do as much as possible on my own. I eventually got pretty proficient at putting on a glove, lubing the suppository, and inserting it.

The first time I was able to do it without assistance was a cause for high fives and jubilation. I was learning! The trick was timing. After it was in, I would lie down in bed for about fifteen minutes until it had had a chance to work. I tried to gauge the impending pressure with what little sensation I still had and then make my way to the bathroom with assistance.

At first, I needed help to transfer to a wheelchair, since I had no gross motor function and couldn't stand. This meant learning how to coordinate paging a nurse a few minutes before I needed help. Sometimes I got the timing right, a few times I didn't.

I hated having accidents; it made me exceptionally angry to not be in control. Within three weeks after the accident, I was able to get to the bathroom on my own. It was usually a major chore to get my bowels to move at all, but the few times they did, it was a cause for celebration.

In those early weeks, I was also catheterized. I never had to worry about peeing since I was already hooked up. I could drink to my heart's content, and I did. In fact, I was pushing so much fluid that my resident MD got concerned that my sodium levels were dropping to the low end of normal. So, for a period of time, I had to back down my intake. I was actually pushing over 3000 cc's per day, which equates to a little over three quarts. I was doing this in the hope that it would help loosen my bowels but to no avail.

At about two weeks out from injury, I approached an important day when the catheter would come out. This would be critical in determining whether I had bladder control and would or would not require periodic, self-catheterization. I was very uneasy about the prospects of having a compromised bladder. The nurses also needed to confirm with a post-void residual (PVR) test that I could sufficiently void my bladder and not leave too much residual fluid (over 150 cc's). Anything greater than that residual amount raises the risk of bladder infection and would require periodic self-catheterization.

The good news was that I did have control, for the most part, although it seemed like I had to go all the time, especially at night. I rarely got more than one to two hours of sleep at any interval before my bladder would wake me up. I established a nightly routine where I would keep two urine bottles, along with some hand wipes, close to my bed on the movable tray table.

Peeing into urine bottles while in bed takes some getting used to. I would have to tilt my lower half to one side, which early on required assistance; get things properly placed; and go, hoping all the while there was a sufficient angle so that the urine didn't drift back out of the bottle. In the five weeks I was hospitalized, I remember only two nighttime pee accidents, but they irritated me nonetheless. Once again I had the feeling of being out of control and making mistakes. Fortunately, I always slept on a waterproof mat because of this possibility.

I talked to the doctors several times about my squeaky bladder, and they tried a couple of bladder control medications, none of which worked. I seemed to be able to get five to seven hours of cumulative sleep a night after that, but it was choppy, and I was always conscious of the clock facing me on the far wall.

During this time of trial and error, doctors presented another idea to help with my nighttime frequency issues—a condom catheter. The idea sounded intriguing: pop a condom on at night with a tube attached to it, flowing down to a U-bag, aka a urine bag. Seemed harmless. Just like an internal catheter in terms of function without the process of inserting it. I enthusiastically agreed to try it.

The night nurse came in to put it on. As she was affixing the condom, I was thinking it would gently go on just like any condom I'd ever used—lubricated and gentle. Instead, the lubricant was replaced with something close to Krazy Glue. The nurse had to make sure it was securely affixed so the seal was solid and no urine would leak out. It worked fine during the night. I think I got a reasonable night's sleep.

The next morning was a different story. Taking that condom off was the single most painful moment I experienced while in the hospital—and I know pain. *This* pain had me whimpering like a baby. It felt like a layer of skin was being torn from my most sensitive organ. After it was over, I dropped back in bed and swore I would never do it again, regardless of the number of pees per night or soiled linen events.

If there was any silver lining, it was that once again I had experienced sensation. I could feel pain, which meant that I wasn't completely paralyzed. Perhaps in the future my waist-level functions wouldn't prove to be completely compromised, but the answer to that question would come later.

. . .

There was never a time in the hospital when I felt good. In fact, I felt crummy all the time. I experienced pain, nausea, fatigue, appetite loss, numbness, lethargy, anxiety, anger, sadness, and later severe spasticity and nighttime extensor cramps. It would have been so easy to just not do anything. Every cell in my body was screaming to stay in bed, and only through great acts of will each day could I make myself do anything. I had to harness more will-power than I had ever used, even on my hardest training rides.

My daily rehab sessions were highly structured. The morning session went from 10:30 a.m. to noon (with PT for forty-five minutes and OT for forty-five minutes), and the afternoon session went from 2:30 p.m. to 4 p.m. The initial focus in PT was getting upright and on my feet. My first time at the parallel bars I was shaky. When I tried to stand, I couldn't feel my legs. I was bent at the waist and couldn't straighten up. My legs and hands were vibrating from the strain. My butt protruded out behind me, and my torso and head were leaning forward. I tried again to straighten, but it was awkward and I didn't have the strength or coordination to accomplish the task.

Everything felt disconnected, detached, and out of balance. Nothing belonged together. I was disappointed and shocked at my level of debilitation, yet undeterred.

Game on.

By the end of the first week of PT, I was standing a little more upright in the parallel bars, though still shaky. I was very unstable. During week two in inpatient rehab, I was fitted with a wheelchair and taught how to propel. I was given gloves to protect my palms and fingers and to help me grip the wheelchair hand rims.

Initially, I didn't have the hand or finger dexterity to put the gloves on myself and had to ask for help. It was frustrating to command my hands and fingers to do something and get no response. I hated asking for help. In fact, I hated it so much, that after a few times of asking for help, I resolved that I would fumble around trying to do it myself until I got it right. Within a few days, I did get it right! This was another small victory, but it was one that seemed very large to me.

One of the charge nurses who gave me great care encouraged me to do more outside my room. Being wheelchair capable meant I could have a little independence on the rehab floor. The nurse suggested I go to the computer desk where I could practice keyboarding. She also suggested I get meal passes and eat down in the cafeteria, which I was allowed to do. She further offered that I could take my wheelchair outside, down to the observation deck by the heliport. The first time I rolled myself outside I felt I had entered an entirely new universe.

Around the third week, my physical therapist decided it was time to challenge my leg function. I was placed in a mobile hanging device, suspended in straps, akin to an adult johnny-jumper. Strapping me in was quite a process. The first time it took three people, and the waist brace gave me a severe wedgie. The machine was adjusted so that my feet touched the ground, but only very lightly. I'm not sure what was more uncomfortable, having a compressed crotch or feeling humiliated that I had regressed to being toddler-like.

The purpose of this suspended device was to get me upright with only limited weight bearing on my legs. The therapists parked me over a treadmill and had me try to walk. I couldn't move my legs on my own when instructed; two therapists moved my feet one at a time, keeping pace with the slow-moving treadmill. It was good to be up and trying to move, but I was very concerned that I might never be able to move my legs on my own. It was utterly exhausting, even though the exercise had lasted only a few minutes.

I soon discovered that my left side, especially my left leg, was significantly more compromised than my right. My left foot tended to flop down, and keeping my foot at a ninety-degree angle, or even lower (meaning greater upward ankle flexion), wasn't yet possible. Going into week three of rehab, the therapists wanted to get me out of the wheelchair to practice standing and walking with a walker. This meant bearing my full weight on my legs.

To attempt this, my PT, Elisa, came up with the idea of wrapping an Ace bandage around my left foot, ankle, and calf to hold it at ninety degrees and prevent the flopping. I couldn't feel my ankle. Even with this adjustment, I had great difficulty elevating and pulling my left leg forward past my right to take a forward step. For a couple of weeks, Elisa had to regularly apply the Ace bandage to that foot to keep it at a right angle, to keep it from dragging.

Looking back, it's hard to believe I survived that time in the hospital. I was always busy doing something—from 7:30 a.m. to 8 p.m. or later, when the last guest left, or the nurse finished inoculating me with a blood thinner, or I said good-bye on the final phone chat of the day with a family member. I rarely had downtime.

I can attribute surviving this period to several things: having been in top physical condition before my accident, leveraging energy forces I couldn't see (more on this later), and my relentless commitment to getting better. I continued on this maniacal march throughout my five-week inpatient stay.

CHAPTER 8

Thou Shalt Not Be Enabled

Early during my stay in rehab, I received adaptive devices. Some were for eating, for example a special knife device or sponges to wrap around my utensils so I could grip them. For mobility there was a wheelchair, walker, four-pronged cane, and a fiberglass foot brace for my left foot. I briefly used a wrist prong to help me keyboard, a seat in the shower for general hygiene, and an elevated toilet seat, to name just a few.

I adopted the following mantra of thought whenever possible: "Thou shalt not be enabled." That was my focus. I did not want to be enabled by anyone or anything. This wasn't possible in the early months, because I had to be dependent, but it didn't mean I liked it. I used all of these devices initially. However, as I developed more independence, I was gradually able to wean myself from almost all of them prior to my discharge from the hospital.

I looked at recovery in this way: I'm never going to learn how to get around without a wheelchair if I am always in a wheelchair. I'm not going to learn how to walk without arm crutches if I am using arm crutches. I'm never going to learn how to dress myself if someone else is dressing me. I'm not going to be able to go without a waist girdle if I'm always wearing one.

Granted, there were times and situations when these assists were absolutely necessary, but I approached these as challenges that I would overcome. No matter how long it took, I resolved that I would eventually stop using these devices. Through dogged determination, I was going to learn to do these things on my own. I refused to give in.

In the weeks following the accident, I became much more aware of the extent of my injury and functional limitations. It was astounding to learn just how intricate our bodies are, as I tried to relearn functions and actions that I had been doing since I was a youngster.

These included everything in daily living, such as getting up in the morning, getting out of bed, using my hands and leg muscles to get up and down from a chair, fumbling my way through clothes, trying to get dressed, putting on my socks and shoes, holding a utensil in my hand—among many others.

I had experienced a complete physicality reset, like someone had pressed the Ctrl-Alt-Del buttons and wiped clean my motor function life. It was a complete restart.

In the initial weeks, a breakfast tray was brought to my room and placed on a side table.

Sometimes visitors, including Diane and friends, would come and bring me breakfast. Left to myself, however, I struggled to eat on my own. With limited fine motor skills, there were a few times very early on when I had to ask for help to peel a boiled egg, open a small cereal box or carton of milk, cut up my food, open a water bottle, or peel off the straw wrapper.

This was in stark contrast to the finger strength and dexterity I previously had. Before my accident I had changed a flat tire on a bicycle, which requires considerable fine motor strength, with ease. Now I had trouble feeding myself. This bothered me a lot. I didn't like the feeling of being enabled, helpless, and dependent. I've always been so independent. Over and over Dr. Jens's words were emblazoned on my psyche—"get independent"—and that has never changed.

Often for breakfast I was given cold cereal in small, single-serving boxes. The first few mornings I did ring the nurse to help me, but one morning I thought *No, I'm not calling for help anymore.* It was important not to be enabled by someone else's well-meaning offer to do things for me.

The first time I tackled breakfast on my own, it took thirty minutes to open the cereal box because I had very limited hand function. I had enough strength in my fingers to get the box in my hands, but not enough to open it.

The commands from my brain saying to pinch the box harder weren't getting through to my fingers. I tried every maneuver I could think of, but nothing worked. Finally I grabbed a knife and tried to cut the box open, but I couldn't hold the knife between my fingers without dropping it on my lap.

I was so tempted to call for help. I finally said screw it, put the side of the box up to my mouth, gripped the box with my teeth, and opened up the box, tearing at it like a wild animal would its newly killed prey. I used the same technique on the plastic liner inside. With some fumbling effort, I managed to get the cereal into the bowl. I was halfway there.

Now I had to figure out how to open a carton of milk. Without finger strength, I resorted again to using my teeth to open it. It was not an elegant solution, but I was utterly determined. I clumsily tilted the milk carton and managed to get most of it in the cereal bowl. Eating was another struggle. I cradled the cereal bowl loosely in my hands, put it up to my mouth, and slowly poured the milk and cereal into my mouth, one gulp at a time. No utensils.

Eating one tiny box of cereal took me one hour. It didn't matter—I did it! Within a couple of weeks, I had built enough hand-finger function to do it in ten minutes.

I desperately wanted to be able to floss my teeth. Placing a blue loop through my upper bridge and then looping floss through it was a big deal. Just being able to hold the blue loop in my fingers and not drop it brought great satisfaction. A few days later, I was able to hold the floss case, break a piece of floss off, string it through the loop, and actually floss. It was awkward and uncoordinated at first, but I kept practicing it. Eventually it became easier and I succeeded.

After a couple of weeks in rehab, Roland, my nurse, said it was time to take a shower, my first one in sixteen days! I am amazed people came to visit me during those first couple of weeks. Early on I was given washcloth baths in bed, along with some crude, ineffective method of washing my hair while lying down. Now it was time for the real thing.

Roland transferred me into the private shower room via wheelchair, and I remained seated. He handed me a washcloth and showed me the soap and shampoo. "Have at it and show me what you can do," he said.

Somehow I managed to turn the water on by clasping both hands together and turning the knob; it was awkward, but possible. At first the water spray on my back felt like needles pricking my skin, the sensation diminished, but it was noticeably uncomfortable. Roland reassured me that this was normal and that those feelings would gradually normalize.

I felt the warmth of the water running down my back. I tried to pick up the soap with one hand and place it on the washcloth to lather up—no good, it fell on the floor. Roland handed it to me, and I tried again, and again, and again. I couldn't grip the soap, and it was frustrating. Once again, my hand strength was insufficient. The proper command signals couldn't get through, and my body was working overtime to build new signal routes around the damaged area.

Undaunted, I decided to use my other hand holding the wet washcloth, and rub the soap while it was sitting in the tray. I finally worked up some lather and was able to loosely touch the sudsy washcloth against my skin and make small circular motions. This first shower experience was a start—clumsy, frustrating, and filled with uncertainty as to what progress I would be able to make—but nevertheless, a start.

I hated the thought of being dependent on someone to shower me and was going to push on to build independence. Over the ensuing weeks, I continued to improve these skills, and by the time I was in the fifth week of rehab, I was showering independently.

Small endeavors could become big challenges but also big successes. I remember one Sunday afternoon when I was alone in my hospital room with little to do. I found a pair of large nail clippers and spent the next ninety minutes eventually clipping all my fingernails. I used every imaginable means to do it, being especially careful not to pierce my skin.

When I finished, I had a great sense of satisfaction and was happy to have found a productive use of my time, rather than just lying in bed.

As I have mentioned, during my hospital stay I felt bad all the time. I never felt like getting up, getting dressed, eating, doing therapy, answering the phone, writing emails, using my wheelchair, doing homework, practicing exercises, or having visitors. I wanted visitors, knew it was important for my recovery, but also knew there was going to be a price to pay.

Doing anything required painful effort. Every cell in my body was still screaming not to do anything. I was only able to function out of the sheer will to get better. I knew that my stay in the hospital would be the best chance for me to maximize my recovery, with all the people and resources in such close proximity.

I'm not sure where my source of will came from. I know I have a stubborn side that refuses to quit. I don't like giving in. It's just like when I am climbing a big mountain pass on a bike, or racing the flats on a Tuesday, or climbing Route 516 on a Thursday. I've had a lot of experience pushing myself and overcoming pain. The same dogged determination to train and race was what I used in the rehab unit.

· · ·

I began approaching each day as a workday, each therapy session as a training ride. I know how uncomfortable a training ride or race can be. I also know how amazing the feeling of satisfaction is when you are done. The rush of endorphins. The feeling of accomplishment. It was like a drug. It was addictive. In sports, the more I experienced it, the more I wanted.

I can't say I got the same endorphin rush in the hospital. The feeling of satisfaction came in different ways. Numerous times I would receive feedback from doctors, therapists, and nurses that my rate of recovery was different from most people in my situation and traveling a steep upward trajectory. I was unusual. Special. That made me feel hopeful.

I remember Dr. LeiLei, my hospital-based inpatient MD, saying "You are a moving target," meaning the goals they set for me in the treatment plan had to be changed frequently because my progress rate was faster than expected. These comments were highly motivating, verbal rewards for the efforts I was making. Hearing these words just added gas to my internal fire to get better.

Dr. Jens visited on multiple occasions, spending time with me, commenting on how steep my rate of recovery was, and how that pointed toward a continued strong recovery. One time when he came by, he watched as I was able to open a small carton of milk, something I had recently accomplished. He seemed impressed and commented on the intricate nerve impulses that are required to do such a seemingly benign task. He then challenged me with something different.

"Try to put your hands together, with your palms together and each of your fingers aligned and touching." I tried but I had no control, and my fingers just flopped. My fingers couldn't sense the contact of each other. The challenge was on, and I worked for days trying to master that seemingly benign task. Before I was discharged, I showed Dr. Jens my new accomplishment. He seemed impressed, but of course he put a new challenge in front of me.

That is the way rehab is. Master one thing and move on to the next. It became the blueprint for how my recovery has progressed to this day and will continue to do so as my journey moves forward. The plan is simple: Master my immediate goal and move on to the next. Celebrate the "win," reward myself, and keep going.

There were times in therapy where the same sense of satisfaction would happen. The first time on the NuStep, a recumbent cycling machine, I cranked out ninety watts. My legs were flopping side to side as I pressed the pedals with my legs. My limbs felt disconnected from the rest of me and needed some therapist assistance to keep them straight. The next time I hit 120 watts, this time with no assistance and more cooperative legs, and the time after that, 150 watts.

I was definitely making progress. Toward the end of my stay in late

July 2007, I was telling my OT, Amy, how I was able to shower on my own, standing up, without sitting assistance. She was impressed. I was also able to handle my bowel program on the regular toilet seat, without having to use the raised chair that straddles a regular toilet. It happened with great difficulty, and I had to use the grab bars adjacent to the toilet seat to pull myself up.

Earlier in my hospital stay, Amy had been trying to figure out what durable medical equipment I would need to take home with me. As the weeks went by the list of items to order got smaller. By the time I was discharged, I didn't require any assistive devices except a cane, urine bottles, and a raised toilet "chair" (which was only temporary).

Into the fourth of week of rehab, I was continuing to have challenges with my left foot and its tendency to flop around. At one point, Elisa decided to bring in the foot prosthesis people, and they made a fiberglass foot/ankle/calf brace that would keep my left foot at a right angle, thereby forgoing the need for the daily ace bandage.

I used the brace twice. I hated the way it felt, and I didn't like the idea of wearing an enabling device. So I willed myself to figure out how to walk better. I had Diane bring me different sneakers from home, which were a half size smaller than the sneakers I had been using. The smaller size seemed to help me stub my left toe less.

There were other signals that my progress was strong. One evening, a nurse I didn't see often came into my room to deliver something, and he asked what kind of neck injury I had. I told him I was a C5-C7 incomplete SCI and he remarked how well I was doing.

"You are atypical and are going to do fine," he said.

My initial rehab evaluation MD, Dr. Recis, came by to visit as well and commented on how much progress I had made since we'd last been together, again saying that this rate of progress portended a strong recovery.

There was a time in PT when Susan, another therapist, wanted to record my walking capability on her digital camera. She wanted me to walk with eyes closed, without a cane, so she could show it to her students for a class she was teaching. I was proud to show off.

. . .

Part of the inpatient rehab focus was to reintroduce me and other patients to activities of daily living outside the hospital. One way they did this was to take us out of our rehab "cocoon" in the hospital and reconnect us with the outside world. After several weeks in inpatient rehab, I had begun to adjust to the routine and my surroundings in the very controlled environment. Immersing myself in the real world again was a necessary part of my recovery process, but it was daunting nonetheless.

During week four of my inpatient rehab, I experienced my first hospital-sponsored excursion to the Seattle Aquarium. I was a bit apprehensive, because we were traveling in an Access van; I was concerned about going over bumps and aggravating my neck, even though I was still wearing a neck brace.

When we were boarding the van (I was using a combination of wheelchair and walker at the time), the rest of the group used the electronic lift to get placed inside. I brazenly asked Susan, the recreational therapist, if I could try to walk up the high stairs of the Access van on my own, with the help of the handrails. She agreed, and I stood up from the wheelchair, shuffled to the side of the van, and stepped up into the van under my own power.

When I reached the top of the stairs, I was met with collective applause from my van mates and members of my family who had come along. After we got to the aquarium, I used the walker about ninety percent of the time, only resting in the wheelchair now and then. I got a great sense of satisfaction from demonstrating my independence. This was the proverbial wind under my sails. All the feedback was positive, and like a drug, I craved more of it. It was a big motivator.

As time progressed in the rehab unit, I experienced a steady progression on other fronts. The little victories of holding a utensil or touching my forefinger to my thumb grew into bigger victories. I was maniacal about doing things on my own. As I continued to build strength and coordination, I was able to abandon the wheelchair altogether and only use a walker.

I used the walker to move around the nursing floor, but being upright and on my feet was not a happy place. My body felt like I weighed many times my normal body weight (165 pounds), and consequently, everything hurt including my feet, ankles, legs, waist, and back. I forced myself to do it, like I would force myself to shuffle to the nurse's station, or to fetch towels and other items from the linen closet as part of my OT homework. But I didn't like it.

I transitioned from the walker to using a four-prong cane and, toward the end of my stay in rehab, was able to shift to a single-prong cane. I even had some PT sessions outside the hospital in a small grassy courtyard. Elisa challenged me to try walking on the grass without the cane. Since the grass was uneven, this required that I lift my legs sufficiently to clear the ground, which tested my balance.

At times, she challenged me to try to walk without use of the cane, and she was always close by to balance check if needed. Even if I did fall, I wasn't afraid, given that I was on the grass. She even had me walk up and down a few stairs, very slowly. She held a strap tethered around my abdomen to help support me if I started to lose balance.

At the end of my inpatient stay, something really cool happened. I had a goal of walking around the outside perimeter of HMC, a total of four blocks. I wanted to do it unaided, with Elisa and another therapist flanking me on either side should I need a balance check. I managed to do it, make it back to my room, and collapse. I had set my mind to do it—and I did it! It was very exciting.

My time was also consumed with homework. Amy in OT had me read excerpts from a book called *Yes, You Can,* which was written for patients with spinal cord injury. I was actually given reading assignments and quizzed on it in OT sessions. Along with this, I was given writing assignments to teach myself how to hold a writing utensil.

This may seem trivial, but when fine motor function is compromised, it is extremely difficult to write. I learned to trace shapes, make letters, and work on writing my signature, which I was eventually able to do, just not very legibly, by the time I was discharged.

I had another goal of being able to keyboard again. As an IT person, I had spent a lot of time on computer keyboards, only to realize in the initial weeks after my injury that I had no finger function at all. Amy in OT outfitted me with a simple device that fastened to my wrist, and extending from it was an eight-inch pencil-shaped device with a small rubber fastener at the end. Its purpose was to allow me to keyboard by using my wrists to move the extender around to touch different keys, press, and type.

It was slow, painstakingly slow, but I used it to type my first email to my concerned colleagues at the company. Within a few weeks' time, after considerable practice and determination, I was able to discard the device and operate the keyboard using just my fingers, albeit with a hunt-and-peck system, like an old-time reporter stabbing at an antiquated Selectric typewriter.

There was so much to relearn. There wasn't much I didn't have to relearn—and I knew I could succeed, as long as I stuck to my unwavering commitment to do whatever it took to become independent.

My approach in inpatient rehab was to maximize every moment, regardless of the monotonous, mundane nature of the repetitive tasks. They all had purpose. The hand exercises were the hardest, but the dividends have been worth it.

My fingers do have some residual deficits, primarily a constant pain in my pinky, ring, and middle fingers. I am fortunate that I have been able to make progress in regard to fine motor skills, which often are the last to improve. Gross motor skills usually advance earlier. For SCI incompletes, having complete hand function is somewhat unusual and a huge blessing.

From ICU to Med/Surg to inpatient rehab, the nurses at HMC were attentive and friendly. The day-shift charge nurse was nice enough to get me transferred to the "hotel room." It wasn't a hotel room of course, but it had all the accoutrements of one. It was another private room, at the end of a hall. I made a request for the "hotel room" about halfway into my stay after I learned about it. It was my room for the last ten days before I was discharged.

It was considered the transition room, more closely resembling a home, set up with table and chair, recliner chair, larger bathroom, two televisions, and a refrigerator. In addition, the room faced west with a great view of the Olympic Mountains and Puget Sound. It was good for my soul to have so much sun exposure. My previous room, though private, faced in an easterly direction with a view of a high-rise apartment building and little direct light.

Each week in rehab we would have "panel" meetings, where in one room, I was joined by the HMC team (everyone involved in my care), which included my attending physician, resident physician, PT, OT, head nurse, social worker, mental health practitioner, recreational therapist, speech therapist, wife, friends if available, and a recorder. The resident MD would run the meeting. The purpose was to review my treatment plan and update my progress against treatment plan goals.

It was also an opportunity for Diane and me to ask questions. My sister Molly, a physician in Portland, Oregon, attended by conference call for the first session. At the end of each session, I would thank each member of the treatment team for their fine care, taking time to look each one of them in the eye. I left each meeting with positive feelings about the progress I was making.

In the last meeting, we talked about what would be needed to accommodate me at home. Diane was quite anxious about the work needing to be done to ensure all would be ready before I came home. We were discussing "grab bars" for the shower and toilet, and someone asked what material should be used. I quipped, "Just make sure if you use wood it's not old growth."

The room broke out in laughter. I didn't think it was that funny, but I think the practitioners were relieved to know that I still had some sense of humor, despite the gravity of my injury.

CHAPTER 9

A Daunting Transition

As part of the process of transitioning from HMC back to my life at home, I was permitted to stay overnight at our house to see how I would adjust. This was toward the end of week four in inpatient rehab, a test period before my final release a week later. Diane picked me up that day in the Ford Explorer. With assistance, I was hoisted into the front seat. I had a cane and walker with me.

Everything about my body felt out of place. Nothing felt right. I had this squeezing sensation around my hips and crotch areas, as if I were back in the adult johnny-jumper. I tried to get comfortable in the seat but couldn't. I wanted to get back out of the car and return to my hospital room, but I forced myself to stay in the car. Diane asked if I was okay. I said no, but implored her to start driving, so we could get this exercise over and done.

I was still wearing the Miami J neck brace and could only look straight ahead. I had a terrible pain in the middle of my back, as if a few vertebrae were out of alignment and all that was needed was a robust chiropractic adjustment to snap them back into place. Of course I couldn't do that, as no thrusting of my spine was permitted, especially at this early stage of recovery.

It was a warm mid-July day. As Diane drove the short fifteen minutes from the hospital to home, I felt like I had taken a step back in time. Everything seemed new, like I was visiting the Pacific Northwest for the first time. It was gorgeous driving east over the Mercer Island floating bridge with Mount Rainier and Mount Baker in their glory in the distance. Unfortunately, in spite of the beauty around me, I was in a lot of pain and suffering during the ride.

My mind was also in flux as I tried to envision how I would be able to adjust to living at home. For the past four weeks, I had experienced the security and predictability of the rehab unit. How would I make it without that? Even more daunting was the fact that this was my first visit home since the fateful day of my accident in mid June—my whole world was different now.

When we pulled into the driveway, it took some doing to get my legs to swing outside the car. With help, I finally, gently, settled my feet to the ground and stood up. Then I nearly passed out. I was dizzy and light-headed without the usual props to keep my blood pressure up.

Diane got out the walker, found me a lawn chair, and set it on the driveway. I settled in to get my bearings, breathe in the fresh air, take in the surroundings, and emerge from my captive stupor. After fifteen minutes or so, with my wife close behind, I shuffled into the house using my walker. Fortunately, I could walk straight into our home because there were no steps inside or out, which made it relatively easy to move around.

After so many weeks in the hospital, it was a shock to be back home, and it made me feel strange. To my surprise, I realized—I didn't like it. I felt displaced, removed from my secure surroundings at HMC to the daunting prospect of trying to adjust to a new life away from what had become my safe place. Question after question tumbled through my mind.

How was I going to get in and out of bed without having all the convenient adjustments of a hospital bed? How was I going to sit in an upright chair after reclining or lying supine for over a month? How was I going to manage to get dressed and undressed, or change positions in bed, without nursing assistance? How was I going to be able to step up and get in the shower?

Some neighbors knocked on the door to say hi and check in. I was so tired from the effort of just walking inside that all I could do was say a few polite words and then ask for their understanding in just letting me rest. They were happy to see me. I was happy to see them too, but any elation I felt about that was quickly displaced by the realization of my new reality. I was suffering badly, and as I looked ahead, I had no idea how I was going to make the adjustment to going home for good, just a week later. I was overwhelmed, anxious, and very scared.

I couldn't imagine making the change away from all the support mechanisms at the hospital to living at home. I couldn't imagine giving up things like an adjustable bed, page-able nurses, overhead television, or food brought to my room, let alone the touch-tone access I had available to reach any one of my providers—doctors, nurses, therapists, and ancillary support personnel. Coming home felt like another difficult episode of "starting over."

I did manage to spend the entire night, but it was difficult. I slept in my usual bed—no hospital bed or special assistance to raise and lower my body; no bed rails to grip and help myself up. It was just a flat, king-sized bed. I slept poorly, more challenged than usual, because sitting up to swing my legs over the edge of the bed in order to urinate into the bottles proved more difficult than I imagined. My core muscles had weakened considerably, and I was in a lot of pain, more so than I remembered at the hospital.

I mostly just lay in bed, drifting in and out, but never falling asleep. Diane didn't sleep well that night either, tuned in to every sound or motion I made. I was too proud at the time to ask for help, mistakenly thinking that doing so was a sign of weakness and dependence, and I wasn't going to go there. I struggled.

Diane and I talked the next day about my fears of coming home and my anxiety about how on earth we were going to make this work. I told her my night at home reminded me of when Kevin was about six months old. Like me, as a toddler he had struggled with skin rashes, colic, and allergies. Most nights in his initial months were broken up with one or more of Kevin's needs.

I reminded Diane of a morning when we got up after a particularly long night with Kevin and remarked, "I think I've reached a new level of exhaustion." The Sunday morning at home after my overnight experiment felt exactly the same. I was spent.

I returned to HMC that morning, anxious to reconnect with the safety of my routine and the familiar faces of the people who cared for me. I was happy to be back in the hospital but discouraged at the prospects of what lay ahead. I didn't know if I would be able to do it. I had the opportunity to take another overnight home visit a few days later, but I came up with an excuse not to do it. I didn't like how I felt at home and was in no hurry to repeat the suffering.

Finally, however, the big day arrived—Friday, July 20, 2007. It was time to be fully discharged, five weeks and one day from the time I had been rushed to the ER at HMC. Strangely enough, the rehab unit at HMC had come to feel like my new home in this new life, and now I had to transfer this new life back to my old home.

My feelings about going home were mixed. I was proud that I had accomplished so much, especially regaining my ability to walk, as well as becoming increasingly independent. I had a strong recovery trajectory in progress, and that was rare in SCI cases. At the same time, I was sad and terribly worried about being able to successfully make the transition to living at home again.

I said good-bye to my inpatient doctors, residents, nurses, and therapists, feeling not emotional but uneasy. I had to sign some discharge papers at the nursing station—the first time I was putting my crude signature to official use. It wasn't very legible, and I could barely grip the pen, but it was more than an "X."

Wheeled out to the car, I was helped into the front seat of the Ford Explorer. It was a difficult process just to pull my legs up into the car and get seated, but I managed to do it on my own, refusing offers of help. There was no turning back now.

It was a fairly short trip, but once we pulled into our driveway, and then got out of the car, I began to feel overwhelmed. I used a walker to move from the car to the house. I didn't use the walker much after that, feeling frustrated that I had to use it at all, but Diane insisted that in the first few days at home we would err on the side of caution.

As I walked up to our house that day, everything hurt, and I felt like I was moving in slow motion. The last time I had been home—besides the one overnight a week earlier—was in early June, before the accident. Back then I had been strong, energetic, and whole. Now I wasn't.

The whole thing was a big shock to my system, especially knowing I was home for good. It took a while to adjust to being in new surroundings and not having the attentive hospital staff around me to tend to my every need. The bed at home was just a flat, normal bed, same as before, without the convenient features of an electronic hospital bed. Consequently, all my movements had to be different.

Instead of eating sitting upright in bed in rehab, now I had to muster the energy to move to the kitchen, sit on a chair, and feed myself. I didn't expect it to be so utterly exhausting; after all, I had been in top physical form a mere five weeks earlier. I couldn't reconcile the chasm between the two versions of myself.

There had been discussion about renting a hospital bed when I went home and using it while my body continued to recover, but I dismissed the idea. I was determined to find a way to make living back at home work, on my own terms, without assistance or accommodation. Surrendering to aid or help felt like I would be going backward, heading down a slippery slope that once started, I would never be able to get off of.

In retrospect, while that mind-set was where my head was at the time, my fears about some things were misplaced. Asking for aid or assistance would have been the right thing to do and wouldn't have compromised my determination to become independent. Instead, the aid would have saved me strength and stamina to apply to other aspects of my recovery.

After I got home, I had a persistent pain in the middle of my back, like there was some kind of subluxation in my spine. It bothered me constantly, whether I was sitting up or lying down. It hurt less when I stood, but standing came with its own misery, so I didn't stand much, unless I was moving to a different place, or doing exercises.

At my request, Diane had coordinated with some work colleagues to set up our back room as an exercise room, with a stretch mat, stationary upright bike, treadmill—even a stationary road bike setup, using my "B" bike attached to a CycleOps "cyclops" unit that allows you to convert a real road bike to a stationary bike. (The B bike is usually a cyclist's "backup" bike, used for rainy days or otherwise inclement weather.)

I used the room from time to time, but as the weeks progressed—with the intense appointment schedule that I was determined to keep—there wasn't much left in my tank to use in the home exercise room. I did use it at times, most often lying down on the stretch mat to see if I could work out the annoying kink in my back. One of my therapists gave me a small foam roller, perhaps two inches in diameter, and I would lie on the firm object, placing it where the pain point in my back would press against it.

At first, I couldn't do this without experiencing sheer agony, so I tried an even more benign setup. I used a small washcloth gently rolled up and placed under my back instead. Even that was a struggle for several weeks, but eventually I was able to tolerate the rolled-up cloth, and then later the foam roller. I never could get the painful kink out of my middle back. I kept longing for someone to give me a back adjustment.

During these initial weeks following my discharge in fall 2007, things got so exasperating that at one point my wife called Dr. LeiLei at HMC inpatient rehab and asked if there was any way I could be readmitted to the inpatient rehab unit again. Diane told her about the struggles I was having and implored the doctor to take me back.

I wanted to go back. Home life wasn't working. I was overwhelmed and needed more support.

Dr. LeiLei explained that everyone who is discharged from inpatient rehab goes through this same adjustment period, some more pronounced than others, and she encouraged me to stay with the program. She said that I would gradually adjust, build strength and stamina, and things would settle down. The truth was, I didn't think I could make the transition. I hated feeling weak and incapable. Dr. LeiLei gave us no choice—suck it up and work through it. Everyone else does.

And so did I. I worked through this initial setback. The transition to living at home was more daunting than I had imagined. Looking back, I'm not sure where I harnessed the willpower and energy to do everything I did in those first couple of months following my discharge. It exhausts me now just thinking about it.

. . .

Once I got back home, I was pushing at every opportunity. I never rested; in fact, I considered it an important challenge not to rest. I still had Dr. Barry's words in the back of my head that the bulk of recovery happens in the first six months post injury, and I felt a strong sense of urgency to go all out.

Every day I was at home I was either fully scheduled with therapy appointments and doctor checkups or doing my homework exercises. These included writing, walking, balancing, stretching, and practicing various fine motor skill exercises—from trying to tie my shoelaces, to dressing by myself, to being able to stand up in the shower the entire time without sitting down.

I worked on sit-to-stand exercises so I wouldn't have to continue using a raised toilet seat. I had social calls with friends. I tried to keep up my appetite, which still hadn't returned. I spent hours trying to work on various upright balance exercises.

During this time, the pain was intense, especially when I was on my feet. I forced myself to stop taking any pain medicine, even over-the-counter NSAIDs and analgesics like Tylenol, Aleve, ibuprofen, and aspirin. I had whittled my pills down to two—both for my bowel program—which were nonprescription.

I was able to do this for two months. Like not resting, I felt it was important to gaining independence not to have to depend on pills, which prior to the accident I had done my best to avoid, except in rare circumstances.

I didn't want my body numbed or enabled by medicines. I wanted to be able to hear my body without the mask of pills. While noble in concept, this choice was not in my best interest. I remember a very specific conversation I had with my outpatient OT, Beth, when I told her all the activities I was doing at home. She had some very prophetic words to share with me.

"Jamie," she said, "there are four very important words I want you to remember and apply in your recovery—planning, prioritization, preparation, and pacing. In your case, the most important word is pacing." She went on to explain what she meant by each of these words, and here is what I took away, although in retrospect, it took some time before I fully understood their application and how I should have applied these much sooner in my daily living.

Planning—For patients like me with spinal cord injury, either complete or incomplete, life moves more slowly. Everything takes more time by a factor of two to three, perhaps more. It affects everything—morning hygiene, getting dressed, eating meals, transport to and from appointments, travel, everything. The key is to take the time to plan out the events of the day, before the day starts, and not commit to doing too much. My plate was going to be plenty full just dealing with symptoms, let alone appointments and transportation. I needed to take the time to think ahead and plan the day with a reasonable amount of activity as well as rest time.

Prioritization—This segues to the process of putting activities in order, from most to least important. Not everything is priority one. I needed to take the time to sort out the "must haves" from the "good to have, but not required," the "nice to have if time permits," and the "totally optional" (i.e., fit it in if I have the energy, but cumulatively won't push me over the edge). At first everything was priority one. It took me until early 2008, almost a whole year post injury, before I finally began to apply this discipline.

Preparation—Everything I needed to do required preparation. For example, getting ready for bed required a number of preparatory steps, including making sure that urine bottles were cleaned and on my night table, teeth were brushed and flossed, medications taken, water glass filled and on the night table, a "catch" cloth placed on the bed in case of bladder or bowel accidents, neck collar gently removed and cleaned, toes lightly massaged and oiled, skin cream applied to dry skin, and skin checked for sores. Sometimes I ended with a nighttime prayer, to say thanks for allowing me to do the day.

Pacing—This was the most difficult discipline to apply and the most important. After a traumatic injury, the spinal cord remains in a state of shock, called "spinal shock," for up to a year. At a cellular level, the spinal cord cells, nerves, neurons, and synapses are trying to reorganize in such a way as to reestablish reflexes and functions impaired below the level of injury.

I know now why I didn't fully absorb these words' importance at the time. I was impatient. I wanted results, now. I felt like the six-month clock was ticking quickly and if I didn't maximize effort now, I wouldn't have a chance later.

This is a very formative time during the recovery process, and it requires a huge investment of physical and mental energy. When physical rehab and other activities are layered upon this spinal shock period, the need for pacing is even more important to avoid experiencing regression or even a substantial setback. Pacing requires listening to the body and paying close attention to the subtle cues it is sending.

As a multisport athlete, I didn't have a good history of listening to my body, especially when it was craving rest. When I was playing a lot of tournament squash in the 1980s and 1990s, I often was on the court six to seven days a week. Squash can be an intense, aerobic and even anaerobic sport, with lots of irregular movements.

I can remember times when my body would fatigue from playing so much, and my performance would decline. There were days when I played poorly for no other reason than being tired. My body was screaming for rest. What did I do? Just the opposite. I fatigued myself more.

After a poorly played match, I would go outside SAC and do wind sprints up and down the block of a very steep street, Virginia Street, with perhaps a twenty-degree gradient, doing up to ten repeats until my legs couldn't move. What I didn't know was that my body was screaming "rest," and I was punishing myself with even harder work.

This was a misplaced mind-set, which took me some time to overcome. When I took up cycling in the late nineties, I had the good fortune to be mentored by my cycling friend, Ben, who taught me several things—one of them being the importance of rest days. He said that I would get the biggest investment payback from my hard training by taking rest days periodically, especially when I felt sluggish. I applied this, and it worked.

However, when I was in the initial months of post injury and feeling a high sense of urgency to push harder with rehab, this advice on pacing went out the window, and I fell into old habits. If I was feeling weak, I pushed even harder.

By November 2007, five months post injury, my failure to follow these disciplines caught up with me. It nearly cost me my life—a second time.

CHAPTER 10

The Second Crash

After I had been home for a while, I started to take short walks in the neighborhood. My goal was to be able to walk around our neighborhood circle, which was one kilometer in length. I started gradually, walking with a single-pronged cane. The walk was flat with little through traffic other than our neighbors.

On one walk, I had gone about two hundred yards, keeping to the side of the road, when I looked up ahead to my right and noticed a lady getting into her car. Her driveway was a short, straight distance to the road where I was walking. Approaching her driveway, I wondered briefly whether she saw me or if I should stop and wait for her to back out. I assumed she saw me and kept walking.

I was about halfway across her driveway when she started backing out, and suddenly, it became clear she hadn't seen me. The trunk of the car was just about to hit me when I lifted my cane and smacked her trunk with it several times. She immediately came to a stop. I wasn't hit, but the motion of swinging my cane threw me off balance, and I stumbled backward, on the very edge of falling.

At that time, I was still wearing the Miami J cervical collar to stabilize my neck. The last thing I needed was to fall and retraumatize that area. Fortunately, I didn't fall. The neighbor got out of her car. I didn't recognize her, but she apologized and asked if she could help. Too proud to say how unnerved I was, I said no, collected my wits, and started my slow shuffling walk back home.

When I got back to the house, I went inside and I sat down on a couch, my heart thumping wildly, and I began to sob. *Why had I taken such a chance? Why had I assumed the driver had seen me, when I easily could have stopped and waited for her to back out first? What would have happened if the car had struck me?*

It had been a close call and a hard, but important, lesson. On every walk I have taken since that time, I am acutely aware of everything around me—cars, bicycles, pedestrians—and especially anything I can hear coming up behind me.

That close call, however, didn't impact my resolve at all to continue to take walks or continue the daily fight to get better. It did, however, make me more fearful and cautious. It impacted me emotionally and manifested itself over the next two and a half years as I became reluctant to push the envelope or go outside of my comfort zone.

There were exercises I wouldn't consider doing during those first three post-injury years, because I was afraid of setting myself back. I did not want in any way to lose the hard-won gains I had made.

I also became more cautious about what I was willing to do and not to do in PT. For example, I was afraid to use a Styrofoam roller to try to stretch and strengthen my back, for fear that it would cause my muscles to seize and cramp. I was reluctant at the time to try the elliptical machine, afraid it would put too much strain on my interior thigh muscles and further constrain walking. I avoided stretching my legs in certain positions, like lying on the edge of a bed and letting one leg dangle off the edge to stretch the psoas muscle.

Frankly, I didn't trust myself. Short and sweet—I didn't want to get hurt again.

. . .

After going home from HMC, the plan going forward was to use the outpatient rehab facilities at the hospital for PT, OT, and any mental health counseling I needed. I decided to forego the mental health counseling—which later proved to be a mistake—and stayed with PT and OT in the Comprehensive Outpatient Rehabilitation Program (CORP). I attended sessions for several months, a couple of times of week.

I always felt terrible during sessions, especially because it meant being on my feet for longer periods of time. The sensation of standing was terrible; my body felt like there were vertical g-forces pushing me into the ground, and pain laced through every part of me. I felt like I had a climbing harness around my waist, pulling up hard against my groin and private areas. With every step I took, my muscles groaned, pushing against the resistance of the involuntary seizing and constriction in my legs. Fear was always in the back of my mind.

Despite these sensations, I pushed on. I was still highly motivated to get better. I even envisioned going on an annual bike ride in Maple Valley with my cycling comrades in the following month, August. Unfortunately, it didn't happen; I wasn't ready.

I augmented the treatments at CORP with a parade of other modalities outside of HMC. These included PT sessions, acupuncture, massage, reflexology, pool therapy, and cranial sacral therapy. In those initial months following my hospital discharge, there were times when I had eight to twelve appointments a week of one kind or another, as I aggressively pursued my recovery.

To improve my fine motor function, I worked on home exercises, everything from trying to shuffle cards to pressing each of my fingers in Silly Putty to improve their strength. I started writing a journal, not so much for content as for the practice of using my fingers to hold a pen and form letters. I spent an hour each morning trying to write at least one page, putting down whatever was on my mind.

Gradually my letters became better formed, and I could construct legible sentences. I kept practicing, and over a period of two years I filled up a couple of journal notebooks, all stemming from the goal of teaching myself how to write again. I also had a laptop that I used each day to practice finger movement as I learned to keyboard again.

For gross motor function recovery, I continued sit-to-stand exercises, increasing the number of reps, and continued with short walks outside. I did balance exercises that involved walking the hallway of our home without assistance, in a straight line.

For another balance exercise, I wedged a couple of books, about six inches in total height, up against the wall. I would stand a few inches in front of the book stack and practice lifting one foot off the ground and touching the top of the books with my toes, then bringing my foot back down to the floor, and I'd alternate, using the same motion with the other foot. As I gained more balance proficiency, I challenged myself by trying to do these movements more quickly, all while trying to maintain my balance.

The purpose of the exercise was to isolate certain muscle groups involved in walking, such as lifting one foot off the ground and maintaining balance on the other. Looking back, I better understand how important that seemingly benign balance check exercise was to my overall ability to walk. Before I was injured, I never thought about the mechanics of walking. I never thought about lifting my foot, or how I planted my feet on the ground, or bent my knees to do so. I just did it.

As time has passed since the injury, and especially as my walking has become more labored, I am mindful of every step I take and have to instruct myself in all aspects of walking. Nothing about walking happens naturally for me, without careful, conscious thought.

Another exercise involved simulated walking strides. The idea was to stand, spread my legs apart, one in front of the other, and rotate my weight forward and backward to elevate up on my front toes and then move my weight back to the foot behind. On one occasion during this exercise, I noticed my right hand starting to vibrate, involuntarily. It was the first time I had experienced involuntary movements, and it scared me. I didn't know why it had happened.

I had thought I was making great progress, and now I was experiencing some weird kind of tremor? I fought back a sudden panic. Perhaps I imagined it. The vibration subsided, and I tried to put it out of my head.

I had a follow-up visit with Dr. Jens in September 2007. He was very impressed with my progress, so much so that he brought several medical residents into the exam room so I could perform for them. He had me walk on my toes, and then my heels. He had me squat using one leg, crouching down into almost a seated position and raising myself back up again using my quad strength, with just enough limited assistance to check my balance. They were all impressed, and I was proud. I wanted to make Dr. Jens proud of me, and I think he was.

During this time, I wasn't working at my job, of course. Diane normally used her time to do volunteer work at a local thrift shop, did periodic caregiving for seniors, and frequently worked food lines at local homeless shelters. However, she committed all the time that was needed to be there to support me, care for me, and love me. She was incredibly generous with her time and always attentive to my needs.

My goal was to return to work within six months of the accident, or shortly before the end of December 2007. Looking back now, it seems overly ambitious, but I knew if I wasn't able to return to work within six months, I would have to go on long-term disability. Fortunately, I had policy coverage for this, but in my personal view, going on disability would mean I was a failure. So I put a lot of pressure on myself to meet or exceed my goal of being back to work as an IT director, my old position, before the end of 2007.

It didn't happen.

In early November 2007, I went out for a walk in my neighborhood. At this point, I had weaned myself off all prescription medicines and was on track to get back to work as planned. One of the walking exercises I was given was to take short steps and try to make quick stepping movements. I tried it for the first time toward the end of the walk, and suddenly my legs started to seize. I could barely move them. It was like they just locked up, and I almost fell over. Fortunately, I had my cane and was able to keep from falling.

I had never experienced anything like this before, and it completely freaked me out. How was it that I had worked my way back to being able to walk with a cane around our neighborhood block and now my legs were seizing up to the point that I couldn't move at all? I stopped for a moment, collected myself, took a few deep breaths, and tried to relax my body. I felt the muscle spasms subside to the point I could at least move my legs a little. I managed to labor my way back to the front door. Thankfully, I had been almost home when this happened.

The possibility of my recovery regressing unnerved me. I had no explanation for what had happened. I went to my room, lay on the floor, and did my usual stretch routine. I could feel tension in my lower extremities, and every movement seemed to be pushing against some unseen resistance. I became more and more anxious, and finally I got up with some difficulty and shuffled into the kitchen, where Diane was chatting with a friend. She asked how my walk went, and I said "fine" and then sat on a stool to try to collect myself.

As I sat there, my mind went to strange places, dark and worrisome places. I was unable to reconcile all the progress I had made and was making with the possibility of regressing. All I knew for sure is that I was feeling something new, something that seemed permanent and inconsistent with all the positive progress I had been making.

At the same time, I was unaware that "neurological spasticity" is often progressive in the first year post injury. In the fall of 2007, I had heard one of my outpatient HMC practitioners, Johanne Lewin, ARNP, use the term "neurological progression" but didn't know what she meant then. Now I know.

Spasticity in particular can be progressive as part of the healing process. I thought back to something that happened when I was staying in the "hotel room" at HMC. I awoke one morning to a strange new feeling in my ankles and feet, which subsided as soon as I sensed it. Then there was the unexpected hand vibration that occurred while I was doing the balance exercise at home. And now I'd had this episode of more pronounced spasticity symptoms when I tried to increase my stepping cadence. Because I had no knowledge of neurological spasticity, this progression was hard to understand.

My mind kept flashing back to an earlier conversation with Dr. Jens in the hospital. "A strong recovery begets an even stronger recovery," he had said. I couldn't make sense of this seizing episode. I was searching for an explanation, and all I could come up with were questions.

How was it that I seemed to be going backward? Why was I regressing? I had never heard anything up to that point about the possibility of things getting worse. *Had I done something wrong and caused other damage inside my spinal cord?* I couldn't get my head wrapped around these questions, and at that moment, sitting in the kitchen, I couldn't come up with an explanation.

I remembered that I'd had an appointment earlier that day with a chiropractor. I had felt like all that was needed to diminish the stubborn pain in my middle back was a brief chiropractic adjustment to my mid-thoracic region. So I went to see my chiropractor, someone I had seen many times before my injury and fully trusted. I had also consulted with Dr. Barry several weeks before about seeking chiropractic treatment for my mid-back pain. He had consented to let me do it as long as there was (a) no thrusting motion and (b) no treatment near the cervical area where my injury was located.

My chiropractor followed the directions I gave him very carefully, applying pressure in the problematic region to try to release my painful back tension. I don't remember coming out of that treatment feeling any better, but I didn't feel any worse either. Everything had felt the same: no new symptoms, no unusual tingling.

As I sat on the kitchen stool replaying that treatment session in my mind, I couldn't find any connection between it and the new symptoms I was feeling. I didn't know for sure if anything had changed inside my body, of course, but my intuition said likely, not. There was, however, still a small voice of uncertainty.

So I started a downward spiral. The more I tried to deal with the situation by attempting to power my way through, the worse the symptoms became. It became more difficult to take walks. I struggled to move my legs. Soon I abandoned the walks because they had become too difficult.

Even walking from the living room to the bathroom became a monumental effort. What was going on?

I was reluctant early on to speak with my practitioners about the situation because I felt embarrassed. I took pride in the progress I had been making, and I knew they were proud too. I didn't want to let them down by reporting I was sliding backward. Perhaps all of this would pass, I reasoned, just as the hand vibration incident had.

But this new situation didn't pass; in fact, it got a lot worse.

This sudden regression continued through November and well into December. I was still going to CORP for therapy, and my therapists could see I was struggling. They tried to calm my anxiety but to no avail. Suddenly, I was having difficulty doing exercises that had come easily just a few weeks before. I tried to disguise my worry by saying I had strained some muscles in my legs and that it would pass. This regression compounded my anxiety, which subsequently turned into depression.

It has taken a lot of reflection over the years to get it clear in my mind why exactly this change in symptoms and depression suddenly happened, especially after such a strong initial recovery. The fears I battled after my accident had been overwhelming. I was afraid—afraid of letting myself down by not accomplishing the unrealistic goal I had of getting back to work full-time within six months, before my FMLA benefits ran out.

My doctors were so proud of my progress, and I worried that they would see me as a failure, someone who had started out strong but couldn't sustain it. This went against everything I was, everything I believed.

I was afraid of failing in my quest to avoid going on long-term disability benefits. I was afraid of losing my position of IT director. I was afraid of failing my boss and coworkers, who were all rooting for me to return to work and inspired by my recovery to that point. I was afraid of failing myself.

My ego and unrealistic ambition had become impediments, causing me to push myself too hard, thinking that I could gut my way through this recovery the same way I would grind through a 120-mile double-metric century ride. As a result of my fears, I hadn't paced myself as my OT, Beth, had recommended, and I was flooded with a new kind of fear that I didn't know how to process.

I wish now that I had approached the situation more aggressively by seeking mental health treatment right then and there. What I needed at this time was a skilled professional to work with me. I desperately needed intensive mental health counseling, especially in the areas of fear, failure, ego, ambition, unrealistic expectations, and the "neurological progression" of spinal cord injury.

If I could go back and do some things differently, seeking out professional mental health help, immediately after being discharged from HMC, would be at the top of the list.

I had never been depressed in my life, and experiencing it for the first time worried me even more. It made me question everything. *What happened?* I kept asking myself. *Why am I going backward? What about all the hard work I've put in? Am I going to make it back to work by the end of year, as I expected?*

At home, not only had my walks stopped, but also I stopped doing everything. I stopped going to CORP. I stopped seeing other practitioners. I stopped all interventions. I became reclusive and confined myself to home. As a result, my pain levels went way up. Everything I did—sitting, standing, lying down—hurt worse than ever. I was suffering, distraught, and depressed.

November and early December 2007 crawled by. I found myself confined to the couch recliner and became a clock-watcher. At breakfast, I got out of bed, limped to the kitchen, and forced down some food. From there I would shuffle twenty feet to the recliner and spend the rest of the day there, only getting up to use the bathroom or have lunch or dinner at the kitchen table. After dinner, I would return to the living room recliner again, waiting until 9 p.m. when it was time to make my way back to bed.

My depression got worse. I felt like I was in a bottomless pit, falling, falling, and hoping someone or something would catch me. I was frightened. My mind began to fill with very dark thoughts, and for the first time since my ordeal began, I didn't want to live anymore. *It's not worth the fight.* I told myself. *I worked so hard only to have this happen, so why bother?*

I felt hopeless, worthless, and useless. I felt the deepest sense of loss I have ever felt in my life, like everything had been reset, and every accomplishment in my life had disappeared. I was just occupying space, doing nothing. I felt like a failure in my recovery, as if all the hard work, appointments, exercises, walks, and treatments had all been for naught. It was as though the fast-forward button had been pressed on my aging process and I was now thirty years older. I felt suddenly old and decrepit.

All at once I felt like I was suffocating in the misery of this relentless and worsening injury. I knew now that there was no way out. I felt very alone, paralyzed by my depression as much as by my injuries. I began to go to dark places in my mind, ultimately planning my suicide. *How might I end my life? What would be the least painful and quickest method to end it?*

CHAPTER 11

Catastrophic Living

My thinking had become circular. The more I obsessed, the deeper into darkness I went, and the deeper I went, the more obsessed I became with taking my own life. One night, as I contemplated my feelings of despair, my mind drifted back to an experience I'd had in the 1980s. I closed my eyes, remembering.

I loved to ski, having grown up in a skiing family. I had participated in the sport my whole life and had the good fortune to ski some of the most magnificent ski areas in the United States and around the world. In 1983, I had the opportunity to partner with some friends, and my sister Molly, and go on a helicopter skiing trip to British Columbia, Canada. The trip was organized by Canadian Mountain Holidays (CMH) and was based out of the village of Valemount, adjacent to the Bugaboo and Cariboo Mountain ranges.

Heli-skiing, as it is often called, is the ultimate experience for many advanced skiers. It is a kind of holy grail event, a journey to skiing's ultimate destination. After receiving special instructions on how to wear and use an electronic transponder (everyone was required to wear one in case of an avalanche), we boarded the helicopter, which was parked just adjacent to the motel where we were staying. We were then whisked high up into the rugged peaks of the Cariboo range.

The chopper carried about eight to ten skiers, and our skis and poles were placed in steel-rimmed baskets attached to the outside of the aircraft. The chopper took us up to a drop-off point several thousand feet above the valley floor. We all jumped out, grabbed our gear, and, under the direction of a guide, followed his lead through the finest untracked powder conditions imaginable. A number of factors—including prevailing wind direction, snow stability, quality of surface snow, sun, and planned pickup point—determine where the chopper drops a group.

The plan was for the group to descend two thousand to four thousand feet to the pickup point, so that the chopper could pick us up and repeat the process. Usually a group is taken to another drop-off point. Depending on conditions, we might get the opportunity to ski wide-open glaciers, or weave in and out of the trees, or both. All skiing is in untracked conditions, usually through one to two feet of "fluffy" snow, which creates a rooster tail of snow behind the skier. It's almost like the water plume created by a water skier weaving back and forth behind a motorboat. It is epic.

Everything had been great on this trip; my friends and my sister and I were enjoying the opportunity to be together, doing something we loved. It was day six of a seven-day trip, with exceptional snow conditions the entire week. This day was no different.

Until I was caught and buried in an avalanche.

I had been skiing down a steep, narrow chute when I heard yelling and a lot of rumbling noises. All the commotion behind me prompted a brief look over my shoulder to see what was happening. A tidal wave of snow was coming straight at me! I looked down at my skis and could see the snow start to accelerate past my legs. The next thing I remember is being engulfed by cold and darkness and tumbling in a churning mass of large ice chunks and frozen debris. I thought I was going to die.

What would it be like to no longer be alive? I wondered, as I was being pulled down into this churning mass. My breath came in harsh gasps, and I knew it was likely that these would be the last few breaths I would ever take. My survival instincts kicked in, and I squelched those thoughts and tried to move my arms in a swimming motion, to see if I could dig to the surface.

I wasn't strong enough. Suddenly, the churning mass of darkness started to slow down, and I could feel the ice chunks start to squeeze in all around me. Before everything came to a stop, I managed to get my hands in front of my face to make a small pocket of air. I knew I had just a few minutes before my breath, as little as I could take in, would freeze the snow around my face and create a frozen pocket. Within a few minutes, I would be suffocating.

I was held motionless in the cold, and everything was strangely still. The ice and snow pressed in on me, squeezing and constraining my movement. There was no way out. I was going to die.

And then—after what felt like an eternity, but was only a few minutes—I heard voices above me, and someone was digging through the frozen snow. Soon an air passageway appeared in front of my face and I could breathe! After that, I was excavated from the icy tomb in which I was buried to learn that fellow skiers on the surface had been able to quickly locate me using their electronic transponders.

I survived the avalanche for a couple of reasons. The width of the avalanche was a few hundred yards wide and the fracture point where it broke loose was over ten feet high. It turned out that I'd come to rest on one side of the avalanche debris field where the ice chunks were smaller. In the middle of the avalanche, the ice chunks were as big as cars, and if I had ended up there, I would have been crushed.

I found out later that the avalanche had also buried another member of our group. The rest of our group was on the surface, away from the debris field. All had their transponders on and were trained to use them. They were able to quickly locate me and the other buried member of our group, who, coincidentally, ended up within a few feet of me.

The avalanche was snow chunks only. Often avalanches take out rocks and trees, and a person commingled in such a churning mess is often crushed. We had been hit by a relatively slow-moving avalanche, which allowed me to maintain consciousness. Because I wasn't knocked out, I was able to put my hands in front of my face, creating a small pocket of air, which bought me a little time and kept me from being immediately asphyxiated.

I was very lucky. I had to be airlifted off the mountain. It took a month for my nerves to quiet down. I did return two years later, with a $1 million life insurance policy, courtesy of my wife's insistence. This time there was plenty of excitement, but fortunately, not from any avalanches.

I opened my eyes. Now, twenty-four years later, I was lying on the recliner, lost, motionless, still, suffocating—just like during those moments after the avalanche when I was buried three feet under the surface. I felt completely helpless.

The difference this time was that I was trapped in depression, and in my own body, with no way out. This time I couldn't even try to dig myself out. Back in 1983, my ski friends had rescued me. Who would rescue me now?

My wife was distraught as she watched me completely unravel. This was new for her. She had never seen me so despondent. I was crumbling. Resourceful person that she is, she found a spiritual healer through a friend in Rochester, New York. I wasn't very excited about talking to a spiritual healer, but I had several phone conversations with a lady named Carla over the course of several weeks.

"I can tell you are suicidal," she said to me, in one of our earlier conversations. It didn't make me feel any better to have Carla validate what I wanted to deny, but there it was. I was suicidal. I don't recall the content of our conversations, but I suppose just the process of talking is what eventually convinced me to reach out to Dr. Barry for medical help. In early December, I went in to see him, and I was a sobbing mess.

"Am I going to be all right?" I asked, with tears streaming down my face.

In his calm, supportive manner he reassured me, "Yes, you will be."

I looked at him closely, examining his body language for any sign that would cause me to doubt what he was saying. It was a watershed moment for me; not just because my tears were flowing, but also because I had a desperate need to know if this slide I was on could be reversed. I was feeling so fragile, vulnerable, and frightened.

But his eyes told me what I needed to know. I really was going to be okay. I'll never forget that moment. He, along with many others, helped save my life. I know now that it was a village that rescued me, especially family, friends, and practitioners.

As we talked, Dr. Barry explained that physically I was experiencing severe neurological spasticity, a very common consequence of spinal cord injury. Muscles seize, constrict, and move involuntarily, which can be triggered by many different things—changes in temperature, physical movement, even by how I think and breathe. Spasticity varies considerably from patient to patient.

Dr. Barry put me on a cocktail of new medicines, including several muscle relaxants for spasticity—baclofen, tizanadine, and diazepam. For neuropathic pain he prescribed gabapentin. For depression, bupropion. For other chronic pain symptoms he prescribed methadone and oxycodone.

He also recommended a different physical and occupational therapist from a company based in Seattle called Pacific Balance & Rehabilitation. The practitioners, Chris (PT) and Chris (OT), work primarily with patients with vestibular or inner ear issues but are also very experienced in neurological therapy. He also recommended pool therapy and seeking out a mental health counselor.

Why didn't I seek mental health care before I reached this "second crash"? My recollection is that while I was hospitalized, mental health care services were provided on an initial basis. I remember a counselor coming in to talk to me a few times in the early days. As inpatient rehab got going, another mental health practitioner, Dr. Charles Bombardier, PhD, came and talked to me a few times, and he also talked to Diane and me together. I think I visited with him on an outpatient basis once or twice, but his focus was on treating me as an inpatient only. He might have given us the names of a few mental health therapists to consult if we needed them.

I don't remember being encouraged to get into therapy. I think this was because they thought, from the inpatient caregiver group sessions I had every week, that mentally I was in a good place. I was making strong progress at that time, weaning myself off medications, and heavily focusing on regaining physicality.

On this first visit, the worst news Dr. Barry had for me was that I wasn't ready to go back to work and wouldn't be for another several months. This meant I would have to go on long-term disability. I had failed to reach my goal of getting back to work by December 2007.

Later, I gained a better perspective on my unrealistic expectations when I did a joint presentation with Dr. Barry at a medical conference organized by Dr. Jens and some of his colleagues at HMC. The top national orthopedic and research specialists in the area of spinal cord injury attended the conference, which was held at HMC in the fall of 2008.

During Dr. Barry's presentation, he showed a chart with the percentage of SCI patients that return to work post injury. Fewer than ten percent return to work within five years, and around forty percent return within twenty-five years. The other sixty percent don't return to work, and most rely on government support. Here I had been on this overly ambitious march to return to work within six months. Seeing that chart and hearing his explanation helped me put much of my behavior and thought process into the proper perspective.

At the time, however, not being able to go back to work was devastating. Going back on prescription medications also felt like a huge setback in my recovery. I had worked so hard to get off medications when I was discharged, and now it was like starting all over again. Mentally, this was a huge hurdle to get over. I hate medications. I hate the idea of having to be dependent on them. Taking them went counter to my goal of being independent.

Perhaps this was part of the denial I needed to overcome. I was, in fact, quadriplegic. I had a severe spinal cord injury, and with that diagnosis comes a range of residual deficits. Some of these deficits require medicinal treatment.

I stayed with the oxycodone and methadone for a couple of weeks. It was a disaster. My weight dropped fifteen pounds from 165 to 150. I felt awful, disoriented, and had a complete loss of appetite and a plugged up gastro system. Finally I called Dr. Barry back and said I was stopping the two opiate painkillers. I told him I would find some way to deal with the chronic pain with over-the-counter analgesics and NSAIDs (nonsteroidal anti-inflammatory drugs)—Tylenol, Aleve, Advil, or aspirin—but would not be taking narcotics again. I stayed with the other medications, and that remains true today.

Even though I was in a deep depression, I didn't seek mental health therapy for another six months, until June 2008. It was a mistake to wait that long, and I should have sought treatment as soon as I hit bottom. In fact, I should have started treatment when I had been discharged several months earlier, but I thought seeking out that kind of help was a sign of weakness. My mistake was in thinking that I could muscle my way through it alone.

There were elements of denial in my thinking, in the sense that I knew I was injured but thought I would be whole again. I knew I had a spinal cord injury. I knew it was serious, knew I had paralysis and impaired function, but at the same time, I knew years of fitness, conditioning, and intense training hadn't been suddenly erased.

Asking for help, especially for mental health treatment, felt like surrendering, and I had refused to give in to what I viewed as weakness. Giving in meant being dependent on someone else, and I was determined to get independent. Acknowledging my weakness would mean I wasn't capable, and I wasn't going to let myself go there.

I refused to even consider the possibility that I couldn't succeed, even if it meant going it alone. I was not going to give in. My thoughts were misguided, but I didn't know it at the time. I needed help, but I wasn't getting it just yet.

. . .

I received many small gifts—cards, printed emails, a CD player, some electronic games, board games, CDs, and a few audio and paperback books—during my first few months at home after being discharged from the hospital. These items were placed on our dining room table and just stayed there while I was consumed with regaining as much physicality as possible.

As time progressed through the fall of 2007, one day, after my "second crash" and slow climb out of deep depression, as I shuffled past the dining room table, a book caught my eye. It was called *Full Catastrophe Living* by Jon Kabat-Zinn. I'm not sure why I decided to pick it up this time. I think I had avoided it before because it looked like a long book, and I didn't like the word "catastrophe."

The word was telling me something I didn't want to be reminded of—I was impaired, my life turned upside down, and I would have to find a way to live and cope differently now. It was telling me that I had to do something different, and up to that point I had held on to the misplaced notion that someday, things were going to be the same again.

They weren't.

I didn't read the whole book. I skimmed sections of it. What stood out to me in what I read was how I could alter my symptoms, and perhaps my healing, by changing the way my mind was behaving. I had been living everywhere except in the moment. I had been looking back, thinking of what life had been like—walking without thinking, hiking trails, cycling to work, skiing the steeps at my favorite ski areas, running around the basketball court with my daughter, fixing things around the house, or going to the office.

At the same time, I had been fixated on the future, getting my life back, getting back to normal, feeling a strong sense of urgency, and pushing, pushing, pushing, thinking I would be back riding with my comrades on the lunch ride before long.

There is a quote from Kabat-Zinn's book that deeply resonated with me:

> Whatever we have experienced and survived, whether it took the form of a big T-trauma, or little t-trauma, our body, our mind, and our heart, which only *seem* separate, constitute a profound resource for healing. If we listen

carefully to the body, it can teach us a great deal about what is most difficult for us to recognize and come to terms with from the past, and how we might approach our hurt with kindness and wisdom. It has a great deal to teach us about stress and pain, illness and health, and about suffering and the possibility of freeing ourselves from suffering. Mindfulness is a key ingredient in approaching and nurturing what is deepest and best and forever unharmed within ourselves.[3]

I thought about this quote and other sections of the book, which expound on being completely in the moment, alive, with a keen sense of interconnectedness and wholeness. *What if I tried to slow things down, take more notice of what was going on around me? What if I paid closer attention to my body, my thoughts, my organs, and all the intricate connections that make living a day possible? What if I thought about the distressing pain in my back and the complex web of fibers, ligaments, tendons, and other muscle groups attached to my spine?*

What if I took closer notice of the sounds and smells surrounding me as I walked around our neighborhood? What if I just let my mind throttle back and idle, cleansed of all the distractions, and just focused on a healing beam of light coming from the heavens, healing the damage in my spinal cord? What if I paid very careful attention to all my movements, whether I was standing, sitting, walking, or exercising?

My hope in all this was to focus positive and healing energy toward these areas. I wanted to be intentional about clearing my mind of the day-to-day clutter. If I could be more measured in my thought process, I felt I could bring healing to the injured areas of my body, which was just about everywhere.

I didn't just flip a switch and suddenly become a polished, mindful person. I did, however, begin a journey in early 2008 of becoming more

....

3   Jon Kabat-Zinn, *Full Catastrophe Living* (New York: Delta, 2007), 186.

present, both inside myself and in my surroundings. I remember taking a walk, a one-kilometer loop, something I was doing on a daily basis at that time around my neighborhood.

It was spring 2008, the flowers were in bloom, there was pollen in the air, I felt a slight breeze, and the sky was dotted with scattered clouds. I remember the day vividly. This was the walk when I said to myself, "Jamie, clear your mind and take notice of everything in this moment."

I did. As I started my walk, I listened intently. I heard birds chirping, a slight wind was audible to my ears, distant jackhammering noises were coming from construction at the nearby high school, and a helicopter momentarily flying overhead drowned everything else out. I felt my heart rate accelerate from the intensity of these noises, and my body began to seize up, sensing fear; I stopped to take some deep breaths, making a conscious thought to exhale the anxiousness that had momentarily gripped me. My legs muscles relaxed.

I took several more deep breaths, feeling my chest expand, thankful that I could breathe, and aware of the oxygen cleansing my lungs as I exhaled. I stood still for another moment as the helicopter passed. The jackhammer noises had stopped. Things became very still. I turned around and looked at my house. I had only walked about twenty yards.

I looked intently at my favorite tree in the yard, a Japanese maple. My mind drifted back twenty years ago to the day we had bought the house and moved in. I thought of how grateful I was to have listened to my wife and decided to buy this house, in terrible condition then but in a perfect location. I thought about all the work that had been done on it. There had been so many improvements; I would be hard-pressed to identify one nook or cranny that hadn't been touched. I remembered in the first six months of owning the home that we had torn up the entire front yard and had it completely relandscaped. The signature item for me then had been the Japanese maple.

The tree had grown so much over the past twenty years, its leaves bathed in maroon, one my favorite colors besides blue. I was totally in the moment, lost in thought, dialed in, appreciative, and feeling a strong sense of connection—to my surroundings, my home, my family, and myself. For those brief moments, the constant, distressing, chronic pain had taken a backseat.

I became aware of my legs seizing again, this time from standing still. Instead of trying to move them when they weren't ready, I took several more deep breaths. I envisioned myself as part of my breath and traveled inside my body, down through my lungs, spreading into my torso, and then into each leg, gently massaging them from the inside, letting them both know that it was okay to let go. Then I returned my thoughts to the outside, snapped back mentally to where I was standing, and slowly the seizing subsided enough so that I could shuffle my way back home.

Another day, I was doing my daily stretch routine at the base of our bed in the master bedroom. I was lying on my stomach, perched on my elbows. This was a common stretch I did to arch my lower back and counter the waist-bent position of sitting. While in this position, my mind drifted, and I tried to put myself in a totally-in-the-moment place, with all my other thoughts and feelings displaced as I focused on the here and now.

I could hear myself breathe. I could feel the slight strain of muscles in my lower back as they stretched while arching. I could feel the rug underneath my torso and my elbows. I sensed the position of my neck, careful to keep it in a neutral position by not looking up or down too much. I formed the picture in my mind of a light beam and visualized it emanating from the heavens, aimed directly at me, specifically at the location of the injury in my spinal cord. I imagined this beam of light containing healing energy, like a surgical laser dissolving the damaged area and restoring it to its original condition.

As I pictured this with great clarity, I felt warmth at the base of my neck—where my injury site is located—combining my heart, mind, and body, connecting to a universal energy source. I pictured myself "plugged in" to this healing energy, visualizing it clearing out the cloud of damaged tissue like a brilliant sun burning off early morning fog.

These two events put in motion an essential part of my ongoing recovery. I have to be in the moment at all times, whether I am walking, sitting, writing, driving, exercising, or sleeping. Nothing below my level of injury (C7, which affects everything from mid-abdomen down to my feet) happens without my conscious thought. I can harness the same mindfulness that allows me to get up early to exercise, and use it to slow down daily life to take notice and appreciate the world around me.

I am by no means a master at this, and my mind often drifts to past regrets and worries about the future. I do know, however, that my mind, body, and heart can work together to enable continuing recovery, do amazing things, and make life worth living.

PART

THREE

ALL

IS NOT

AS IT

SEEMS

CHAPTER 12

The Daily Routine

Behind my athletic-looking, easygoing appearance lies another life rarely seen by anyone with the exception of my wife—and even she doesn't hear the thought stream in my head all day long. I'm giving you a backstage pass to what life is like with a spinal cord injury. This is my "second life," the ticker tape stream of consciousness dialogue that provides a glimpse into my behind-the-scenes invisible world.

SCI is cruel, punishing, and relentless. Overcoming this affliction every day takes an act of great will, effort, and conscious thought. To use Dr. Barry's words, SCI is "an unimaginable injury." A strong recovery from an incomplete SCI masks the reality behind that recovery. This is the invisible made visible.

Everything I do each day comes at a cost. There is a price to pay in everything—mentally, physically, socially, recreationally, and financially. Living is a grind that requires a constant determination to accomplish anything and everything. Life moves more slowly, with greater strain and energy depletion. And it always, always requires constant mental attention.

This description of my day is from the perspective of spending the morning at home, going to work, and coming back home at the end of day. Usually, four to five times a week I am up early and will go to the gym for several hours before heading off to work on the days I am scheduled to be there. Everything I'm telling you about here would be applicable for whatever setting I am in.

Pain

My body's natural tendency is to try to manage pain, which, on a ten-point system, always runs between three and five. It can easily spike higher to a nine or ten, depending on what I am doing. Standing in place, for example, is progressively painful if I do it for more than a few minutes. This is due to my muscles seizing, constricting, and squeezing. They don't know how to let go, unless I break the pattern with some kind of movement.

The pain I live with is distressing, on my mind all the time, and I am constantly trying to manage it. Position and activity make no difference in my pain profile, except for the one hour after exercise when my endorphins peak. This is one of the reasons I frequent the gym and stay as long as I do. I need that time—it offers relief and reward.

I hate being in pain. It is chronic and constant. So many times I want to crawl out of my body and separate myself from it. Of all the issues I deal with, pain is the worst. It has the biggest impact on my quality of life; it is the strongest headwind I face when choosing to do anything, because anything I do is going to hurt. It is just a question of how much suffering I want to endure.

Pain is a mental and physical drain, and it depletes my reserves. Some days I can successfully compartmentalize it, set it aside, and treat it as background noise, like "white" noise. Other days it grinds on me and makes me angry and impatient.

What helps? Ice, heat, massage, stretching, meditation, exercise, and over-the-counter medications like Advil, Aleve, Tylenol, or aspirin. I have tried opiates but won't go back to them because the side effects are too severe. I even use medical marijuana, in vapor form only, primarily at night just before bedtime.

Getting out of Bed in the Morning

For the most part, getting out of bed is pretty straightforward, although my mind is usually fixated on being very careful not to strain any joints, ligaments, or other body parts. I always worry about yanking tendons or damaging my Achilles, both of which would significantly set back my mobility and rehab program.

I am very stiff when I first swing my legs over the side of the bed and put my feet on the ground. My feet are "flopped" and stiffly bent forward. Straightening them, until my ankles are at ninety degrees, takes some careful maneuvering. I am conscious of my right ankle in particular, because I seem to have a harder time flexing it. I worry about doing anything that might aggravate this problem.

After a few minutes of work to get my body into a standing position, I'll then gradually squat down twenty-five degrees or so, to slowly stretch my ankles. In this way, I can take my first step, knowing I have broken through the "spastic lock." This is a process I repeat throughout the day, before I'll walk up or down steps or stand up from a seated position. I follow this process frequently during my bathroom routine, before the medications are taken and active.

Many times when I first wake up, and after I stand, my feet feel like stumps, and I have no feeling in them. My brain hasn't received signals that my feet are even there, and because of this it's as though I have no heels, toes, or metatarsals. I'm mindful of every movement, step, twist, or bend I make. I don't make a move without first thinking it through.

Standing

Before I stand, I think about how my weight is distributed on my feet, trying to make sure that it is distributed evenly and won't unduly stress either side of my hips. I look at my toes and can see some of them, primarily the ones next to each big toe showing hammertoe symptoms. A hammertoe is a form of contracture where the middle of the toe tends to bend upward and get stuck in that position. In my case this is because my toes are desperately trying to feel and sense the ground so that they can send proper signals back to the brain. This feedback to the brain from my feet is essential in helping my body balance itself and for it to recognize where it is in space—a medical term called *proprioperception*. It is about the body's overall sense of position in relation to the spaces around it.

As I begin to move forward and start walking, I try to lift my feet up to clear the carpet as each foot comes forward, but sometimes my weight shift is off and I end up in lunging into a hip flexor, usually on my left side. As a consequence of the gluteus muscle and hamstrings not doing their job to support me while I'm upright, the hip flexor muscle, which wraps around my waist, absorbs the stress. This is not supposed to happen.

My hip flexor muscle isn't built to do this and, as a result, is sent into a state of severe spasticity. The muscle seizes and constricts. For up to thirty minutes afterward, it is even more difficult for me to walk. The hip flexor incorrectly compensates because the gluteus muscles, which are supposed to do the work, don't fire. The nerve commands from the brain are not getting through the damaged area, to the appropriate nerve endings. When I remember, I'll touch the gluteus muscle with my hand for tactile stimulation, to try to wake it up.

They don't know how to fire properly. It's one reason my gluteus muscles have shrunk so much. Sag creases are now visible on my buttocks. Seeing those creases annoys me, because they are another reminder of my condition. When I stand up from a reclining or sitting position, my body feels like it weighs many times its current weight. My ankles hurt. My hips hurt. My feet hurt. My legs feel completely disconnected from my torso.

When I walk, my body often leans forward first to initiate movement before my legs try to follow along. If I don't catch myself in this posture—in other words, realize what I'm doing—I will invariably stub a toe and fall down. In the past nine-plus years, I have fallen well over two dozen times; fortunately, none was so traumatic that it required an ER visit. A few did require follow-up visits with my internist, but they resolved within a few days.

Bathroom Rituals

First thing in the morning after I get out of bed, I walk (shuffle) with measured steps to the bathroom with urinals in hand. Sometimes I use the other hand to touch something—the wall, dresser, or bed—to help maintain my balance.

In the bathroom I do the typical rituals. When I take my clothes off and they fall to the floor, I have to consciously think about bending down slowly. First I evaluate whether I am square to the ground or straining a muscle. Sometimes I'll take a deep breath and, after I exhale, I can bend down a little farther. I'll repeat several times until I can reach the clothing on the floor. I then consciously think about pulling in my belly button, tightening my core, and slowly rising up, making sure I don't aggravate anything in my lower back. At this time of the day, I haven't had my morning medications yet, so I am twice as cautious.

If I'm home (not at the SAC) and use the shower, I have to step up twenty-four inches over the edge of the bathtub. But before I attempt this, I perform a squat to flex my ankles, and then I gingerly lift my right foot and step into the bathtub. Because of the height I have to clear, I use one of my hands to help elevate the leg I am lifting. I then slowly follow with my left foot, mindful not to put too much torque on my right ankle. I follow these preventive measures in bathing, all the time, every day, out of fear and caution.

Once I'm in the shower, I check my body for any nicks, cuts, or blisters that could be portals for the dreaded Methicillin-resistant Staphylococcus aureus (MRSA)—and other bacteria, which can cause blood infections. I have had MRSA twice as well as two blood infections, both in my feet, which required IV antibiotics in the ER and visits to an infectious disease doctor.

If I see something suspicious on my skin, I will immediately put some Bactroban ointment on it (a powerful, prescription antibiotic version of bacitracin or Neosporin). I've learned my lessons about infections the hard way. I always have a clean towel under my feet when I move around in the bathroom to keep germs, bacteria, and fungus out of my toes. I do the same thing in the bedroom before putting on shoes. If I am at the gym, I always make sure to thoroughly towel off my feet before putting on my socks with the same objective of minimizing exposure.

I have diminished sensation in those areas, so keeping them clean and unexposed is important. Once showered, shaved, and dressed, which I can do independently, I'll pause in place, take some deep breaths to try to relax my tight ankles, and then walk very carefully down the hallway to the kitchen.

Walking Inside My Home

The distance from my bedroom to the kitchen is about forty to fifty steps, small steps, no more than a twelve- to eighteen-inch stride. I know I can fall at any time. I generally do not use a trekking pole in the house. Since the accident, I have this long-held notion of "getting independent." These words, in large part, have guided my recovery.

I view walking around the house without assistance as an ongoing challenge. I'm not going to learn how to walk without trekking poles if I continue to use trekking poles. I have used the same approach at every stage of my recovery. I do believe that every motion, every movement, is having some rehabilitative effect. I do these movements without aid inside the house with measured risk. I could easily fall, trip, or catch a toe. When I do fall, my body is rigid, akin to a tree falling in the woods. There is no bending; it's just one straight body catapulting toward the floor. All landings are hard, awkward, and painful.

I proceed down the hallway, thinking about each step, I am constantly asking myself where the pressure is on my feet. Am I walking on my heels first? Am I striding heel to toe? Could my stride be longer? If I stride longer will I yank my adductor muscles, which aren't flexible? Can I lengthen my stride without pulling some muscle in my groin? Am I initiating movement with my upper body or lower body? Am I sagging into my hip flexors? Am I slumping forward with shoulders down or am I standing upright? Is my chest up and chin back? Am I looking straight ahead or at the ground? Are there any objects I need to move around or step over? Am I scuffing my feet? Am I clomping on the floor flat-footed? Am I tightening my core for stability? I feel like a beginning golfer learning how to hit the ball and replaying a laundry list of instructions in my head.

When I pull in my core, stand straight, and pull my shoulders back, my interior thigh muscles groan from tightness, causing my feet to scuff the floor. Tightening that area to correct my posture makes it more difficult to bend my knees and pull them through as I stride. I find this especially annoying.

All of these thoughts flow through my head for the minute or less it takes me to move down the hallway to the kitchen. I sometimes ask myself—*what if I cleared my head of all these thoughts?* I've actually tried this on occasion, and it always gets me into trouble. My body doesn't do these things automatically without conscious thought. If it did, I wouldn't have to continually prepare myself to do them. Every time I walk down the hallway, I've already preplanned this walk and have it scheduled in my brain, knowing that I'll be in discomfort and fear for a little while. I've budgeted the energy and will for this purpose, but doing this all the time is incredibly draining.

Breakfast

Once I sit down at the table, the first thing I do is take my medications and supplements. I take six medications and seven supplements. The morning dose of medications is for spasticity (diazepam 10 mg; baclofen 20 mg; tizanadine 4 mg), neuropathic pain (gabapentin 1200 mg), depression (bupropion 150 mg), and high blood pressure (lisinopril 10 mg). For supplements I take CoQ10, alpha lipoic acid, low-dose aspirin, magnesium, zinc, men's multivitamin, and vitamin D.

I hate taking medications, because they are foreign substances, chemicals introduced into my system and all filtered by my liver. I know they allow me to function. I worry about their long-term effects on my organs, especially liver and kidneys. One of the blood tests done as part of my annual physical is for kidney and liver function.

For the hour it takes for my medications to take effect, I'll read news—mostly sports.

After the medications begin working, I get up, using the same deliberate ankle stretch–lean forward–stretch calves approach, and once I feel ready I stand up. Being in the kitchen requires a lot of moving, turning, twisting, bending, leaning over, and changing directions. When I get a plate out of the cabinet, silverware from the drawer, food out of the pantry or refrigerator, a hand towel from a different drawer, or wash my hands—these all require multiple movements in different directions, which must be done slowly because all my muscles are rigid, especially from standing.

Moving slowly allows my groaning muscles to acquiesce enough to allow movement without undue strain on muscles in my legs, waist, back, or feet. When I get dishes from the dishwasher, I have to bend down and to my left side, which causes my rigid muscles to groan more, and I have to rise slowly for the same reason, to not unduly strain muscles that are already seizing. If I have to pick something up off the floor, I have to do it carefully and thoughtfully, especially rising back up mindfully, so as not to cause problems with my lower back, which is already hurting from the strain of being bent over.

I am conscious of not making quick turns, because my interior leg muscle adductors can strain easily. My body feels very heavy when I stand, and my ankles and feet ache. I go slowly. I have a planned route that I take around the kitchen to minimize the amount of up time I spend on my feet and to facilitate turning and changing directions.

Cooking

Moving around the kitchen to make a meal is very painful. Standing for any length of time, even for just a few minutes, even with an intermittent sit-down, is painful. Even sitting down causes pain, just in a different location. Cooking involves numerous directional changes, which I can't do quickly. I have to be very mindful of quick directional changes so I don't aggravate or pull an adductor muscle. I don't cook very often because my pain level becomes too high (eight plus). I can do it, but I am not always willing to pay the price. In recent months, I have prepared breakfast and dinner more frequently on my own, because my schedule is different from Diane's. Food preparation always hurts.

I have cereal, fruit, and yogurt on a typical morning. I eat eggs, toast, and protein bars on occasion. I think about my intake, what am I eating, if I'm getting enough protein (80 to 120 grams), fiber (25 to 35 grams), and water (100 to 128 ounces). I have to be especially vigilant about my fiber intake, or I will pay the price.

Eating

Moving my hands is a slow endeavor, and it takes twice as long to feed myself than it did before the accident. When I cut things with a knife, I have to be very careful not to cut myself, especially on the pinkie, ring, and middle fingers. Those fingers on both hands are constantly numb from paralysis. When I eat, I sit and, therefore, experience middle back pain. To numb the pain in my back, I often pull out a Ziploc bag of frozen peas and lean against it when I'm sitting. The numbing sensation helps temporarily.

Sitting

I always have pain in my middle back. Chair, recliner, couch—it doesn't matter. I always have pain. When I sit, at home, in a restaurant, at work, or in a car, having something cushioned at different pressure points helps. I've tried different positions, heating pads, posture, ice—anything to distract or numb the pain. I have several Ziplocs with frozen bags of peas inside that I pull out of the freezer and use to ice my back and hips. I generally can't sit for longer than twenty minutes without having to get up and down. If I don't, my lower half will go into spastic cramping and my ankles will stiffen. I have to rock back and forth to break up the seizing in my ankles and calves before standing.

Office Work

After breakfast, I move to my office, retracing most of my steps back down the hallway. The same thought process orbits in my mind as before. Once in my office, I sit down in an ergonomically designed chair. As soon as I sit, my middle back hurts. My back hurts intermittently in other positions sometimes but always when I sit. The pain is generally in the lower half of my back and focused on the large muscles that support the spine, called the spinal erectors. This is a set of muscles that allow the back to straighten and rotate.

Padded seating is essential to help mitigate the pain but it never takes it away. Hardback seating is brutal and intolerable for longer than ten minutes. If I know I am going somewhere with that kind of seating, I will bring a cushion with me. Sometimes I also bring ice bags with me to numb the pain.

I have a tendency to slouch and let my neck lean forward and my core loosen when I'm sitting. When I catch myself doing this, I reorient my position to sit up straight: plant my feet flat on the floor, pull shoulders back, pull stomach in, and steady my forearms to be level with the keyboard. It is all a conscious effort and something I have to continually remind myself to do.

When my body tires of this and unconsciously slides back to a slouching position, I will reorient myself, and it often dawns on me that I am repeating this process again and again. It is hard work. Often I will stand up in front of my desk for a few minutes to just move, roll my shoulders, walk in place, stretch my back from side to side, and then sit again. I check my calendar for any events I might have that day.

Sometimes I am fine with being alone, so there is a part of me that is happy when the day is open.

I have a VersaBall in the office, which I use at times to stretch out my back, by lying either face down or face up. Lying on the ball is easy. It is more challenging to lie on my back, feet firmly planted on the floor, allowing my head to recline backward. I am very cautious about trying to arch too far, and I make sure my feet maintain secure contact with the floor. It would be easy, without careful attention, to have an inadvertent roll, which could result in injury.

My energy levels vary while I'm in the office. Sometimes, because of my medications, I am yawning a lot by 11 a.m.; other times I am buzzing along, knocking out "to do" item after item. Sometimes recurrent questions flow through my mind like a Wall Street ticker tape. *What am I doing with my life? What is my purpose? What is my life's work? What will make me happy?* Other times, I just want to zone out and listen to music on my headphones.

Sometimes my hands ache terribly, more than usual. Sometimes the pain is so bad that I lean forward and lay my forehead on the desk, wishing the pain would go away. Sometimes the pain makes me so angry that I just scream in anguish.

This is variable, but on days when pain is a dominant feature, I feel very impaired and, consequently, despondent. I just want to curl up and crawl out of my skin. This feeling also makes me angry, because I can't readily determine why I am hurting so much on one day and not so much on another. It makes me angry because I can't come up with an explanation. I may get up from the desk and sit on the adjacent couch. It is comfortable for a few minutes, and then the pain in my middle back returns.

Walking for Exercise

I always preplan walking for exercise. I have to mentally prepare myself before I do it, but the preparation is akin to having a blood draw. You know it is going to hurt and, in a way, have to kind of "rev yourself up" to deal with it, even though the pain will be short-lived.

For me, it's also like exercising at the gym. I know it is going to be uncomfortable and, in many cases, is going to hurt. I rev myself up mentally to do it and can do it, knowing I will hurt in the process. I know the hurt will pass, but it doesn't make the mental preparation any less necessary.

I know walking is going to be painful. I also know there is going to be a risk of falling because my balance is so precarious. My movement is slow, labored, and stiff; my body feels like it has multiple g-forces placed upon it when I am vertical. I grind my way through it, but it is not automatic, and it is never without pain or fear.

Walking (if I had been a gymnast) might be akin to walking on a balance beam, with poor balance and blurred vision, and it's a carefully choreographed process that holds the ever-present risk of falling. When I was walking outside a lot for my first three post-injury years, using trekking poles, I worked up to walking two-plus miles, several times a week. After a while, my walking had improved so much that during the last four hundred yards, I would challenge myself with speed walking, amping up my speed to go as fast as I could, timing myself in the process. Today I walk much less, because my exercise focus is in the gym.

Swimming

In the first three years of rehab, I spent a considerable amount of time in a therapy pool. Toward the end of my time with the pool therapists Linda and Debbie, I started to try swimming with the aid of abdominal flotation. In addition, I was assisted with snorkeling gear so I could keep my head facing down and not have to rotate it when taking a breath. In December 2013, we took a family trip. At the hotel pool, I fixed myself up with a round tube that helped elevate my head, neck, and abdomen above the water, which gave me enough clearance to move my arms in a paddle stroke and kick my legs at the same time.

I could move my legs up and down, but robotically—in a very stiff and rigid way. I took a couple of short, successful laps, and then, with assistance, came out of the pool. I stood up but wasn't able to move my legs. Moving my legs up and down while swimming had triggered an intense spastic response, and they were completely locked in spasticity. I asked Diane to find an assistant with a wheelchair. I was wheeled back to the room so I could take a muscle relaxant, baclofen, to quiet the spastic response. The medicine began to work within thirty minutes and allowed me to gingerly walk again.

Driving

While I was doing outpatient OT at HMC in fall 2007, I practiced simulated driving on a special device. In particular, it was designed to measure reaction speeds. After several appointments, my reaction speeds consistently passed the tests. Several months later in spring 2008 I re-passed my driver's test through the Washington State Department of Licensing. The only restriction is that I have to drive automatics only, no stick shift.

My reaction speeds are very good when called upon. I've had to hit the brakes quickly to avoid a car or pedestrian multiple times. I can move my right leg from gas to brake and back to gas without restriction. I can now retract both legs on command, but not well enough to drive a stick shift with multiple gear-shift changes over the course of a trip. I typically drive twenty to thirty minutes at a time, but if I travel longer, which is infrequent, I have to load up on over-the-counter (OTC) pain relievers and make frequent stops to get through the trip. Driving is also a challenge because if I do it for longer than forty-five minutes, it causes me intense discomfort in my hips.

Nap

I usually nap two to four times a week on average. I nap in the recliner in the living room, where I can rotate backward to get in a comfortable position. Occasionally, I'll nap in bed. In recent years, I have been more open to napping in bed. I didn't nap in bed previously for silly reasons, thinking I was somehow giving in to the injury. I don't feel that way anymore, knowing that my body needs rest and I need to respond to it. Naps are a good news–bad news event. A nap typically lasts an hour, primarily because my bladder or pain wakes me up. When I first recline, it takes some jostling around to find the right position, and then sometimes I just daydream. My thoughts could drift anywhere.

Sometimes I think about what in my remaining years would make me happy, really happy. If I could do anything to make me happy again, what would I do? Would I travel? Would I go on cruises? Would I drive to national parks? Would I sample jobs I would never think of doing before? Would I buy a motorcycle? Would I rent a motor home? What other things are there to consider, and how do I find out about them? What do I really like to do? Sometimes it is hard to answer these questions, and I think I lack imagination. But other times I just get lost in these thoughts and go to sleep.

When I awaken, I hate how I feel, which is very lethargic. I don't want to do anything initially. I could just lie there all day and do nothing. My body is sluggish, and it is difficult to move. All my limbs have gone dormant and have to be reawakened. I know it will be at least an hour before I feel like I did before the nap. When I do decide to get up, I go through basically the same process I went through that morning when I got up. I rely on faith from previous nap experiences that the same metamorphosis will happen again.

During and after a nap, my body often has momentary extensor cramps where my legs shoot out from under me or go rigid, pulling and yanking. I have to try to regulate the intensity of the cramp so I don't pull a hamstring. My only recourse is to try to breathe through it or rub the area to distract the response. Sometimes I am successful, sometimes not. It subsides, and I get up. The first time I put my feet on the ground, I lean forward to stretch my ankles and calves and then I push to get up. I remind myself to use my legs to get up. I remind myself to feel my heels and push up. I worry about straining my ankles.

My first try is often unsuccessful, so I sit down again. Knowing that my limbs have been dormant takes a couple of efforts to reengage them to do what they are supposed to do. Once I'm standing there are times when I can feel that my lower body still has extensor spasticity. I'll squeeze my butt to try to trigger a mild extensor cramp for a few seconds and have it recede. If a cramp occurs, sometimes it can force my heels up and put me at risk of falling forward. I can't control what the extensor cramp does. If I'm successful, it releases the muscles. I can then walk, usually to the bathroom first.

Nighttime

I keep two thirty-two-ounce urinals on my bedside table at night. There is no way I could walk to the toilet at night because of spasticity, visibility, and poor balance. When I have to pee at night, I swing my legs over the side of the bed, stand upright very slowly—mindful of allowing my ankles to first sufficiently flex at ninety degrees—and then I use one of the bedside urinals. It's not elegant, but it is my reality.

Once I have taken up a position in bed at night, my body stays in that position and doesn't move. It is encased in spasticity. It is like I am cemented into that position. As a result, when pain or bladder needs awaken me, I have to be very mindful of starting movement without triggering the dreaded extensor cramp. An extensor cramp is not a charley horse, or muscle spasm. It is a wave that starts at my toes and swells toward my chest.

Lifting my arm to scratch the back of my head, for example, can trigger a very violent extensor cramp. When I experience an extensor cramp, my body contorts into positions over which I have no control. My right wrist could pull backward to the point of straining tendons. My back could twist, causing vertebrae to pop. My legs could shoot straight out and become extremely rigid. However my body reacts, there is fear and pain. To an observer it might appear that I am having a severe seizure that lasts a few seconds to a half a minute. It often startles my wife.

Any movement at night has to be carefully done to avoid having the swell turn into a violent cramp.

Sleep

Bedtime is usually between 9 and 10 p.m. I fall asleep pretty quickly. Typically I sleep in one- to two-hour increments. I am in bed between six and seven hours a night and average about six hours total. My sleep is always choppy. I am up four to eight times, sometimes even more. Pain, extensor cramps, and bladder needs are the culprits preventing me from getting continuous sleep. Fortunately, after I have to get up, I can usually fall back to sleep within just a few minutes.

While asleep, I use three positions—both left and right sides and on my back. Unfortunately, I never have restorative sleep. I can count on two hands how many times I have slept three to four hours straight. It feels great when it happens but is rare.

Mindfulness

I think of mindfulness as being "in the moment." To me, mindfulness means being keenly aware of my surroundings, thoughts, feelings, and sensations. It is "stream of consciousness" awareness. I have learned that mindfulness is also the process of finding acceptance in our space, in our environment, and in everything around us.

All activities, times of day, or feelings described in this chapter require being dialed in at all times. Prior to my crash, I never had conscious thought about walking. I just walked. It was automatic. The same goes for sitting down, or standing up. I never thought about it. I just did it. With regard to sleep, I never went to bed prior to the injury with thoughts of managing pain, bladder, and extensor cramps all night long. I just went to sleep and woke up eight hours later.

Today, mindfulness is in play at all times, keeping me mentally vigilant about every movement, activity, and feeling. My system is always "on," except for very brief moments. The journey in this area for me is in continuing to find acceptance for these moments. Over a great deal of time, I have come to the difficult realization that I am quadriplegic, and all that comes with this, but accepting my condition feels counter to my whole approach of fighting the good fight. I'm sure there is a balance to be found there, but at this point, it still remains elusive.

Sometimes, only briefly, I get to forget about my body. For the thirty to sixty minutes after exercise, when I have had a good sweat, my endorphins are flowing and I am lying on my back on the stretch mat feeling good. There have been times after exercising when I have relaxed to the point of falling asleep. I can say the same for the brief thirty to sixty minutes of naptime when I'm reclining on the couch. The same holds true when I am immersed in a dream at night and not aware of being on watch for bladder, pain, or extensor cramps. I dream practically every night. It is a welcome distraction. The only other times I feel that my body is not "on" is when I am fully in the moment of what I am doing, distracted, and enjoying life.

My first post-injury trip when we traveled to Cabo San Lucas as a family is one time that comes to mind. Alana and I went as a pair doing a paragliding tour. It was so much fun, elevated high in the air and taking in 360-degree views of Medano beach on a gorgeous sunny day. I forgot about everything other than enjoying a special moment with my daughter.

On that same trip, Kevin and I went out on a Sea-Doo watercraft for the first time, shooting around the harbor in the same area, canvassing all around the point, around the cruise ship moored in the area, and racing with other similar watercraft. I was totally lost in the moment, oblivious to my infirmities.

What keeps me going despite these difficulties in everyday life is my unwavering belief that things can and will get better. As an example, I am often asked why I don't walk with both trekking poles all the time, use a cane, or use elbow-supported crutches to reduce my risk of falling. My answer is that I believe that every challenge I take on, such as walking without assistance when in the gym, is at some level teaching my body how to better walk.

While I can't provide scientific evidence that this occurs, I can say anecdotally that at some level it does. Perhaps I get some benefit by overcoming fear. Perhaps at some cellular level, it is helping to rebuild a new circuit around the damaged area in my spinal cord that may over time improve my balance. It is what I choose to believe, and I think the progress I've made in so many areas over the years is proof that it works.

What keeps me going is being there for my family. It is important to me that my wife and children see a father who leads by example. I frequently talk to my children about the need to work hard, to persist in the face of challenges, to have goals and strive. I talk to them about the hardships that life throws at us, its unfairness and occasional cruelty, and about persisting in the face of loss; how they can find a way to take these experiences and turn them into something meaningful in their lives, in a way that benefits others.

It is important to me for Diane and the children to see that I can overcome; I'm diligent, persistent, reliable, and relentless. I can deal with all the issues of this injury and thrive. These are life experiences that are not taught in any school. They are modeled by parents and are vital to their children's futures because they, too, will face unwanted challenges and need to be equipped to handle them. If I leave no other legacy in this world, my wife and children will know how deeply I loved them and that I gave everything I had to provide them with an example of what is needed to thrive and leave this world a better place than they found it.

What keeps me going is feeling that this injury is "bigger than myself," that as a consequence of this injury, there is something beneficial for me to do for others. Perhaps people may find something useful from my story—hope, inspiration, belief, and possibility. Possibly making a difference in people's lives keeps me going. It has taken some time for me to accept that I am impaired, disabled, and part of a community that I wasn't anticipating joining. I realize now that everything I have learned over the past nine-plus years is not just for me. There is benefit for others from what I have been through, managed, and accomplished.

Frankly, it would be selfish of me not to write or talk about it. There are people I don't even know who may be able to take something away from my story and apply it in their own lives at some level that could help. I believe this after numerous experiences I've had talking to people I know, and even people I don't know, who have remarked directly or through others that they are inspired by my story. They've seen what I am doing, what I've done, how far I've come, and they want to know more. That inspires me to keep going.

I have an innate dislike for quitting, surrendering, or giving in, and that keeps me going. I'm not one hundred percent sure where my dislike for quitting comes from other than just plain, dogged determination. I'm reminded of a story that happened when I was attending junior high school in Weston, Massachusetts. There were football tryouts. The only football I had played at that point was backyard touch football with my neighborhood friends. I thought I was pretty good.

On the first day, we had to go select our equipment from a gym room where all the gear was laid out—shoes, knee and hip pads, shoulder pads, helmets, pants, and jockstraps. Heck, I didn't even know how to put on a jockstrap so I just suited up in my underwear. The helmet I selected was oversized, in part because of my narrow, somewhat large head. Because my head was narrow, the helmet wasn't very secure when strapped on. After I managed to get dressed, I was the last one on the field, and practice was already in progress. They were doing tackling drills.

When it was my turn, I attempted a tackle and, in the process, my helmet rotated on my head so the front of the helmet was facing the back of my head and I couldn't see anything. Everyone laughed. Humiliated, I straightened out the helmet and ran as fast as I could back to the locker room. I took off my equipment and left, never to return to the game again. I quit. I think of that experience with great disdain, and perhaps my fire to never see that repeated had its origins on that fall afternoon.

Once I've made up my mind, as in this cycling-injury case—making the decision to define my terms, take a stand, and choose to win—there is no turning back. I will never quit. I will prevail.

CHAPTER 13

The Weight of So Much Loss

Having all my faculties impaired as a consequence of this catastrophic injury has been brutal. I have experienced so much loss on so many levels. It is a cruel reminder that life never promised to be fair, without difficulty, or without pain and suffering. Bad things can and do happen to good people.

Losing control of so many aspects of my life and fighting to rebuild has taken monumental effort. It continues to challenge me, and I'm certain it always will. Nothing comes easy. Nothing is automatic. Nothing happens without conscious deliberate thought.

I was doing everything right in my life, but something terrible still happened. It is difficult to rationalize. I wasn't doing anything reckless, unless riding a road bicycle the way it was supposed to be ridden can be considered "risky behavior." I could possibly rationalize it if I had been injured while skydiving, bungee jumping, heli-skiing, or free climbing, as such, but safely riding a road bicycle? No.

In the first year following the accident, I could find no other explanation than wrong place, wrong day, and wrong time. Obviously I knew *what* happened. I didn't know the *why* other than incomplete, inaccurate guesswork and explanations from various people. I wouldn't know why this accident happened for several more years, not until a lengthy process of information gathering and detailed analysis was completed. Until then, I was living under the mistaken belief that "shit just happened" that day.

Since the day of my accident, my losses have grown until, at times, they feel insurmountable. There are so many things that I loved doing that I can no longer do. Many relationships I loved having in my life are now gone. These losses are sometimes almost more than I can bear.

Professionally

I had twenty-eight years of progressive IT experience prior to 2007. Starting off early in my career as an analyst, I worked in several industries, including health care, real estate investment, and retail, and then made my way into IT management. Eventually I moved up the ranks to higher IT positions including supervisor, manager, director, and VP. I was proud to be good at what I did.

Like everyone, I had my improvement opportunities, which were constructively addressed as they came up. My performance was consistently recognized as "exceeds expectations" and "exceptional." I received recognition and several awards. The work I did had a positive impact on the companies I had worked for and had navigated at all organizational levels. With my last company, and shortly before the crash, I was under consideration for an officer level or VP position. All of this professional progress came to an abrupt halt for me in June 2007.

I was out of work for thirteen months and returned to work in July 2008 on a limited, eight-hour-a-week, part-time basis, working from home. While doing so, I continued to work my hardest to build greater physical ability. My new part-time role as an individual contributor (as opposed to a director) was a big step down from where I had been before my accident, and it felt like defeat.

However, being back at work, having a work schedule, and doing something productive, adding value, and having social interactions were very important in my recovery. Shortly before I returned to work in July 2008, I started mental health therapy with a clinical psychologist, Dr. Roberta. We worked together for about two years until the summer of 2010 with visits two times a week. Our work together was internally focused, intense at times, and very helpful. In early 2009, I was slowly building up my weekly work hours. I brought up the idea to Dr. Roberta of starting to work at the office one day a week. Dr. Roberta countered and said, "Jamie, have you considered trying to work *three* days a week at the office?"

"No," I answered. "I hadn't and didn't think I was ready for it yet."

She said encouragingly, "Why don't you give it a try and see what happens? If it doesn't work out, you can always go back to supplementing your work hours from home and working at the office when you can."

I hadn't considered it before, because I thought there was no way I could make that work. But I valued her advice and agreed. "Okay, I'll give it a go."

Shortly thereafter, I worked my way up to being at the office three days a week, strictly because of her encouraging me to take some measured risks. The risk in actuality was minimal, because I had the option of returning to telecommuting, but that wasn't necessary. Taking that measured risk came at her suggestion, and it paid off.

As my strength and stamina improved, so did my capacity to work additional hours, starting in small increments from eight to fourteen, and eventually rising from twenty-four to twenty-eight hours a week, over that four-plus-year period. It was important for me to transition more of my work time to the campus to get into the energy flow of the company and enjoy more face-to-face interactions.

By the end of 2009 and early 2010, I was working all my part-time hours from the campus. Being fully engaged in the company's activities and the hustle/bustle around the office contributed significantly to my mental and physical recovery. At the same time, I felt like I had taken a big leap backward in time, to the days when I had first started working as an IT systems analyst.

No longer responsible for a team, I no longer navigated in the same influential circles that I had before. This, too, was a big loss and felt like a huge failure on my part. However, while working as an individual contributor, I continued to provide exceptional value to the company in terms of dollars saved and efficiencies gained.

I worked on various projects where I, and company management, thought I could add the greatest value. I did add value, saving the company hundreds of thousands of dollars. In one case, I secured a $225,000 refund due to a previously undiscovered overpayment. Still, being in a junior position made me feel "less than."

I no longer attended IT leadership meetings or annual company management conferences. I didn't run committees as I had before, nor did I interact with people at the higher levels of the company. I was now under the thumb of other managers, some whom had worked on teams I'd managed as part of my pre-injury organization.

The work I was doing was referred to as "keeping the lights on" in IT-speak; in other words, it was basic IT operational support. As Dr. Jens had said, working was important to my recovery, but the loss in title, stature, span of control, influence, personal value, and working relationships left me with stinging feelings of being left by the wayside; feelings that were hard to shake.

In many ways, I was self-conscious in my new role at the company. It felt very different moving around campus, knowing that others knew I had lost my old position and was now an individual contributor. I was a staff person, doing assignments, and for the rest of my time at the company, I had someone else directing me. It felt embarrassing, even humiliating to consider myself a nonentity.

For so many years, I had fought and worked hard to build the reputation I had, only to have it erased in a flash with a catastrophic accident. It was as if I had accomplished nothing, and life's Ctrl-Alt-Del buttons had eradicated my track record. Others may not have viewed it in that way, but I did. This was my new reality.

It was very hard to adjust to these losses—loss of respect, loss of influence, loss of stature, loss of importance, loss of admiration, and loss of responsibility. It was good, however, to be working again and to be able to make valuable contributions. Even with my limited hours, over the next four years I completed a variety of assignments that were meaningful and valuable. Although the work was comparatively pedestrian compared to what I had been doing as a senior IT leader, it was still purposeful.

I made the best of it, put on a good professional face, did as I was told, played team ball, and did my best to keep my attitude up and stay positive; still, the change was extremely difficult. At times I felt very lost, not knowing who I was anymore. So much of my identity—who I was and how I thought about myself—was wrapped up in the job and company.

As time progressed from 2008 to 2012, especially in the latter half of 2012, my work assignments and engagement with the IT Security team lifted my work spirits considerably. I liked the work I was doing, and especially enjoyed the team I was working with. I was adding value and received numerous commendations from colleagues about the project I was managing. It was unfortunate to be involuntarily separated from the company in December 2012.

Relationships

My relationships with friends and family, as well as coworkers, have been affected by my accident, and of all the areas of loss, this one hurts the most. Relationships I had made at my last company, the company where I worked for eighteen years, suffered the most. I built up many professional relationships over those years, and many of those people came to visit me while I was hospitalized. Others expressed well wishes with cards, letters, and emails.

My cycling community was largely linked to the company. I cycled with many of them every workday during the lunch ride. We rode local organized rides as well, many of them century rides, some shorter, others longer. Some in the area included Chilly Hilly on Bainbridge Island, Tour de Blast up Mount Saint Helens, Sunrise Century in Wenatchee, Seven Hills of Kirkland, Flying Wheels in Redmond, Seattle To Portland (STP), Millersylvania Double Metric Century in Tumwater, Ride Around Mount Rainier in One Day (RAMROD) in Enumclaw, and Kitsap Color Classic on the Kitsap Peninsula.

We trained together in the Cascades, riding the major passes around Mount Rainier, including Paradise, Chinook, Cayuse, and Sunrise. Many of us rode together in France and climbed some of the major mountain passes featured on the Tour de France, including the Col du Glandon, Col du Galibier, Col d'Izoard, Col de Sarenne, Le Mont Ventoux, Les Deux Alpes, and L'Alpe d'Huez. We had a group that raced together at the motor speedway in Covington, Washington, known as the Tuesday night series. I loved every minute of the time I spent on the bike and the bonds I formed with my cycling comrades.

Today, a number of those relationships no longer exist. I have a pretty good idea why and to some extent I can understand. In another sense I don't, because I imagine if a similar situation had happened to any of them, they would likely have pursued a similar course of action. I'll never know for sure, but the loss of those interactions and relationships has been difficult. I know I need to let go of these losses and move on with my life, and for the most part I have.

I had established many relationships outside of work as well, and generally, those have not been impacted. I still have many friends that I talk to, visit, have a drink with, or enjoy meeting for dinner. However, it's not easy to maintain these relationships, because there are a lot of limitations in my ability to function, and there's always the penalty of pain.

When I go out to dinner with someone, it is important that I use a chair or bench with a cushioned back. If I don't, after a few minutes, my pain spikes to an 8 or 9. I'll suck it up and deal with it, but it limits my time to two to three hours before I can't take it anymore. I have purchased a back cushion to take with me on these outings, and it does help when seating is uncomfortable. Hard seats are also uncomfortable because my buttocks have lost so much muscle mass; what's left is a lot of skin and bone.

We don't entertain at home very much for the same reason—it is painful. I can do it, but I have to prep and rev myself up for events. This doesn't come easy, but I know how important these social interactions are, even more so for my wife. She feels constrained because we don't socialize a lot and would like it if we did more of it. The answer is for me to suck it up and make it happen. Of course, given the choice of suffering a lot or a little, I prefer to choose the latter. This usually means quiet days by myself working on projects, home business, or financial activities; things I can do at my desk.

I have built some new relationships and rekindled some old ones, largely through my SAC community. It has been gratifying to reconnect with old friends with whom I used to play squash. I have met some fascinating new people at the club as well, and I'm sure these relationships will continue to grow. The club offers me solace, purpose, and fulfillment.

While losing relationships has been difficult, I continue to push myself to maintain my existing relationships and build new ones. It would be easy to become a hermit and isolate myself. That would be the path of least resistance. There is no easy path coming back from this injury, and like everything in life, it takes effort. Just like pushing through pain to do an exercise circuit, building and maintaining relationships requires the same amount of determination.

Of course, some of the biggest relationship changes have taken place within my own family. These haven't been easy to weather, but I never had any doubts about their love or continued support as I did with my working/cycling community. The next chapter is dedicated to my loved ones and the challenges they have faced while remaining steadfast by my side.

Recreationally

I have always been a sports buff and enjoyed many different activities. Of all the sports I enjoyed, I was strongest as a skier. I had the good fortune to grow up in a ski family. My parents and all four of my siblings were skiers. I grew up in New England and became intimately familiar with hard-packed, icy, frozen-granular conditions.

I did the bulk of my skiing in Massachusetts, New Hampshire, Vermont, and Maine. I took many ski trips out West to Colorado when my sister Molly was going to medical school and getting her doctorate, and many subsequent trips when my brother Rob moved to Boulder and ultimately settled in Fort Collins. I was also fortunate to ski several times in Europe, primarily in Austria and Switzerland.

After moving to the Pacific Northwest in 1981, the Whistler Blackcomb area in British Columbia, Canada, became our home base for skiing. It is where I taught both my children how to ski. I also had a group of high-octane ski buddies who skied more aggressively than any group I had ever skied with, and we went to places like Alta, Snowbird, and Jackson Hole. I've also been very fortunate to heli-ski on two occasions, the peak experience for the skiing enthusiast.

None of this is possible for me today. I miss the adrenaline rush of standing at the top of the "steeps" at Jackson Hole with my heart pumping, watching my expert comrades take the run before me. I miss skiing the trees at Steamboat Springs, weaving in and out of the saplings, shaping finely cut turns in the fluff at Snowbird, effortlessly caressing the bumps at Squaw Mountain, or racing down the corduroy of the finely groomed, wide-open slopes of Sun Valley.

For now, the hard reality, given my residual deficits, is being unable to ski many of the expert runs like Blackcomb Glacier, Ruby Bowl, or Spanky's Ladder at Blackcomb Mountain, and this is an enormous loss for me.

After the crash, I always held on to the belief that I would ski again. I haven't ruled it out because I refuse to rule out anything in my recovery, but doing so would be off the charts in terms of achievement.

I miss it. I miss it terribly, and the loss of these experiences that brought me such great joy and fulfillment leaves a big hole inside of me. I feel the same way about cycling. I love the outdoors and was fortunate to do a lot of day hiking and camping in New England when I was a teenager.

The summer after my freshman year at Ithaca College, I had a chance to do a five-week outdoor expedition in the Wind River Range in Wyoming through an organization called National Outdoor Leadership

School (NOLS). It was a thirty-five-day outdoor wilderness expedition teaching a broad range of skills—camping, climbing, leave-no-trace, cooking, first aid, topographic map reading, and survival skills.

We packed all the food and gear. We were re-rationed twice during the entire trip, once by horse packers and the second time by buried cache. We stargazed at night, lying on our backs looking at the constellations. They felt like they were on top of us. We made bread, built custom saunas, slept under "fly" covers, and learned many disciplines of protecting the environment. I learned about navigation using topographical maps and how to follow game trails (made by native animals, not people) to get from point A to point B.

On July 4, 1976, America's bicentennial, we stood atop the highest mountain in the Wind River Range—Gannett Peak. I felt like I could see Chicago; it was such a clear day. The outdoors was a special place to me, peaceful and comforting. There was something about being in nature, viewing its splendor, and facing its challenges and teachings.

In my early teens, I took a two-month summer trip to a canoe camp in northern Ontario called Keewaydin. Both of my brothers, Tom and Rob, had been to Camp Keewaydin and raved about it. It was my turn. At the camp, I learned everything about canoeing, portaging, even how to pack and carry wannigans, a simple wooden box used to carry cooking gear and provisions. I had a great time.

Now, after years of rehab, I could try canoeing, kayaking, or some other paddle sport without much risk. The challenge is staying stationary in a fixed position, which triggers severe muscle spasticity and seizing. It is on my goal list to at least try canoeing and kayaking in the future.

I developed a passion and love for the outdoors when I was young that continues to this day. The hard reality is that I can't enjoy it like I used to, primarily because it is so painful to be upright and on my feet due to spasticity. I also have challenges with balance; my ankles don't have the flexion to make going up and down inclines doable. It would be easy to roll my ankles due to diminished sensation. I have tried to hike in the outdoors, just a little distance, but the price paid is too high to do it on a recurring basis, or even to want to try it. I know I will suffer, and I always have to weigh that fact against the benefit.

I also used to enjoy going to sporting events, especially professional football, baseball, and soccer. I went to a lot of Seahawks, Mariners, and Sounders games. Since the injury, I have been to two professional sporting events. One was a Seattle Sounders soccer game. I was a guest and had exclusive club seating and easy in/out access to transportation. At the Sounders game, I enjoyed overcoming my infirmities to be there, but I suffered the whole time. I sucked it up and felt proud that I did it, but on the fun meter, the event didn't rate very high.

I could have used a wheelchair; after all, most professional sports venues have accommodations in terms of seating and service. Perhaps in the future I will seek more assistance, although the thought of requesting additional help runs counter to my primary goal in rehab—to get independent. Using a wheelchair, even in that situation, feels like going backward, and I don't want to find myself on that slippery slope, seeking more and more accommodation.

Emotionally

I have come a long way from where I started. From the first few days in ICU to inpatient rehab, outpatient rehab, the setback crash, deep-dive depression, recovery phase II, and forward from there, my journey has been filled with extreme ups and downs. My emotional state has run the gamut, from suicidal thoughts to feelings of great joy when I overcome an obstacle. Depression, anger, anxiety, lethargy, and fear are ever present. They manifest themselves in different ways at different times.

When I get angry, it is usually with myself. This usually happens when my body doesn't function the way I expect—like when I try to walk, but don't lift my legs correctly, and end up scuffing along the floor. I get mad because I feel like my body is betraying me. I'm trying to command my legs to lift, bend, and move forward correctly, but sometimes they don't listen.

Sometimes I have berated myself, saying, "You dumb ass, lift your damn legs like I taught you how to do!" Sometimes I just scream in anguish, imploring my body to do something. Still, compared to the early years, post injury, my mind in general is in a much better place today. I attribute that to years of professional counseling, medication, mindfulness, and determination to be as positive as I can. It doesn't always work out the way I would like, but my focus is unchanged.

I continue to work at being the best me I can be, accept the hand I've been dealt, and make the most of what I can do and not dwell on the things I can't. Most importantly, I take it a day at a time. I set goals, I set milestones, and I try to make every day better than the previous one.

Retirement

Retirement is something that was on my mind back in 2006 when I took my second cycling trip to France with my cycling comrades from work. On the first night of the trip, we were on our way from Geneva airport to Grenoble and stopped along the way, by happenstance, at one of the most beautiful places I had ever seen—Lake Annecy. It is a gorgeous lake, nestled in a recessed area surrounded by mountains and gently rolling hills. The lake itself is about thirty miles around and has been used as a Tour de France stop for time trials in the past.

We found a little restaurant and had the best fondue I can remember. I vowed to come back some day and look for a possible retirement location. My dream at the time was to find an older home, perhaps needing some work—with a stone exterior, one floor, and about 2,500 square feet—set somewhere on a gentle rolling hill, with a beautiful veranda overlooking the lake.

It would be a place that Diane and I could work on and turn into a long-term retirement spot, with enough land to build a small vineyard and fertile ground to plant a garden and grow our own produce. There would also be cycling roads everywhere, which would allow me to explore surrounding areas, take long rides, bask in the countryside, take in the lavender smell, or venture into town for another fondue meal. That was my dream.

My retirement dream is different today. The harsh reality is that gardening, landscaping, remodeling, building out a retirement home in France—none of these are practical goals, as much as I would like them to be.

Due to my condition, I need ready access to highly specialized medical practitioners. The best are located in the Seattle area. Redirecting my dream for retirement is another area of loss in my life, and I've had to come to terms with it. For now, my quality of life is best in Seattle. I have lived here for nearly thirty-five years, have established relationships, enjoy the climate, and have access to the best medical care needed for my injury.

Instead of France, I am searching for a new retirement dream location. I still dream of building that single-story home of 2,500 square feet, secluded on a rolling hill, with a gradual sloping landscape with finely cut green grass, a small garden and vineyard, and a veranda wrapped around the house. I imagine sitting on the deck in a padded rocking chair, enjoying a gin/tonic/lime and sharp cheese at dusk, watching the sun set, admiring the view, and drinking in the fresh air to rejuvenate my soul.

Spiritually

Many people seek the healing power of prayer and the comforting power of their Christian faith. We walked the Christian path for many years, beginning in the 1980s, when we were first introduced to Christian believers in a small group setting. We repeated the prayer that Christians pray when committing their lives to Christ: we admitted being a sinner, invited Christ into our lives, and committed to a walk in faith.

I don't think either Diane or I really knew what saying such a prayer meant, or what we were in fact signing up for, but it seemed like the right thing to do at the time. We were considered "born again." We joined a Baptist church in Seattle, where we were Sunday regulars for the most part. We participated in many activities in the church—small group meetings, retreats, and I even chaired a committee when the church was looking to modernize its computer systems.

We weren't evangelical by any stretch, didn't broadcast our faith, and generally kept quiet about it. When we moved from Seattle to Mercer Island in 1989, we joined a local neighborhood church that had a much smaller sanctuary, with a smaller membership. I would describe it as a more conservative Christian church, rooted in reading and deepening our understanding of scripture. It also offered a variety of programs, dinners, small group meetings, and retreats.

I would describe myself as a "fringe" follower, not an outsider, but I kept my distance and didn't become fully immersed. I didn't lead small groups, or speak up much at events, but I did continue my walk as a Christian, intermittently reading scripture and regularly attending Sunday services and retreats. I was active with a good friend, helping work the technology board in the back of the sanctuary, ensuring that all the video, sound, and lighting was synchronized with the service.

We very much liked the pastor and his wife. The pastor spent a number of sessions with Diane and me, helping us work through some marital and child issues, for which we were very grateful.

As with the prior church, I wouldn't say my faith deepened to the point of wanting to be overly public about it, to invite non-Christian friends to church, or to evangelize my faith to others. I believed in prayer, as I still do, but questions always nagged at me—How did the Bible come to be constructed? There were many books to choose from, but why are these sixty-six books the ones that compose the Bible?

I had many other questions as well. Why are some prayers answered and some not? Why is suffering in our world so rampant and allowed? Why is following the narrow path to salvation the only path? Is salvation and eternal life only possible through Christian faith? What about other religions? Do they have it all wrong? What about hell? Does everyone who doesn't go to heaven end up in hell? My father wasn't a believer in the strict "born again" Christian sense, and I have a very hard time believing he has been relegated to eternity in hell.

Even with all my questions, I continued to consider myself Christian. I never considered myself an evangelist, or even a fundamentalist in my beliefs. I believed in God, Jesus, and the resurrection but couldn't get past the complexity of the Bible.

In the early 2000s, the pastor and his wife left our church on Mercer Island, and soon after so did we. We sought out a new church family and ended up at another conservative Christian church in the area with similar belief systems to the church we had left—or so we thought. We were members there for several years, up until a few months after my crash in 2007.

I participated in a couple of small groups and attended Sunday services pretty regularly. I still considered myself a "fringe" member, not fully engaged in the social activities of the church but still on a walk with my Christian faith. My belief system came into serious question in late winter/early spring 2007, right before my accident when I was critically injured.

The church family we had been a part of turned on us because of a very complex and misunderstood situation. Church leadership went on to make false statements, including saying we had a pattern of being kicked out of churches, which was pure fabrication. This whole experience brought my faith in the church community and Christian belief system into even deeper doubt. I had listened to the head church pastor talk for years about the importance of keeping its "sheep," aka Christian believers, within the cozy and safe confines of the "body of Christ" or church membership. I had listened to this pastor standing on his elevated pedestal, espousing that pastors like himself will be held to a higher standard come judgment day.

The head pastor of the church even said to my wife that she was an evil person, who was "marked" and destined for a one-way trip to hell for standing up for herself during this difficult time. This tension continued right at the time of my accident, while I was hospitalized, and for several months after, at which time the church said we were no longer welcome. That is when my whole belief system in the Christian faith became broken. This was a substantial loss, and it was insulting, humiliating, and embarrassing.

I still consider myself a believer, but my belief system has been molded through experiences that have led me to believe there is no single way to salvation. I believe if you live a good and honorable life, display honesty and integrity in all your actions, love and serve others, give more than you receive, and follow the golden rule of treating others as you would like to be treated—then those are the things that make up a life worth living and are why we were put on this earth in the first place.

I believe there is a spiritual afterlife, but I am unclear as to whether I will ever see my loved ones who have already passed or who will pass before me. I believe in the power of prayer and the mobilization of energy that taps into this universal energy force. Perhaps this force is a God force, a "Jedi" force if you will, a force for good that is not restricted to any particular religious domain such as Christians, Buddhists, Islamists, or Jews, but that, instead, is for everyone. That is the force I hold on to and that anchors my belief system. It is not encumbered by one singular religion.

The loss of our church community and, frankly, our disdain of that particular community with its religious hypocrisy and dogma were artifacts of this time in my life. Now they have been replaced with a straightforward belief in the power of good over evil.

In the first few months after being discharged from HMC, I would spend a few moments in quiet reflection, sometimes prayer, thanking the Divine for getting me through the day. During the fall of 2007, I had a massage appointment with a practitioner, Renata, whom I had known for many years. During the session our conversation turned to the difficult experience my family and I had had with our last church. She shared her perspective on religion, church, and prayer.

Renata talked about this universal energy source and her belief that it connects all of us and knows no boundaries of religion, church, culture, or ethnicity. She said this energy is available to all of us, so that we can tap into it. What she said made complete sense to me and put in motion a change in how I thought about faith. For me now, prayer is a form of concentrating energy and enabling my connection to this universal energy force that binds us all. It can be leveraged in many ways to heal people, and I increasingly embraced this approach in the way I visualized my own healing.

While I connect with this force more through visualization than through prayer, I do use both. Regardless of method, I believe it does connect me to something larger, more powerful, and more loving than I can comprehend. I do believe it exists and know that, at some level, it has enabled a remarkable healing process in my life.

Physically

Today on an overall basis I continue to get stronger. The scheduled therapy appointments I have had over the past nine years number in the thousands. I have invested countless hours in the gym working out, sometimes with friends, other times by myself. It has been an agonizingly slow and difficult journey, and if I had known ahead of time what I was in for, I might never have been able to do it.

The eating-the-elephant-one-bite-at-a time analogy applies here—one step at a time; one exercise at a time; one session at a time. I have achieved some amazing milestones that I am extremely proud of, and I continue to pursue new goals.

The biggest loss of all is how my body "feels." I feel like my body leapfrogged thirty years in the aging process, like I stepped into a time tunnel and came out the other side much older and more frail, with more aches and pains, more limitations, more risks and vulnerabilities, more falls, and slower movements. It feels as though I have lost three decades of my life, as though my life has been shortened, though hopefully not. As a result, my sense of urgency to do meaningful things with my remaining time has become much stronger.

In some ways, like upper body, arms, and core, I am stronger than I was prior to the accident. In other ways, I am considerably weaker, especially with hip, gluteus, and hamstring muscles. I have faculties today that are more impaired than they were even four months after the crash. For example, I can't walk as fast as I used to, or for as long. In the early years post injury, while working with Chris at Pacific Balance, I worked my way up to walking three miles per hour on the treadmill for ten minutes, without holding on to anything for support. Today, I would be lucky to walk half that speed.

During that same time, I could walk up stairs, hands free. Today I can't do that. While I have experienced an abundance of positive accomplishments, there are places where I have regressed, and those losses concern me at times.

My physiatrist, Dr. Barry, once told me he envisions that I will be wheelchair bound by the time I reach age sixty-five. That's not my plan, but I also know he has worked with countless SCI patients and has pretty good insight into the neurological progression. However, I have not made it a practice in my recovery to be like everyone else in the SCI population studies. I have my own program and expect to be different.

I have had slightly increasing numbers of bowel and bladder accidents that I never had before. I certainly didn't wear adult diapers in the early years, post injury. I have been on walks with my trekking poles and often came upon seniors with their walker chairs, and sometimes we would joke about who could walk faster. I felt like I was part of the senior community, and we could relate to one another because of our infirmities.

This is a sad feeling in a way, knowing that I most likely have permanent impairments (but remember, I don't rule out anything). On one hand, I have experienced a deep sense of loss over my reduced physicality. On the other hand, there are a lot of really cool things I can now do, thanks to all the time investment I've made in the weight room.

Overall, I do take stock of certain ways I have regressed and loss patterns that I try to manage. I also know they could worsen. The fact that I can't just stand up without being in pain and going severely spastic is the most disheartening of my maladies. I fight these feelings by focusing on things I *can* do, like living independently with almost no accommodation, including personal hygiene, cooking, eating, dressing and driving.

I focus on all the different exercises I can do in the gym with weights, balls, bands, kettlebells, and various cardio and strengthening machines.

I will continue to build on the things I am able to do and strive for new goals. My primary focus is on the possible, not on the ways I might be regressing.

I am teaching myself that the aging process is natural, and as an impaired individual, everything has a cumulative effect. I deal with it by following the same mantra I came up with nine years ago in a lonely hospital room:

Define your terms. Take a stand. Choose to win.

CHAPTER 14

It's Not Just About Me—Family

I know this accident hasn't just affected me. It has been a challenge in many ways and has had a very deep impact on my wife and children. All of my family has been incredibly supportive throughout this journey, and I wouldn't be where I am today without them.

Yet I know that all of our relationships have had to change. Much of my energy is devoted to just being able to "do the day"—to get up and work on my independence and my routine of exercise and rehab. Consequently, I don't have much left in the tank for my family. I've struggled for years trying to balance my life, but there is so much on my plate.

My mind is constantly filled with managing distressing pain, monitoring my efforts, being mindful in everything I do, being mentally conscious of every step I take, trying to avoid a fall, prepping and revving myself up for every endeavor. All of this selfish commitment worsens if my body is imbalanced in any way—through sickness, infection, injury, temperature, or any exacerbation of symptoms.

Alana

In 2009, my daughter Alana was in high school, and Kevin was another year from finishing up college. I was working part-time, primarily telecommuting from home. Alana and I shared the same home office. One afternoon I came into the office and sat down at my desk. Alana was at her desk, with her back to me, and I could hear some soft sniffles. It sounded like she was crying, and I asked if she was okay. She didn't respond.

I got up, walked over, and put my hands on her shoulders. Her shoulders shook, and I sensed tears were streaming down her face, although she wouldn't turn and look at me. She didn't want to talk, so I just stood behind her, painful as standing was, and tried to just be there with her. Eventually she did turn around red-faced, still crying as she looked up at me.

"Dad," she finally said, "I hate seeing you in pain and would do anything to take it away from you. It makes me hurt when I see you hurt."

Her words really touched me, and I teared up too. "I know how difficult it is to see me in pain," I told her. "I would feel just as bad to see you suffer. It's that way with loved ones. I want you to know, though, that you don't need to carry around that weight on your shoulders. It is a boat anchor that you don't need."

I thought for a moment and then continued. "I need you to trust me, to know that I can deal with the pain, and that you don't have to take it on yourself. I'm not going to whitewash it; this pain sucks. It really does. Sometimes it gets to me, which is natural, but you should know that I can handle it. It's not a burden you need to carry." I gave her a big hug, and she seemed relieved.

Alana has a big heart for others. She cares so much about people. I'll never forget that brief talk because it made me aware of something I hadn't thought of before. We, our family, are all trying to protect each other. In one sense this is a good thing. We all care about each other. We all love each other.

We've struggled, however, with respecting each other's boundaries and trusting that we can each deal with our own infirmities. We've all heard the axiom "misery loves company." That's kind of what was going on with our family at this time. In our desire to protect, we weren't respecting each other's boundaries and capabilities.

How did we work through this? Today, we are still working on it. This is not an easy process to figure out. Each of us has sought professional help, both in one-on-one sessions and in group therapy. This has helped, but we are still trying to figure out how to consistently apply some of the principles—like not overcompensating (doing for the other person what each is capable of doing for him- or herself) when it's not needed, as well as trusting, not doubting each other, and respecting one another's space.

I suppose it is natural to feel the impulse to take away another person's suffering, but carrying that boat anchor can inhibit your own life and even affect your health. In Alana's case, I think to some degree it has impacted her health. The stress of my injury isn't the only thing that has affected her health, but it has been a component.

Unfortunately, at the age of nineteen, after many years of undiagnosed severe abdominal pain, multiple ER visits, and a large number of tests and exams, she was ultimately diagnosed with an autoimmune disease. She had abdominal surgery in 2014 where the diagnosis was confirmed, and it resulted in the removal of some lesions in her abdomen.

Later her symptoms returned, and she had to have a second laparoscopy in March 2015.

This time she was diagnosed with an advanced stage of the disease and had to have over ten lesions removed. She had a third surgery to remove her appendix as well as additional lesions and scar tissue in December 2015. All the lesions removed in her surgeries were benign. Alana's symptoms are difficult, persistent, and unpredictable. The prognosis on several levels is unclear, depending on the course this disease takes. It is unknowable and difficult to process.

She continues to suffer ongoing symptoms of this incurable autoimmune disease. Like everyone with this condition, it will be something she has to manage for the rest of her life. There is no question that my injury is a stressor that has in some measure added to her health problems; it's not the only cause but is likely a contributor.

One day while I was in the inpatient rehab unit at HMC, Alana came to my room for a visit. She was in seventh grade at the time and had given a presentation to her class as part of an assignment to research and talk about a topic in her family history. She chose to research my wife's great-grandfather, Sir Henry Bessemer, who invented the Bessemer Steel Process that Andrew Carnegie acquired and brought over to the United States from the United Kingdom. It was an important part of the Industrial Revolution at the turn of the twentieth century.

Alana asked if she could replay her presentation to me. I said, "I would love to hear it—do you have your notes with you?" She said, "No, we were asked to present without notes if at all possible, and so I didn't use any."

For the next twenty minutes, she delivered her presentation like a professional—no pauses or "umms" and "ahhs"—as if she was reading out of an advanced novel. Her sentences were perfectly structured, her cadence on point, and the content perfectly woven together. She did it all extemporaneously. I had never seen anything like it and was stunned.

"Alana," I said, "that is the most amazing thing I have ever heard. You have an incredible gift, and I'm not saying that because I'm your dad, but what you just did was off the charts! That, my dear, is an incredible talent."

As she pursues her professional ambitions, there is no doubt in my mind that she will be reaching many people in need of hearing her medical story and giving hope and inspiration to thousands of women who are struggling with this terrible affliction. The power of her public-speaking skills will take her to some awesome places.

Alana was a strong cross-country runner in middle school, in the top three of her class. About nine months after I returned home from the hospital, I came out to her school to watch her compete in a track-and-field event. She was running the four-hundred-meter race. As she came around the last turn in full stride, leading the pack, her left foot landed on a clump of mud on the track, awkwardly twisting her knee, and she went down.

She got back up and limped to the finish line. I saw the whole thing. She was proud to have me there, and I was proud too. Seeing her fall to the ground felt awful, because I know how hard she was trying to win.

Three knee surgeries later, she could possibly have ongoing knee challenges in the future because a lot of her meniscus has been removed. It was one of those random things, but I still feel some guilt, as if somehow

I'm responsible for her injury because I had made a special effort to be there and she wanted to perform for me. She has never returned to running in the same way she had before that track meet. Perhaps my feelings of guilt are misplaced, but they are real and sometimes challenging for me. I feel in part some responsibility, and just as Alana had longed to take away my suffering, I would do anything to take away her pain.

She is a tremendously gifted daughter, very smart, and a high achiever. Graduating with a combined undergraduate and master's degree with honors, summa cum laude, all before age twenty-one, is a testament to her talents. From my injury standpoint, I'm clearly not the only one affected. It has been difficult to work through these challenges—how best to support her, and how best to manage my own intermittent feelings of guilt and responsibility.

Kevin

Kevin was the first person to be contacted about my accident, and he had the difficult job of discovering Diane's whereabouts so that she could be contacted. He also had to deliver the news to Alana. During the first year post injury, Kevin had to step up as man of the house, assisting Diane and Alana in multiple ways including household chores, driving Alana to school events, etc., in addition to holding a part-time job, working on his community college studies, and being captain of the cross-country team. Once he transferred to Seattle University as a boarding student, his involvement in our household needs became less as my condition stabilized.

Since spring 2011 Kevin has been out of the country during most of my injury recovery period. He hasn't seen all the ups and downs of my recovery process, because he has lived in China for the past five years. My injury has touched him, but not in the same way as Alana. I know, however, that he misses the athletic things we used to do together, especially skiing. Before my injury, he was passing me in ability, and I was the one trying to keep up with him. We've had some epic ski runs together.

Kevin and I spent a very special moment together a few days after I was first hospitalized in the acute care unit. Because I was completely bedridden with no movement from my mid-abdomen and down, Kevin came over to my left side. Tears were streaming down his face. He didn't know what to say. I asked him to pull the curtain over the middle of the bed to shield us from other family visitors so I could spend a moment alone with him.

We were both quiet for a while. I asked him to come closer to me so I could reach his face with my hands. I could move my arms and elbows to extend my hands to his face, but no hand or finger movement was possible at that time. My hands were slightly curled inward in the shape of a "C," but otherwise they were without function.

He leaned over the bed railing, and put his head on my chest, and I laid my arms on top of his back. We didn't say anything. At that moment, our hearts were touching, and there was this unusual exchange between us—spiritual, energizing, and moving. He lifted his head, and we looked deeply into each other's tear-filled eyes, practically touching each other's souls.

I said to him, "Kevin, I'm very badly injured. I'm scared, more frightened than I have ever been in my life. I don't know what the prognosis is; I don't know where this is going to go. Things are going to be different, and it is going to require a lot of time and adjustment. What won't be different is this—I love you. I love you with every ounce of my being. You are so important to me. I admire you, respect you, and know that you are destined to do great things in your lifetime. You are going to have a great impact on this world, I have no doubt about it."

Kevin smiled at me and said, "I love you so much, Dad, and thank you for believing in me. It must be so hard to think about someone else when you are in this condition."

As we exchanged these words, he held my hands up to his face and curled them around his cheeks. I was unable to feel the tears streaming down his face. It was a special moment, one that he replayed two years later in 2009 when we were celebrating Father's Day at home.

We went around the table and each said words of gratitude that were initiated by Father's Day but that included everyone. Kevin said that conversation in the hospital room on Father's Day 2007 had touched him profoundly. He said it had ignited a fire inside him like nothing else ever had in his life.

Kevin was at Seattle University majoring in environmental sciences coupled with a minor in Mandarin Chinese. He was keenly interested in climate change. After our talk that day in the hospital, he immediately launched an effort to build a coalition of American and Chinese youth interested in making a difference. He traveled to Copenhagen, Denmark, for the 2009 Global Climate Change Conference and followed that up the next year with a trip to Cancún, Mexico, for the same conference.

I had long coached him on the power of networking, building relationships, and creating what I loosely termed a "portable rolodex" of contacts. He came back from the first conference in 2009 with over three hundred business cards and many stories of meeting influential people, including a brief visit with the US Secretary of Energy Steven Chu.

Kevin went on to build a US-China Youth Climate Coalition that met again in 2010 in Cancún and was the primary impetus for his moving to China after he graduated in 2010. In recounting our hospital-bed conversation that Father's Day, he said the words I spoke had played over and over in his head and that it energized him in everything he was doing.

There is no doubt Kevin is destined for great things, and his gifts will touch many people in incredible ways during his lifetime. He said the words I spoke to him were the fuel that stoked his engine and that continue to do so to this day. I couldn't be prouder of him.

Diane

My wife, Diane, has had understandable difficulties in dealing with my injury. She has witnessed all these changes from a very different perspective than that of our children. The challenges span multiple areas. For one thing, she has residual anger and resentment about the defective bike I was riding when the crash occurred. Her anger is still somewhat unprocessed, even today over nine years later.

She has some bitterness about my accident, and I am concerned that her anger could be toxic to her system. I want fervently for her to find a way to process her anger and be able to completely let go and move on. To that end, she has finally consented to seeking professional help, and I'm hopeful that she can find some strategies to cope in this regard.

Diane has been a steady caregiver and has been attentive to my needs, which, over time, have become less. I can do most things on my own, but she handles most of the household chores, grocery shopping, and other errands. I generally make my own meals, breakfast and dinner, simple fare to give her time to pursue her own interests.

In the early years after my injury, she did all the driving, took me to appointments, massaged my feet before going to bed, put on and took off my compression socks, cleaned my neck brace collar every night, took care of all our home living responsibilities, and was basically tethered to all my needs. This was incredibly hard on her. There were times when she was extremely distraught, resentful, and frustrated with me, my injury, and the defective bike, and she no doubt contemplated finding a different life for herself. She lamented on a few occasions that this wasn't the life she had signed up for. I understood her feelings and knew they were completely normal.

The changes in our lives have affected our relationship. My body doesn't feel like my body. It is strangely different, with my bodily sensations muted, diminished, obscured. The truth is my waist-level functions have been impacted. This entire side of my life, and the impact it has had on our marriage, can't be understated.

Despite all of this, Diane has stayed by my side, has advocated for me, supported me, and been a relentless caregiver. I could always depend on her to do what she thought was right. She has continued to love me, even when I've been unlovable. She has tolerated my moodiness, my periodic frustrations with my dysfunctional body, and my occasional outbursts. Somehow she has insulated herself from acutely feeling my pain, in a different fashion than Alana has. Diane has learned to provide me with space and alone time when I have needed it. In many ways she deserves better than I can provide, and I have had some guilt feelings emerge because of this. I am impaired, and it has affected our relationship, yet she has stood by me throughout these struggles. Her love has indeed helped bring me back. Bring me back from what? Bring me back from the edge, from being my own worst enemy, and she has kept me from falling off a cliff. It could have easily happened if it hadn't been for Diane.

Coming to grips with our new marital reality is still ongoing. Of all the issues associated with the injury, this has been the most challenging. To date we haven't been very successful doing this on our own. In some ways, I've just wanted to sweep it under the rug, not worry about it, reluctantly accept it, and just forget about it. Dealing with these emotional scars feels more daunting to me than dealing with the physical side. This area needs attention, but I've been risk averse in tackling it. I'm sure it is best to deal with it through counseling and some deep, reflective conversations.

But the risk is months of intense counseling that will likely open floodgates of unprocessed emotions. I recollect my days as a toddler, wrapped in gauze bandages like a mummy due to skin eczema, oozing blisters, and then having dried bandages torn off with skin attached. That's the kind of pain I envision will be a part of intensive couples counseling, and I am reluctant to go through that again. But I will do what it takes, on my terms, to win this battle too.

. . .

Diane and Alana have often wanted to do family things together (while Kevin was living in China with Viki), but they are also mindful that anything we do causes me pain and suffering. It's a difficult conundrum because they miss doing family activities but also want to protect me from pain.

Last Thanksgiving, Diane and Alana talked me into participating in a hot yoga class at the local studio. The studio had arranged special classes on the holiday morning with fees being contributed to a local charity. I have long considered trying yoga but hadn't felt I was ready, given my balance issues and limited range of motion. I decided to take a big step out of my comfort zone and consented to join them in the class.

Hot yoga is done in a heated studio, which was helpful for me in terms of loosening up my seizing muscles. Diane and Alana were so excited to have me there. It was an hour-long class, and I managed to stay with it the whole time, often with balance assistance from the wall grab bar. I found I could do most of the strengthening exercises, but I struggled, predictably, with those requiring balance. I was dripping with sweat at the end of class.

Diane and Alana were so proud (and so was I) and were excited to introduce me to the instructor, fellow classmates, and the studio owner. I guess it was rewarding for them to showcase their disabled father/husband and what I was capable of doing. I was exhausted but feeling a pleasant afterglow from the effort. As anticipated, I paid a significant price in pain after the endorphins from the workout wore off, but I used ice and ibuprofen to manage it.

This experience and others like it, although infrequent, are a kind of family therapy that would benefit us if done more often. While I can occasionally muster the will and energy to do them, they invariably come at a price. I wish I could do these and not suffer so much afterward.

. . .

My son Kevin and wife Viki moved back from Shanghai to Seattle early in 2016. We had purchased a second condominium on Mercer Island prior to learning of their intention to return to the United States. It was also fortuitous that we had furnishings in storage that we had brought with us a year ago when relocating from the Phoenix area back to Seattle.

There was a confluence of events—Kevin and Viki moving, the condo purchase, and furnishings in storage—that made their move to Seattle pretty much turnkey. All they had to bring with them were their clothes. They have done amazingly well getting acclimated and working diligently to start their own business.

Now that Alana is employed she wants independence, understandably, and is aggressively looking for an apartment.

As in any family, there are often challenging dynamics. What makes these struggles so challenging for me is that layering these issues on top of my daily living difficulties causes my other family members to want to insulate me from everything that is going on. They do this under the misplaced notion that they are protecting me. Eventually I learn what is happening, to some extent happening behind my back, and then I do my best to be objective and help bring understanding to all family members.

We've tried to keep our lines of communication open and stick to some semblance of family togetherness. We do this by having a family dinner, all of us, at least once a week, at Kevin and Viki's condominium. It doesn't hurt that they are both masterful chefs and that their meals are five-star restaurant–caliber meals. Their meals are incredible. Family communication during mealtime is sometimes chatty, and other times quiet, even emotional. The point is being together and continuing to work as best we can to hear each other out, whether we come to agreement or not. It starts with dialogue and can build from there.

Dealing with family issues, and there are plenty of others, requires considerable energy and focus on my part, and I only have limited energy cycles to do what I think is best. I feel a loss in my ability to influence, and it leaves me with a very bad feeling of parental impotence. To deal with this and other family issues, I know the best approach is professional counseling, which after many years is beginning to happen. Most of us are engaged in counseling with different practitioners. The way forward is to build on that and bring us together as a group in family counseling.

In spite of the difficulties and obstacles we each have faced, love of family, and love from family, has been the wind under my sails, lifting and keeping me up, helping me feel needed, purposeful, and hopeful. I am regaining the "dance" again, and love is the "music" propelling me. Even though I may be impaired, love still transcends all—even in our darkest times.

PART

FOUR

IN

PURSUIT

OF A

NEW

NORMAL

CHAPTER 15

The Solace of Memories

I've always loved sports, especially those played outside. My sports favorites included skiing, golfing, squash, running, cycling, and rowing crew. At every step of my recovery, I would spend time combing through my memory banks of my own memorable sports moments. It was a helpful distraction from all the trauma and suffering after my injury. I found myself lost in these memories for hours when I had time to myself. I would even daydream about them while lying in bed at night, visualizing what it would be like to do them again.

When I was in college, I took up running, in part for cross-training purposes. It slowly grew on me, and following college and for many of my adult years, I continued to run until I took up cycling. When I would run, especially while in college, my distances rarely exceeded three to four miles. I ran often, usually every day, and generally would run hard. I'd make the workout anaerobically taxing, and if I didn't finish feeling like I was on the rivet (on the edge), then the run seemed incomplete. I'd resolve to make the workout harder the following day.

I was sort of a masochist, seemingly driven to push myself to the point of being punishing, straining for breath, chest burning, and legs wobbly. Strangely, that's what I wanted. My mind-set was, "I'm not going to get better if I don't push harder." Funny how that came in handy when I was injured and had to fight ever harder to make progress in my recovery.

There were many long-ago memories that brought me comfort during the days I spent in the hospital. I thought back about how I had learned to row crew on a whim and then joined the Ithaca College rowing team. For three years I rowed for Ithaca in College Division III crew, which changed everything about my college experience.

Freshman year I had been lost, treading water without any clear direction of what I was doing or what I wanted to achieve. Crew changed all of that. Sophomore year, I met my new roommate, Andy, completely by chance. He turned out to be a very talented oarsman. We roomed together for three years and to this day still stay in touch. My grades improved as I became part of a community, and most important, I developed a lifelong commitment to fitness, diet, and exercise. Crew changed my life.

We won a lot of races and medaled in others. One race occurred junior year rowing in a regatta on the Schuylkill River near Philadelphia, Pennsylvania. The event was called the Dad Vail regatta, named after Harry Emerson "Dad" Vail for his years coaching at the University of Wisconsin–Madison. It is the largest intercollegiate regatta, drawing crews from over one hundred colleges and universities.

We were rowing in the semifinals of the lightweight eight, and I was stroking the boat, the person in front of the coxswain who sets the boat cadence consistent with the calls of the coxswain. The top three finishers would make it into the final. We were nervous going into the race because we were up against some very tough competition, including a top crew from the University of British Columbia (UBC), as well as perennial powerhouse Trinity College. We rowed the race of our lives, everything was clicking, and we came in second, just behind the boat from UBC and ahead of Trinity.

I'll never forget the shocked look of the Trinity team. Unfortunately, we didn't replicate the same performance in the final and did not medal. That semifinal race was the most exciting race I rowed in those final three years at Ithaca and is a special memory I will always cherish.

. . .

I had the good fortune to grow up in a ski family. My father taught all of us kids to ski during our early teenage years on Mount Whittier in West Ossipee just south of the White Mountains of New Hampshire. The Mount Whittier Ski Area operated on Nickerson Mountain. The ski runs we grew up on closed in 1985, but when we were younger, we often traveled there as a family and stayed at the local Tamworth Inn in nearby Tamworth, New Hampshire. The building unfortunately met its demise in 2013 and was replaced by a local brewery.

But that's where I developed my love for skiing. Over the years, I've skied many of the most storied ski areas in the world. These include locations in Europe like St. Moritz, Crans Montana, and Zermatt in Switzerland, and St. Anton am Arlberg in Austria. Growing up on the East Coast allowed me opportunities to ski at numerous areas like Loon Mountain, Killington, Waterville Valley, Stowe, Balsams, and Big Bromley. With my brother and sisters, Molly, Allyson, and Rob, all having lived in Colorado, I also had the opportunity to ski Vail, Steamboat, and Mary Jane (part of Winter Park).

Of all the areas I have skied, I still believe the snow quality in Utah is the best, especially in places like Alta, Snowbird, Brighton, Solitude, and Park City. In terms of overall mountain experience—snow quality, steeps, vertical—it's hard to argue that Jackson Hole doesn't top them all. I sampled other locations out West, including Big Sky in Montana, Heavenly and Squaw Valley in California, Sun Valley in Idaho, and Mount Bachelor in Oregon. Spending over half my life in Washington, I often skied Crystal, Stevens Pass, Alpental, Snoqualmie Pass, and Mission Ridge.

However, the area where we spent the most time skiing was Whistler Blackcomb in British Columbia, Canada, where we raised our children on skis. Both of them went on to become advanced skiers.

I always skied hard with maximum aerobic effort. My layers were always soaked. I enjoyed the groomers and bumps, steeps and cruisers, but what brought me the greatest thrill was finding untracked snow through the trees. A close second was any of the steeps, and many of these ski areas had plenty of them, especially at Jackson Hole. Corbet's Couloir ranks right up there, as does Ruby Bowl or Spanky's Ladder at Blackcomb. Without question the steepest slope I ever experienced was Tuckerman Ravine on Mount Washington in New Hampshire.

There is no lift. You hike it, which is daunting in itself, look down, close your eyes for a moment, pray you don't catch an edge, and *go*. The runs off Tuckerman Ravine vary in pitch from forty to fifty-five degrees, which is so steep you can stand sidewise to the downfall and reach with one arm and touch the downslope. I made it. Once was enough.

. . .

Experienced skiers crave powder like crack addicts crave their fix. A snowy overnight forecast with twenty centimeters of "fresh" interrupts sleep faster than six cups of coffee before bedtime. I've had countless powder experiences, but one stands out. My son and I were at Blackcomb a few years before my injury. The particular forecast I mentioned here materialized, and we were at the base lift fifteen minutes before opening.

Twenty or so chairs back from the first group, we made our way to the top of the Wizard Express. Almost everyone continued on to take the next chair higher up, called Solar Coaster. Kevin and I went the other way and skied back down to the bottom through eight inches of untracked snow, he to the left, me to the right. As we made our way down the run, underneath the Wizard chair, we could hear the chorus of screams, hoots, and jealous hollers of those skiers still making their way up on the chairlift. Kevin and I were cutting turns in an untouched canvas landscape of dry snow, creating our own snow painting, albeit briefly, of perfectly drawn S turns down the slope.

Before other skiers carved it up, we had a few moments to hug each other and look back up the slope and admire our work. Like an etch-a-sketch, our work was gone in moments. What a sport. Up until my bicycling accident, I had been able to feed my skiing passion that began from the days I learned as a child on Mount Whittier, New Hampshire, to so many ski days at Whistler Blackcomb and Crystal.

. . .

My father taught me how to play golf at a local nine-hole course at our summer getaway in Dublin, New Hampshire. I continued to play golf most of my life until I was injured. I was a golfing enthusiast, but I can't say I ever got really good at it. At best, I had a thirteen handicap. Typically my handicap was between sixteen and eighteen. I really enjoyed the camaraderie and friendly competition and being outside.

One of my favorite memories, and photographs, is of Diane and me on our honeymoon in Hawaii. The year (I better get this right) was 1980. We were staying at a resort called the Mauna Kea on the Big Island. This was without question the most opulent resort in which we have ever stayed. The resort beach was exquisite, horseshoe-shaped with perfectly tender, white-grained sand. The resort also sported an exceptional beachfront golf course.

We were standing on the tee of a par three hole, and we asked a nearby guest to take a picture of us. Most of the picture is shot over water with the golf green nestled on a small peninsula sticking out into the ocean. The sun is setting, ocean in the background, and our faces are lit up from the sun's rays. This framed picture adorns our home entryway.

I've had some very special golf experiences. A very memorable one was being invited to attend a Pro-Am celebrity golf tournament played outside Las Vegas. There were celebrities everywhere, including golf coach legend Butch Harmon (coached Tiger Woods for many years); baseball legends Greg Maddux and Barry Bonds; tennis legend Pete Sampras; football legends Jim McMahon and Terrell Davis; musical artist Kenny G. (born in Seattle!); LPGA professional Natalie Gulbis; and others. Our amateur foursome got paired up with Natalie, and besides her beauty, we admired her effortless swing as she carded a sixty-seven.

For many years, whenever I traveled, my clubs came with me. My friend Bob and I would often travel to Las Vegas for a few days of golf, shows, good wine, and some time at the card tables. One year, just after arrival, we were at the baggage claim at Las Vegas airport collecting our golf clubs. We met a guy named Tracy who was also collecting his clubs and introduced ourselves and had a brief chat. At the car rental station a few minutes later, we bumped into Tracy again, and did so a third time while checking in at the same hotel, MGM. While walking the long hallway to our room a few minutes later we saw him a fourth time.

The chance meetings were more than coincidence. Evidently, he and a cadre of other friends from around the country would get together for a three-day golf tourney in Vegas every year, and Tracy invited Bob and me to join them. That was about twenty years ago and the tradition continues today. Although I haven't attended since my injury, Bob has been to most if not all of these events. Perhaps in one of these coming years, I'll make an appearance again. Time to start visualizing!

These guys are all jokesters and love to have fun, on and off the golf course. They are all very good golfers. No one was insulated from some friendly ridicule when making a bad shot. I was no exception. On one round, Bob and I were partnered with Tracy and a friend. I duffed my tee shot, barely dribbling it past the ladies' tee. The other three crushed their drives two hundred-plus yards straight down the fairway. As we drove our carts to my ball, which was next shot, Tracy quipped, "Next stop, ladies' lingerie!" We all busted out laughing. That year I won the trophy for having the worst (highest) collective score over three days. At the final evening banquet, I was an honored recipient of the "Last Place Bitch Award." What an honor.

Tennis was another staple sport of my family. My father was a very active tennis player, often in different competitions playing both singles and doubles. I remember my dad teaching me how to play at our summer getaway in Dublin, New Hampshire. The courts at the Dublin Lake Club were clay—a deep dark maroon that would quickly discolor the white tennis balls as soon as they were uncorked from a new canister.

My brother Tom and my father were quite a tennis duo, competing in doubles tournaments and often placing well. Tom was a top high school tennis player and went on to teach for a number of years. In 1969, Tom and his tennis partner were state high school doubles champions in Massachusetts.

I also had the opportunity to experience playing on grass, as my dad kept a limited membership at a tennis club in Chestnut Hill, Massachusetts, called Longwood Cricket Club. During the summers we were allowed to go to the club once a month. Playing on grass is very different from clay or hard surfaces, because the ball bounce is very low, and instead of maroon, the balls quickly turned green.

Longwood during those days in the 1970s hosted a professional tennis tournament, US Pro Tennis Championships, which was held on grass courts as a lead up to the US Open at Forest Hills, in New York, also held on grass surfaces at that time. For many of the pros, it was considered the US Open warm-up. In 1976 we had a chance to get tickets and watch one of the tournament matches that included notables Jimmy Connors and John McEnroe.

During the tournament that year, Tom and I were sitting in the stands, and right next to us was Bud Collins, a famous tennis broadcaster and pundit during those years. (Sadly, he passed away in March 2016.) I overheard him talking to someone next to him about McEnroe, this young, brash talent just entering the pro scene. He was talking about McEnroe's serve, being a lefty and how his fast, arching serve would spin away from right-handed players when serving to their backhand. He predicted that McEnroe would soon displace Connors as the premier player of that genre, which he eventually did.

I played tennis recreationally through high school and college, but soon after moving to Seattle and joining the SAC as a charter member, I was introduced to a new sport called squash. Figuring I had a lot of childhood experience with a tennis racquet, I thought squash would be easy to pick up. It wasn't easy, but I learned it fairly quickly. A squash racquet could best be described as something between a tennis and badminton racquet.

In the early days, the SAC had two eighteen-foot-wide courts used for the "hardball" version of the sport. Squash is both similar and dissimilar to racquetball. By comparison a racquetball court is twenty feet wide, and you can use all surfaces of the court. In squash, there are court lines drawn on the floor—front, side, and back walls—within which the ball must remain to be in play. In racquetball, when you watch the very best players, it tends to be a power sport, and the objective is to put the ball away by hitting it very low against the front wall without first touching the floor so that the other player can't return it. Usually it is less than a handful of exchanges and point over.

In squash, because of the lines, especially in the frontcourt, it is harder to put the ball away and win a point, so rallies tend to be longer and thus more aerobically intensive. When watching the very best players, it's easy to see that squash requires incredible agility, consistent misdirection and irregular movements, aerobic conditioning, and finesse. Rallies last much longer, often thirty exchanges or more. That requires amazing physical fitness.

I played hardball for a couple of years, and then the SAC transitioned to standard international squash, building out several twenty-one-foot-wide internationally dimensioned squash courts and switching everything to softball. I became a passionate and dedicated squash player for almost fifteen years, playing almost every day of the week, at lunch, at night, and during weekends. I got involved in tournament squash and competed locally and in two national tournaments at my ability level (there are competitions for different ability levels).

Eventually I moved up to A level at the SAC, but for national competitions I was at a B/C level. I built a number of relationships over those years, and squash became my community. I had to give up squash at the SAC when I changed jobs and my employment took me forty-five minutes away, making it impractical to continue there. I had a lot of great years playing squash and developed some long-lasting relationships that still exist today.

. . .

While living in Seattle, I got involved in a number of organized runs and resolved to train and run a marathon with Tom, who was living in Maine. He suggested I train and run the Maine Coast Marathon, 26.2 miles. I took a conservative approach: I trained for three months, ran thirty to thirty-five miles per week, and every two weeks would take one long run starting at twelve miles, and in two-mile increments, worked my way up to twenty. My goal for the marathon was to finish stronger than when I started. I started the run at eight-minute miles and finished at seven-minute miles, for a time of three hours and twenty-three minutes (3:23).

Tom's plans changed, and he decided to join me on the run for the first six miles and then planned to connect with his wife, Kyle, to be picked up, and then meet me at the finish line. Tom was dressed in his tennis sneakers, had done no training, and had not eaten or hydrated, thinking it was only going to be six miles. For some reason, Tom and Kyle didn't connect, and Tom, amazingly, ran the entire 26.2 miles! He finished behind me, but I was beyond amazed at what he was able to do with absolutely no preparation. I figured if I had even five percent of his genes, my chances of becoming a decent runner were very good.

I primarily ran 10K races after that, and sprinkled in one half marathon. My best 10K averaged 5.37 per mile splits. I thought about training to become a triathlete, but could not commit the time, and more importantly, was a challenged swimmer. I was able to swim, but it was always labored. I could never get my body to relax enough to breathe properly and would become quickly anaerobic.

I stayed with running up until 1998. At the company where I worked, I ran at lunch from 1994–1998 with a triathlete named Ed, and he worked me hard. Often we would run this eight-mile route around the Kent Valley, which included a very steep hill, in the fifteen percent to twenty percent gradient range, which itself lasted a mile. The flat, final mile back to campus was an all-out sprint, and once we were in the parking lot, I quickly found a grassy area and collapsed.

Running soon segued into cycling. Besides runners, there was a cycling group that rode at lunch, and someone suggested that if I wanted to protect my joints longer from the high-impact stress of running perhaps I should consider cycling. I decided to buy a bike, a starter bike from the company I worked for, Italian manufactured. It was a steel bike called a Bianchi. I knew nothing about cycling gear, bike fit, mechanics, or apparel—nothing.

I ended up buying a pair of mountain bike shoes, not the right shoes for a road bike. The bike came with all the protective componentry like reflectors and other air-resistance devices that competitive road cyclists have removed. I must have looked like quite the "gomer" when I first joined the lunch ride. The group varied in size, from as small as five to as many as twenty, and sometimes more. During my first set of rides, I stayed at the back of the pack because I knew nothing about riding in a group.

Slowly I got the hang of it, made some mistakes, but learned proper etiquette—riding in a pace line, rotation, hand signals, call outs, climbing, descending, cornering, etc. I had a pretty good base of lung and leg strength and had plenty of experience in being able to push myself.

The group had a traditional ride they did during the late summer, a ride up Mount Rainier to Paradise, an ascent of about 3,500 vertical feet over twenty miles. The ride started and finished in Packwood, Washington, a loop that covered over eighty miles. Known as the TdP, or Tour de Packwood, the group started at a gentle pace up Skate Creek Road, a road connecting Packwood to Ashford, which connects to the Nisqually or west entrance of Mount Rainier National Park.

At the top of Skate Creek Road is usually when the games began, attacks, bridges, counterattacks—fun cycling strategies to mix it up. I was hanging on for dear life, trying with everything I had to stay with the group, bobbing on/off the back. Once into the park itself, we stopped for a quick break and then started the real climbing. This was my first time climbing Mount Rainier on a bicycle.

A few miles into the climb the pace began to push up a notch; some riders fell off the back, but I managed to stay with the main group. As we passed Longmire the pace began to amp up another notch, this time jettisoning a few more riders off the back. Not long after that, I found myself with four of the strongest riders, breathing heavily, oblivious to what was ahead or to how long this pace would continue. I had no idea where the top was.

Soon, it was just two of us on the front; all the other riders had fallen off the pace. The other rider then dropped back as well, assuming, I suppose, that I wouldn't be able to hold my pace and would consequently "blow up." I was suffering terribly, anaerobic, legs and lungs burning, looking up, anxious to see if I could find the top. This went on for another thirty minutes until I finally reached the top, still in front, and came to a stop in the parking lot. I felt absolutely awful, dehydrated and nauseated from not enough fluids and food.

I made my way to the water fountain, then went and bought some food, and took the next thirty minutes trying to recover. I walked back to the parking lot where other riders were assembling as they finished at the top. Brian, one of the strongest riders, came up to me and said, "Osborne, I don't know how the hell you do it."

I think he was remarking about the fact that all the other riders were riding lightweight, aluminum, tricked-out bikes with all the "goodies" in terms of cranks, drive train, and other carbon fiber componentry. I was riding a heavier steel bike, triple ring (which is not a racing configuration), with bike shoes that weren't even designed for the bike I was riding. I had no idea what I was doing, but from that moment on I was hooked.

As time went on I began to hear some secondhand comments about my cycling strength, and potential, which only fueled my passion for the sport. The next decade up until my accident in 2007 offered some of the most satisfying years of my life. I loved cycling, training, camaraderie, and friendly competition.

In 2004 I made my first of two road cycling trips to France, joined by Mike, a company colleague. We took part in an organized seven-day outing through a company called Experience Plus out of Fort Collins, Colorado. This trip involved doing a number of the storied mountain climbs in the French Alps, as well as following certain stages of the Tour de France (TdF). While we were in southern France in Provence, we had the opportunity to climb the famed Le Mont Ventoux. Technically it's not part of the Alps, because it stands monolithically by itself against the rolling hills and landscape of that region.

There are several ascent routes up Mont Ventoux, and we started from the less frequently used route out of Malaucene, the climb from that point being five thousand–plus vertical feet over about fourteen miles—straight up, no breaks, with multimile stretches of ten percent gradient and greater. The guide said he would be surprised if anyone could finish the climb in under two hours. That was all the motivation I needed.

It was a long, arduous, beastly climb under sunny skies, with little to no wind—which is rare. I went through multiple mental phases but never gave in. The closer I got to the top the stronger I felt. I finished in one hour, fifty minutes. I didn't mention my time to the guide or anyone else, because I wasn't looking for recognition; I just relished the personal satisfaction of having done it. It took some time to recover and get my bearings, and Mike and I decided to make the descent down the route to the small village of Sault.

It was an epic descent, taking us through fields of blooming lavender. We stopped at one point to take in the views and intoxicate ourselves in the smells and sights all around us. When we reached our pickup point with the guides, one asked how my day was, and I said, "bar none, the best day I have ever had on a bike."

In 2006 a group of us from the company traveled to the French Alps again for eight days of cycling. It was during July when the Tour de France was in progress and we stayed at a small holiday cottage, which in French parlance would be referred to as gite (pronounced jeet). It was located just outside the village of Bourg D'Oisans, one of the most famous stage locations of the TdF.

From that location there are at least ten or so famous climbs within a thirty-minute drive, many easily accessible by bike from the gite where we stayed. While we did many climbs on that trip, the one I'll most remember was the last day of the trip when we were scheduled to pack up and drive back to Geneva to catch our return flight home the next day.

Four of us got up and on our bikes before 6 a.m., descended into the village of Bourg D'Oisans through a cool, morning mist, and started the famed climb of Alpe d'Huez. It wasn't the first time I had done this famous climb, but it was the first time I started at the break of dawn. It is 3,500 feet of vertical ascent at an average gradient of eight percent over eight-plus miles with twenty-one hairpin turns. There were very few cyclists other than us that early in the morning, with light fog in the valley and clear blue skies above.

I was exhausted from six days of nonstop climbing and wasn't sure I had any more gas in the tank. After the first mile, which is abrupt, steep, and a rude wake-up call, my blood started circulating, my legs and lungs warmed up, I had my food bars and energy drinks at the ready, and I buckled down for the approximately sixty-minute ascent. The further I climbed the better my body felt.

Ben was off the front, to be expected, and I dropped Brian, which was not. Dan was slightly in front of me, and eventually I passed him about two-thirds of the way up. Dan is a very experienced and competitive cyclist, and I knew in the back of my mind that he wasn't going to let me go without a fight. With less than one-quarter mile to go to the finish, he caught and passed me. I wasn't surprised, even though I did everything to try to hold him off.

We all said our good-byes to the famous climb and began the descent back to our gite. The sun was just peeking over the glacier-topped mountains, and I had this incredible feeling of well-being and peace. The others descended quickly, but I took my time to soak in everything around me. Part of the descent involved riding a cat-walk traverse along the side of the mountain, still perched about 2,000 feet above the valley floor.

As I slowed my descent to a walking pace, I looked at the view below, took several deep breaths, looked up at the sky, and thanked the universe for giving me this moment. I can't recall many times in my life being so happy.

Reflecting on all of these moments brought me a lot of comfort during times of incredible distress and sadness. They also gave me considerable motivation to fight for as much recovery as possible, and the idea that with consistent, determined effort I may perhaps do some of them again. They became vectors, lighthouse beacons, to guide my recovery efforts. I have goals and am always focused on possibilities.

The solace of memories, besides giving me comfort, continues to give me hope and motivation.

CHAPTER 16

Recovery Phase II

My employer invited me to visit the company campus shortly before Christmas 2007. A department meeting was being held, and some friends had suggested I make my first return visit that day to attend the meeting and visit some colleagues. I was nervous, after having been away for six months, I had limited mobility, and I was just at the tail end of a very difficult period.

I was still depressed and had started the long process of a second recovery. I had a lot of ambivalence about going into the office that day and almost didn't do it. I knew I was in a transitional period and still very fragile. My wife, and some close coworkers, encouraged me to make the effort and see the team. They thought it would be good for my depressed state of mind to be around people who cared for me.

It was quite a visit. The meeting was held in an upstairs open area with about fifty people in attendance, including the CEO and CFO. I remember speaking to the team and sharing some of my journey over the prior six months, along with some of the insights I'd learned along the way.

I told a story of being awake one night in the hospital after a visit from Dr. David, my acupuncturist. I shared a conversation we'd had that culminated in this statement: "When you distill all of life to its bare core, it comes down to this simple axiom—love and be loved."

When I was finished speaking, I don't think there was a dry eye in the room, including mine. I remember looking at the CEO and CFO and both had tears in their eyes. It was very moving and touched me deeply.

This was the beginning of what I like to call "recovery phase II." I had physically crashed in June 2007 and mentally crashed in November 2007. This time my approach to recovery was going to be different. A combination of things helped keep me in my new recovery phase. First and foremost, I had the unwavering support of family and friends. Knowing they are there for me is something that has meant more and more to me as the days, months, and years have passed.

Sometimes it was just the little things that meant the most and helped buoy me up during this hard time. Diane introduced me to pedicures shortly after I was injured, because I had a lot of difficulty with range of motion. It was tough for me to bend over to reach my nails and, at the same time, be able to hold and squeeze the large nail clippers.

In December 2007, before Christmas time, Diane invited her specialist to bring all his equipment to our house and give me a pedicure in the living room. She did this to surprise me, lift me up, and perhaps bring a little happiness to my life. She knew my mobility had regressed considerably and also knew how much I enjoyed having my feet massaged.

On another occasion when there was a football game on TV, Diane invited two of my friends to come over to the house and watch it with me. Although I wasn't in a social mood, and I didn't talk much, my friends stayed for the entire three hours. They were just with me. Their company meant a lot, and they provided some healing energy just by being there. This was the beginning of reengaging with people after being so alone and isolated. I resisted it at first, but Diane and the kids persisted and helped bring me out my shell.

Alana and Kevin wrote special letters for me over the Christmas holiday. The first time I read them, I was unfortunately still in the throes of my depression, and thus disconnected from the heartfelt meaning in their words. However, I reread those letters several times during the ensuing weeks, and the love and caring in their words increasingly touched my soul and helped bring me back.

Working with Chris at Pacific Balance was another big boost to phase II. Chris and the people in his practice are filled with positive energy and played a big part in getting me back on my feet after my second crash, as did two wonderful pool therapists, Debbie and Linda. All of these medical professionals were extremely patient as I struggled to climb out of the funk I was in; they helped me slowly regain the functional progress I had made prior to this terrible setback.

My feelings of failure over not being able to return to work as I'd planned and having to go on long-term disability were things I had to come to terms with in order to continue my recovery. Because I couldn't work for another seven months, until July 2008, my position as IT director had to be permanently reassigned to someone else.

Losing my position was hard to accept, and the loss was profound. I had worked very hard and done great work for the company to earn that position. I had a solid track record, had earned the respect of my colleagues, received the company's top leadership award on two occasions, had circles of influence throughout the company, and was respected.

I had good working relationships with people at all levels of the organization, from the CEO to frontline staff. I navigated in multiple circles and had the ability and stature to influence decisions that were in the best interests of the organization. I loved the company, the culture, the people, and the opportunity to be of significant value.

The business had to function, and I recognized they had given me time to try to recover and regain that position; in fact, they held it open for me for nearly nine months before making the decision to replace me. While it was extremely hard, I understood the business decision had to be made. It also helped that one of my close and respected colleagues, Carol, was assigned to the director position.

As recovery phase II progressed, I resolved to stay consistent with the new medication cocktail, sans the opiate painkillers. Being dependent on prescription medications was a big adjustment for me, but I realized if I was going to climb out of this deep dark hole of depression, then I was going to have to make some changes in how I thought about things.

Instead of thinking I was losing control by being dependent on meds, I reversed those thoughts and began reminding myself that I'd had a very serious injury and these were tools I needed to function. Perhaps I'd be able to wean myself off the drugs at a later time; but for now, this was what I had to do. Today I take half the dose of bupropion I was originally prescribed, but I use all the others to help maintain my progress and health.

I remember when Dr. Barry first discussed with me the idea of taking an antidepressant. I hated the thought of having to take it, thinking that this meant I wasn't capable of managing my own mental health. I have difficulty with feeling a loss of control and being dependent on people, devices, medications, etc. This was something I had to learn how to get past.

Dr. Barry considered several different options for my antidepressant, including SSRI medications (selective serotonin reuptake inhibitors) like Prozac, Zoloft, or Paxil, but these were contraindicated because they could worsen my spasticity. After his research, he recommended bupropion. Reluctantly, I went on the medicine and was pleased to find I had no adverse side effects from it.

After a month or so of taking bupropion, I noticed a change in my mood, and the feelings of darkness, isolation, and despair began to give way to hope and possibility. My energy level and motivation improved, and I didn't feel as despondent. I began to pursue more healing modalities, including mental health therapy.

Receiving regular assistance from a mental health practitioner, which I continued until just recently, was another critical element in my continuing recovery. In retrospect, I should have started taking antidepressant medication and sought mental health therapy while I was still an inpatient or shortly thereafter.

I rededicated myself to my new phase of recovery by including one big change: listening to my body. I realized that in my hurry to get back to work, I had put enormous pressure on myself, trying to accelerate my recovery process. In doing so, I ultimately ended up with diminishing returns. I had dug a huge hole that almost cost me my life.

Before my second crash, I had been on a frenetic schedule with eight to twelve appointments per week. That was exhausting, but I also hadn't allowed myself to rest during the day. The couch recliner was always there in the living room beckoning me, but I had refused to use it. I'd considered it a badge of honor at that time to get through the day without resting, reclining, or taking a nap.

The recliner couch became my friend during this second recovery period, which started in January 2008. I rested when my body said rest. I had to learn that it wasn't failure to rest; in fact, it was just the opposite. As Linda, my physical therapist who worked with me in the pool, would often tell me, "less is more."

My climb out of the hole of depression was slow and steady. The recovery phase II physical trajectory was not as steep as the first recovery, and by January and February 2008, I knew I was making progress, retracing recovery steps I had made before and even breaking some new ground. In addition to pool therapy twice a week, I worked with Chris three times a week at Pacific Balance.

Chris helped me in many ways, slowly challenging me with new, innovative exercises and offering a positive energy that was infectious. We worked together for two years, which was about the same length of time I worked with Debbie and Linda of Mercer Island Physical Therapy. I continued with acupuncture treatments, but not as frequently, because I was trying to limit my recovery program to one therapy visit per day.

This turned out to be a more tolerable pace. When I felt the energy to do so, I would also go for a neighborhood walk. I was getting stronger again and becoming more accepting of the fact that I was really impaired, disabled—an incomplete quadriplegic. For a long time before this, I had always thought I would one day be my old self again, just like I was before the accident. I had been fighting so hard to get back to the person I used to be, but I now knew that I was actually on a journey in pursuit of a new normal.

. . .

After the severe setback I experienced in November 2007, my entire mental and physical constitution was severely shaken. I was afraid of taking any kind of risks. It took me over two years of very conservative OT and PT—first through HMC, followed by Mercer Island Physical Therapy pool therapy and Pacific Balance, as well as mental health therapy from 2008 to 2010—to restore the gains I'd made in my initial post-injury months (before I began pushing myself too hard). It was time to take some measured risks again, but I was very afraid of repeating what had happened in November and December 2007.

Taking measured risks wasn't just about the physical side. The mental side also required risk taking, particularly stepping into the discipline of psychoanalysis, which was foreign to me. I had attended marital counseling sessions in the past but never one-on-one clinical psychoanalysis with someone I didn't know.

Grappling with feelings of deep depression was a foreign experience to me, and during the next six months I continued to try to process all of it without professional psychological intervention. However, in June 2008, I approached the mental health side of my treatment for the first time. I faced a measured risk with psychoanalysis in exposing my vulnerability and, over time, revealing my deepest, innermost thoughts that had been buried for years—in some cases, decades—to a virtual stranger.

Part of finding my new normal was beginning mental health therapy one year after my bike crash. Seeing a mental health therapist was one of the most important parts of phase II. Participating in mental health care helped me extricate myself from isolation and become social again.

While I am an introvert by nature, I was reminded again how important social interactions are to recovery. They keep the brain active and provide a sense of belonging. I had been hibernating in my own world for too long, and it was time to come out again.

As mentioned earlier, I started with a clinical psychologist, Dr. Roberta. I had never had mental health counseling before and wasn't sure what it would involve. I was initially impatient, wanting to know at the outset how long this process was going to take, when would I see results, and when would we be done. I think Dr. Roberta may have considered me a little off the wall and unrealistic about what the process would entail.

After a bit of a bumpy start trying to understand her process and meshing it with my expectations, we settled into a twice-a-week pattern for two years. Clinical psychology involves a lot of internal work, navigating all sorts of psychological paths, with no direction, just talking about whatever was on my mind.

It was hard work, and the first months spent with Dr. Roberta required my understanding and acceptance. As time went on in my two-year treatment program, I became more comfortable with the approach. Often in our early sessions I would start talking, taking myself down a path, only to abruptly stop and turn around. Dr. Roberta would ask why I had stopped going down that particular path and I'd tell her I didn't want to go there.

"When you do that," Dr. Roberta would patiently comment, "you prevent us from learning what's further down that path."

I struggled a lot with this concept, but slowly over time I was able to keep going down certain paths without stopping. I got more comfortable going to uncomfortable places, especially when the topic concerned my early life. All of our focus was not explicitly on my accident or injury. This was an internal journey that explored many different paths in my life. We dove deep down into my psyche.

I was soon able to explore facets of my life that I had initially refused to look at. I overcame the risk of opening my inner self to Dr. Roberta and establishing a trust, a place of safety and confidentiality, which only belonged to the two of us. Once established, I found I was able to go even to the dark places and share my feelings with her—some very painful ones that evoked years and years of repressed emotions.

Intersections of these pathways began to emerge, which revealed different themes about my life and how I process the world. It turned out to be a very revealing method, and more than anything it helped me understand myself better, why I think the way I do, and why I choose to do the things I do. She helped me explore why I have, for most of my life, pushed myself past my strength and endurance to the point of pain, as a kind of punishment. We talked about my mother and how her emotional and physical absence had impacted me.

Pain and suffering had characterized much of my life since I was a toddler with severe skin problems. I grew up feeling like I deserved to suffer, because that was all I knew. For many years, exercise—hard, strenuous exercise—served two purposes. It was both exhilarating and punishing. The exhilaration was the challenge, the "carrot" in front of me, tapping my competitive spirit to see if I could do it. The punishment was the pain, hurt, and suffering that accompanied it. I wanted to hurt, to burn the anger and frustration out of my system. I never overdid it to the point of needing medical intervention, but I would push so hard, hurt so much, and then push even harder.

In recent years, my approach to exercise and fitness has been moderated, although I still challenge and push myself. What's changed is that I have lightened up on myself—somewhat. This effort is not so much driven by a sense of deserving to suffer but more by a need to prove that I can overcome, not allowing my impairments to be an excuse. Now I'm willing to do the work, without a warped mind-set of intending to punish myself. Dr. Roberta helped me understand this.

Dr. Roberta also helped me unravel much of the connection I had with my company and realize that too much of my identity was wrapped up in my work there. Exploring this part of myself helped me find a way to decouple that connection to my work so that I could move forward with my life.

She also challenged me to do some things I would not otherwise have done. It was hard work, unpleasant at times, occasionally tearful, and always revealing. I'll always be grateful that Dr. Roberta and I worked together.

On the physical side of things, I was very far from any managed risks for quite a while. I started working with Chris from Pacific Balance in early 2008. He took a conservative approach to exercises and was careful not to push too hard and put me at risk of experiencing yet another "crash." His work, along with the work I did with Linda and Debbie in pool therapy, helped me rebuild my fragile constitution and slowly regain some modicum of confidence. The work was gradual, deliberate, risk-free, and slow going.

We did push boundaries at Pacific Balance and Mercer Island Physical Therapy pool therapy, challenging different areas and breaking new ground. In the pool, for example, we worked a lot on range of motion, flexibility, and core strengthening. Chris and I did the same thing using different exercises and coupling those with exercises with full weight-bearing walking, balance, and core and leg strengthening.

The progress trajectory of my recovery continued upward, which was encouraging, but it was nowhere near the steep path I had traveled in the first few months post injury. One of the cool things Chris and I worked on was walking up and down stairs until I could do it without having to use handrails. I even practiced doing some high stepping as I climbed upward.

The Pacific Balance building had five stories, and often after our session, I would go by myself and practice more reps up and down the stairs. We pushed the envelope a couple of times, but Chris was always close by to spot or arrest a fall. Pushing the envelope with Chris meant primarily trying to do speed work up and down stairs. We were testing my limits to determine when spasticity symptoms would be invoked. When that occurs, my muscles seize and movement becomes very difficult.

As time went on, I did a number of exercises with Chris with my eyes closed, which challenged my proprioperception deficiencies. It was easy to lose balance. We practiced balancing on one foot at a time and used a leg extension machine to improve quad strength. These exercises, along with those in the pool, were all measured to meet me where I was at the time, which in retrospect was significantly limited compared to where I am today.

These early years were absolutely crucial in establishing a foundation of mental and physical strength on which I could further build. I could never have joined the SAC or enjoyed the progress I have today without the time I invested with Chris, Linda, and Debbie. In addition to the physical side, their positive and encouraging energy helped me climb out of a very deep, dark hole that could have easily thwarted the significant progress and milestones I've made over the past six years.

Working with the three of them, using conservative approaches, was assuming a level of risk that was right for that period of time in my life. In the same way, but at a different level, I had to be gently nudged and supported to get out of my narrow comfort zone in order to push boundaries. The payoff has been enormous growth and progress.

. . .

In the summer of 2010, three years after the bike crash and two years after I started working with Dr. Roberta, Chris, Debbie, and Linda, a number of things changed.

Chris and I had reached a plateau in our work, and over the next several months he effectively graduated me from his practice, saying, "You know all the exercises, Jamie, go join a gym. Check in with me periodically if you have any issues or just want to update me on your status."

I also brought pool therapy with Linda and Debbie to a close. We, too, had reached a bit of a recovery plateau, and they agreed with Chris that I was capable of continuing therapy on my own. Dr. Roberta wrapped up our clinical work together as well.

Since summer 2010 until just recently (spring 2016), I partnered with a behavioral psychologist, Dr. Diane. Dr. Diane is trained in, among other things, working with people who have suffered traumatic injuries. She diagnosed me with post-traumatic stress disorder (PTSD), depression, and a few other things. We took a one-year hiatus between fall 2012 and fall 2013, thinking I had made enough progress to continue on my own. In December 2012, I was separated from my employment, and we resumed work together about nine months later.

Behavioral psychology is more externally focused, examining practical life issues from the behavioral standpoint of how best to deal with them. Unlike clinical psychology, which is more internally focused, my work with Dr. Diane has provided a number of practical approaches to managing issues such as PTSD, depression, anger, anxiety, fear, loss, and lethargy—all issues I grapple with to varying degrees.

While the type of psychological work we did together was different, some of the measured risk taking was similar. This involved establishing rapport, trust, and a safe environment where I could be vulnerable and reveal deep, sensitive feelings and emotions. It didn't take long. Dr. Diane is a special practitioner, whose experience working with patients with significant physical trauma was very helpful in quickly coming up to speed on my case.

We have covered a broad range of topics, dealing with loss, betrayal, confidence, and self-esteem. Her steady hand has coached me through some difficult losses, and she has provided practical suggestions and resources. Some of these include modalities like eye movement desensitization and reprocessing (EMDR), a process of dealing with trauma and emotional stress and lifespan integration by creating new neural networks when faced with difficult situations.

Most importantly, she has helped me learn to be willing to take additional measured risks—in this case, regarding my next life's work. She has been a gentle advocate for encouraging me to consider doing something different with my life, something perhaps a little out-of-the-box, but important work that could benefit other people and myself. She, along with others, has been part of the universal force nudging me in the direction of sharing my story of injury and recovery, so that I could potentially impact the lives of others.

I have been open about my fear—of something new, of the unknown, of failure—of doing this. She consistently reassures me that these are natural feelings and to start gradually and see where it goes. She encourages me to embrace fear and use it to my advantage, to use it as a catalyst to overcome the fear itself. She has urged me to apply myself to my psychological recovery in the same way that I have applied myself in the physical realm to overcome my infirmity and loss of function—with hard work and dedication.

I am grateful to Dr. Diane for many things. She helped me restore my self-confidence, which through all the phases of loss I've experienced as a result of the accident, injury, and job loss has taken a beating. With her focused guidance, she has continued to lift me up, helping me look at myself in the mirror and be reminded of the talent, skills, and gifts I have to offer.

If there is one lesson in all of this, it is this: If you experience any kind of loss—either through relational separation, disease, injury, or other tragedies—seek professional help. I made the cavalier mistake of thinking that needing help was a weakness. It is not. We all need professional intervention at times in our lives, and being willing to accept help to get you through depression is actually a sign of strength. It is nothing to be embarrassed about, and in fact, today I proudly talk about my time spent in therapy.

CHAPTER 17

Getting Back My Life

These past six years, from 2010 to 2016, are a considerable contrast to the early years of my recovery in 2007 to 2009. As Chris suggested, at the end of our sessions, I joined a gym in the spring of 2010, or in my case, rejoined a gym I had previously belonged to when I was a very active, tournament squash player—the Seattle Athletic Club.

I had been a charter member there from 1982 to 1995. I had taken a fifteen-year hiatus from the SAC from 1995 to 2010 because my employment location had moved to the Kent Valley in 1994, and it didn't make sense to continue using a club facility located in Seattle. This time returning to the SAC meant I would be spending most of my time in the cardio and weight rooms and on stretch mats, instead of the squash court.

When I first returned to the SAC, I sought out the services of a personal trainer, a lady named Barbara. We had a couple of sessions together. Among the many trainers at the SAC, Barbara appeared to mostly work with people like myself, who were impaired and who had functional limitations. She worked patiently and gradually, careful to listen to my fears about doing too much and understanding how desperately I wanted to avoid incurring any setbacks.

A few weeks later, I bumped into an old friend Sam, a squash colleague and fierce competitor on and off the court. He is unbelievably strong and very knowledgeable in the weight room. He works out twice a day. Watching him work out reminds me of one of those super athletes you might see in a Cirque de Soleil performance or on TV's *American Ninja Warrior.*

One day he watched me doing some lame, limited wrist strengthening exercise and asked where I'd been and what I was doing back at the club. I told him about my injury and that I had just finished with PT and been advised to join a gym to continue my therapy.

He asked me if I would like to work out with him, indicating he was frequently at the gym. I said, "Why not, let's go for it." Little did I know what I was getting myself into—in a good way.

Sam kind of adopted me as a project. He committed a lot of time and effort to working with me over the next several years. He—and another friend, Samantha, an amazing woman with three young boys, also super fit—helped me "learn the ropes" in the weight room and taught me a lot about different exercises, techniques, and proper form. I had come from several years of PT and OT, but it was nothing like what I was about to experience in the weight rooms at the SAC.

Early on, both of them worked with me on a number of exercises initially focused on strengthening my very weak core. I once used the word "abs" and was quickly admonished that the focus was on strengthening my core, not to have pretty abdominal muscles. All I could think of relating this to was the golfing quip, "You drive for show and putt for dough." In my case, core strengthening was learning the fine art of putting complete concentration on the most important part of the game. A strong core is central to everything in physical recovery just as putting is to golf.

To provide a sense of where I was starting from, Sam had me lie on my back on the weight room floor. Once I was in a complete supine position, he asked me to raise my right leg. I said, "Don't bother asking me to do this because I know I can't."

Undeterred, he said again, "Squeeze your butt muscles together, pull your belly button in to the floor, and lift your right leg." I couldn't do it.

I said, "See, I told you—I don't have the strength."

He got on his knees next to me, took his hand and jabbed his fingers into my abdomen, just below my sternum, kept them there, and said, "Now tighten those muscles where my hand is so I can feel it, and lift your right leg off the ground." I still couldn't do it.

Sensing some impatience, he took both his hands this time, jabbed them into my mid-abdomen, held them there, and implored, "Now do it!"

I said, "Man, you're pissing me off!"

"Good!" he said. "That's what I want to hear, now do it!"

With all I could muster, I jammed my lower back into the floor, tightened my butt muscles, squeezed my inner thighs with what limited feeling I had, miraculously raised my right leg an inch or two off the ground, and then put it back down to resting position.

"See," he said, "I knew you could do it! Now repeat it, this time with your left leg, and this time go higher than what you did with your right leg."

His hands were still jammed into my abdomen. Slowly my left leg rose off the ground, eventually reaching a couple of inches, then it quickly collapsed back down to the ground. I was astonished.

It was a very surreal experience, because my upper body felt totally disconnected from my lower half. Sam would give me these instructions, but neurologically the signals weren't sufficiently transmitting from my head to my lower extremities. This is where neuroplasticity comes into play.

My body is physically impaired, and to do what I used to be able to do without thinking now requires intense mental focus. The brain has an innate ability to reorganize itself. Knowing that my spinal cord is damaged, with six out of eight traffic lanes permanently blocked, the brain's plasticity kicks in to figure out how to reorganize and create new routes, or new circuits, around the damaged "lanes" to accomplish its objective.

I had my baseline. My core was dreadfully weak, but at least I had a starting point. This was the process we followed with countless exercises, establishing baselines on everything from push-ups, sit-ups, pull-ups, and a host of other exercises. I remember a pivotal moment early on in our working together. I said to him, "Look, when I tell you enough is enough, you have to trust me."

Sam responded, "No, you have to learn to trust yourself."

His words stopped me in my tracks. Sam was absolutely right. The single biggest impediment to making progress was fear—a lack of trust in myself. I was so scared of doing something that might cause an injury and set me back. I did not want to repeat the terrifying experience of crash number two. Fear was holding me back.

There was more progress to be made—as time would reveal, *much more progress*—but I had to get over the fear, or at least figure out a way to manage it and not have it manage me. For too long, fear had gotten in my way. It is understandable to some extent because our bodies are programmed to protect themselves, especially after injury. In the process of recovery, though, there comes a point where fear becomes a limiter and is no longer a protector. I was at that point and ready to move past fear.

"Trust myself" were the words I needed to hear and apply. It changed everything about my recovery and allowed me to go places both physically and mentally I had only remotely imagined. This was the start of regaining much of my life.

Working together was almost an everyday event. Every time I saw Sam in the weight room, my stomach churned with anxiety. I knew working out with him was going to be hard, very hard. His approach to fitness and strengthening is a little—different. He sees free weights, machines, weighted balls, bands, VersaBalls, and kettlebells—everything—through the eyes of a creative engineer. Very rarely does he use a machine, for example, the way it was designed. He'll come up with some creative way to use equipment and to construct an amazing, unique challenge. And his challenges do not disappoint.

Sam never looked at me as impaired, and he certainly was not sympathetic to my whimpers and injury excuses or any other complaining I did in those early months. I finally got the message: just be quiet, try to do what's asked, put forth maximum effort to see what you're capable of, and push in and out of "the zone."

The zone is that place where my neurological symptoms become visible. My legs shake. My legs go rigid. My hands vibrate. We all learned together how to toggle my efforts in and out of the zone with the objective of raising the bar when I was in the zone. In other words, if the tenth push-up sent me into the zone, causing my legs to go rigid and stopping me from continuing the exercise, then in the next set, I would do eight. In the set after that, I might shoot for twelve push-ups, with the challenge being to see if entering the zone might be two push-ups further away.

This is the philosophy that allowed me to meter my efforts, challenge myself, and push the envelope without pushing me over the edge. The process paid big dividends in terms of the progress I was able to make. Yes, it was an incredible amount of hard work. It took consistent effort and a willingness to work hard. I was willing to put in the work because I could see I was making progress.

Sam worked me very hard, much like he works himself. He doesn't leave anything behind in terms of effort, and he expected the same from me and anyone else who worked out with him. If I wanted to work out with him, I had to do it his way. Competitor that I am, I was up for the challenge. I was only interested in competing with myself.

Of course, I always paid a price in terms of suffering, during and after workout sessions. I often had to ice my aching muscles after workouts to control inflammation. Sometimes ibuprofen was necessary after a session.

Almost like clockwork, if I had a very vigorous session, my body would most acutely feel the aftereffects thirty-six to forty-eight hours later. It was just something I had to get used to, part of the price I paid. Given the dividends I was getting from the investment, I was willing to make the sacrifice. To this day that scenario hasn't changed.

I remember one session in particular in the fall of 2010, where we spent seventy-five minutes doing push-ups, only push-ups. In this particular session, it was the three of us plus an additional friend, Spencer. We each had a small piece of paper and pencil to count our push-ups. It was thirty push-ups every sixty seconds for seventy-five minutes. At that point in my recovery, I could only do push-ups on my knees. My goal was to try to do ten or more push-ups in each segment, while the others were doing thirty, and they were doing full-on push-ups from their toes.

After a brutal, memorable, and completely exhausting seventy-five minutes, I went home barely able to move. After applying ice bags all over my body, I counted the number of push-ups I'd done. It was just over one thousand. I wrote both Sam and Samantha a text message saying, "neither elegant nor manly, my push-up count exceeded 1,000."

Their responses were quick, and both said how proud they were of me. I was proud, excited, and surprised. When I had first joined the gym, I couldn't do a single push-up, not one. In six months' time, I had transformed into someone I could never have envisioned becoming.

I had also eclipsed the third year post-injury gains. In contrast, according to some of my medical staff, recovery for SCI patients generally plateaus after one to two years. I was proving myself to be an exception, and that will continue. The takeaway here is that the brain's plasticity, along with exercise, is a powerful combination.

Fear, while it serves a valuable purpose in protecting us, can also be a deterrent, a roadblock in the recovery process. Both Samantha and Sam helped me overcome that fear by challenging me just enough to test my capability and desire, but they were mindful not to go too far.

Sam seemed to have a sixth sense, and in a way seemed to know my body better than I did. He pushed me places I would never have gone alone. Crazy places. These were exercises you don't see people doing in a gym, unless you're with him. I have an example that was actually filmed on a friend's mobile phone.

It was a triceps-core exercise. Sam asked me to lie on my back on the weight room floor. He brought over a flat bench commonly used in the weight room. It was about eighteen inches high and four to five feet long. He pushed one edge of the bench so that it was just over the edge of my forehead. The bench was aligned as an extension of my body. He placed a six-pound medicine ball between my calves and asked me to tighten my core and squeeze my legs together, to hold the ball in place, and then raise my legs a foot or two off the floor and hold them there.

Sam sat on the bench and then had me raise both hands and place them on the edge of the bench. In this position, my hands were slightly above and behind my head, with elbows bent to challenge the triceps muscles. Now in position, he had me straighten my arms to raise that end of the bench up and down twenty times, including the weight of his 160-pound frame sitting on the bench. It was brutal.

In typical fashion, all his exercises are designed to challenge multiple muscle groups, almost always involving the core. I discovered some amazing things about myself, especially the exhilaration of raising the "zone" line, pushing new boundaries, and achieving some incredible milestones.

While I undertook several over-the-top exercises that could have caused serious harm if I'd had a problem, both my mentors were there to spot me on the ones I felt were overly risky. For example, Sam had numerous variants of doing push-ups. He often described push-ups as "the mother of all exercises," because it emphasizes, when done correctly, numerous muscle groups.

One variant involved using a large VersaBall and two six-pound weighted balls. The idea was to get in a push-up position with feet perched and elevated on the large VersaBall, in a plank position, facedown, with each hand on a six-pound weighted ball. The VersaBall is about three feet in diameter, with the weighted balls being about eight inches in diameter. This position created a downward sloping "plank" position for my body, with my feet straddling the top of the VersaBall, and my hands clutching the tops of the two weighted balls.

Once in position, being intentionally unstable because the three balls could roll in any direction at any time, the objective was to challenge stability in my body position by tightening core, gluteus, and inner thigh muscles. Just being able to establish that stationary position required considerable strength and concentration in those areas, as well as in my hands, shoulders, back—pretty much every muscle group. Once stable in that position, the next step was to bend my arms at the elbows and lower my body down, with my chest nearly touching the floor, and then raise myself back up again by straightening my arms—doing a push-up. All other parts of the body were to remain flat and stationary.

Unlike a typical push-up where the body is stable, with feet and hands touching the floor, this exercise was intended to multiply the difficulty by creating unstable conditions (i.e., feet and hands on balls and activating core and adjacent muscles to challenge stability). The risk, of course, was losing concentration or muscular failure and having my hands and/or feet roll off the balls.

The goal for me in this exercise was twenty push-ups. Sam and Samantha could easily crank out thirty. I was lucky to be able to do a few. I don't have good control over my lower half and can't just readily jump off the VersaBall if I feel like my muscles are about to experience momentary muscular failure, which was why both my friends were close by, to spot or catch me, in case I lost balance or my arms gave out. After a lot of practice, I can do ten of this style of push-up at a time.

All the workouts with my gym mentors involved pushing boundaries in ways I could never have imagined, and many involved some small elements of risk. I did have some falls—nothing that required medical intervention, but all sufficiently unnerving to get me thinking about whether or not I was pushing too hard. I couldn't argue with the results, though, and that is what kept me coming back.

I was willing to put in the work, challenge my fear, push my capabilities, trust myself, and accomplish some very cool things. Both Sam and Samantha taught me a lot about different exercises, form, technique, and numbers of reps. In the past couple of years, I have been able to take these and other things I have learned and apply them on my own.

We don't work out together as often as we did the first three years after I rejoined the SAC because of our different schedules, but their guidance and teachings will be with me for a very long time. They both know how much I appreciate what they did for me. By teaching me how to trust myself again, conquer my fear, and manage risk, they gave me back a very big piece of my life. For that I will always be grateful.

· · ·

There is no question that the effort and strain I've placed on my body in the past six years is considerable. I can't, however, argue with the results, which have been significant, opening up so many doors in terms of mental health, confidence, emotional well-being, physicality, and community. When I contrast this time period with the first six months post injury (when I was pushing too hard in my recovery, which resulted in a physical and emotional crash), I can see many differences.

For one, my mental state is considerably different. In the early months after the injury, my mental state was very fragile, unsettled, uncertain, and unrealistic. I thought I was in the right place mentally, but as the second crash proved, I clearly was not.

In 2010, when I heard Sam say, "You need to trust yourself," it was like a big mirror had been placed in front of me that said, "Jamie, you need to get control of your fear, or it is going to continue to control and limit you." I can't overstate how important those words were. They were as important as the words Dr. Jens spoke to me in the hospital: "Jamie, get independent."

Also, in my initial recovery period in 2007, I was still in a state of "spinal shock," which I have since learned can last up to a year. My body during that time was still unstable, fluid, malleable, and fighting hard to find some kind of equilibrium, or a new baseline. My body was still vulnerable and fragile, and my mental and physical constitution was weak. I was very afraid.

Three years later in 2010, when I started this new program at the SAC, my constitution was different. Better. I had been in mental health therapy for almost two years and had a much better handle on my feelings and emotions. Although I hadn't yet conquered fear when I began working out at the SAC, things changed significantly over the ensuing year. I discovered I had much more capability and potential than I thought. My confidence in exercise, fitness, and strength conditioning has continued to progress in a positive direction, and I've experienced many breakthroughs.

Medication management has also played a significant role. While I don't like taking medications, and in the early months after injury was doing everything to get off of them, in retrospect weaning myself off of everything turned out to be the wrong decision.

After my second crash, and for the following nine years, I have been on a consistent regimen of medication management. Before I go to the gym now, and ever since I rejoined in 2010, I take my medications, which give me a time window of four to six hours where I am more mobile and able to exercise—to work on strengthening, cardio, and range-of-motion exercises.

The muscle relaxants I take—including diazepam, tizanadine, and baclofen—are especially important. They allow the severe spasticity I deal with every day to acquiesce enough so that I can get warmed up on a stationary bike or elliptical, work up a sweat, and transition to more challenging and aggressive exercises.

My fitness foundation is considerably stronger now than it was in the fall of 2007. I didn't realize in those early months how quickly my body had weakened and the time it was going to take to rebuild that strength. Today, and even in 2010, my body was stronger, I had better stamina, and consequently I had a foundation on which I could build.

Having been through the painful experience of crash number two, I was much more aware of my body and the need to provide rest when my body said rest. In those early post-injury months, I still considered myself a very fit cyclist and was rather in denial about my injury. I felt I could power my way through anything.

I've written how I viewed even taking a rest in the recliner during the day as some kind of bad thing, a failure, like I was letting myself down by allowing my body to rest. I know now how misplaced that kind of thinking was, and how important it is to take rests during the day when they are needed. I've done it for years now without giving it a second thought, certainly without any sense of guilt.

Since I rejoined the SAC, it has been especially helpful to once again be part of a community of like-minded, fit individuals. When I receive positive compliments about my progress, or determination, or even in some cases unsolicited expressions of admiration and inspiration, it is incredibly motivating to keep going and make the best of what I can do. I don't look for these expressions, but they are always welcome and meaningful, and I appreciate all of them.

My road cycling community is gone. I no longer connect with many of my old comrades; it's not that I don't want to, but unfortunately so many things have changed. Not having that community in those early years post injury left a huge void in my life. That's why I made the choice to reconnect with my old community at the SAC. Becoming reacquainted with old friends at the athletic club, as well as meeting many new ones, has been a rising tide that has raised my boat, lifted me up, and encouraged me more than I can say.

When I first came back, I'll never forget seeing one of my former squash friends, Jim, an amazingly fit individual, who looked at me and unabashedly said, "Jim, great to see you . . . you look like shit!"

I'm sure I did, even with all the progress I had made over the previous three years. I know the perspective he was coming from, and it only stoked the fire in my gut. I couldn't wait to get going and see if I could raise my game.

These friends at the SAC have been incredibly inspirational to me, and it means a lot to have a place to go where I am known by name, welcomed, and engaged. I enjoy greeting and being greeted with smiles in the morning. I love seeing people work out—hearts pumping, sweating, grunting, pushing—and seeing their faces. It is the wind under my sails.

CHAPTER 18

The Upside of Alternative Medicine

Mother's Remedies

My mother has had a lifelong interest in alternative health. In many ways, she was way ahead of her time. As youngsters, all of us (my siblings and I) were exposed to her novel approaches to diet, nutrition, and health care. I remember in my preteens when Mother would invite a massage therapist over to the house and one by one we would each have our turn with Flo Gilman.

It's amazing that I can still remember her name today. I remember her using this very thick skin cream as she massaged, which felt great to me because I grew up in my toddler years with severe eczema and even as a preteen still suffered from dry, flaky skin.

Mother had us see our regular internist for standard physicals, but she also had us see an osteopath named Dr. Miller whose primary aim was treating and strengthening our musculoskeletal frameworks. I vividly remember the doctor having me stand up as straight as I could against a white wall while he took pictures. Reviewing the pictures, I was appalled at my posture, especially the appearance that I was listing to my right side, the slumping shoulders, and the protruding belly. I needed a lot of work, and some of those issues still persist in various forms today.

Another time my mother took me to a practitioner who performed colon cleansing, aka colon hydrotherapy or colonic for short. One of

Mother's theories about the root cause of my eczema was that my colon function was suboptimal and lined with sludge, or "toxic butt" as she called it. The colonic was to cleanse out the junk and was followed by a diet rich in good bacteria to repopulate my colon and restore proper function. It was uncomfortable having the device inserted and then feeling the very strange sensation in my gut of an internal shower. I don't think the treatment achieved any noticeable changes, but I was a good sport about giving it a try.

The most bizarre attempt Mother made in trying to treat my eczema was based on some readings she'd done speculating that the root cause was a malfunctioning gallbladder. The treatment she read about and proposed was to clean out the gallbladder sludge with a regimen of olive oil and lemon juice. More specifically, every hour on the hour for eight hours, I would swallow a shot glass of virgin olive oil chased down with a shot glass of freshly squeezed lemon juice.

I was so excited about the idea of clearing up my eczema that I was willing to try anything. She joined me in taking the concoction for no particular purpose other than to keep me company. We started at 2 p.m. and finished consuming everything at 10 p.m. By ten, I was completely distended and doubled over in pain, still hopeful that the process would work. I went to bed shortly thereafter but never slept.

For eight hours, I was coming out at all ends and suffered miserably. It turned out that Mother did too. I don't know about my gallbladder, but my dry skin condition never improved from that treatment. I've been open to trying some of her other ideas.

Post injury, she recommended that I use a special water-filter device that would turn tap water into alkaline water, with no acidity from a pH balance standpoint. The theory is that alkaline water would be very beneficial to improved health and eliminate the possibility of contracting any virus, bacteria, germs, or other sources of infection because those bad guys can't survive in an alkaline environment. The theory was impressive, but from a practical standpoint did not work for me. I abandoned the unit after a couple of months.

In our elementary school days, Mother got into wheat grass, so much so that she would grow trays of wheat grass in our laundry room. This room had unobstructed sun access and plenty of moisture from running the washer/dryer. From the grass she harvested, she even baked home-made wheat grass bread. She would also juice the grass herself.

She had read about its numerous health benefits, and for several years it became part of our morning breakfast routine. Mother would set out five shot glasses of wheat grass juice next to five glasses of freshly squeezed lemon juice. We all had to down one of each, and anything else she had laid out before marching off to the bus stop.

I have no doubt that years of dental maintenance can be attributed to the lemon juice acidity, but with regard to the wheat grass, she may have been on to something. It is interesting today, some fifty years later, that I see wheat grass trays everywhere—organic grocery stores, juice bars, athletic clubs, health food stores, and even in people's homes.

She was into juicing—juicing any and all types of fruits, veggies, spices—pretty much anything you could put into a blender. The Vitamix blender and associated advertising had its roots back in those days, and perhaps that's what prompted her interest. Juices became part of our daily diet.

She always packed our lunch boxes before school, but our lunch boxes didn't contain the same things that other kids' lunch boxes did. When it came to lunchtime at school and kids wanted to trade—candy, chips, sodas—I had nothing to trade because nobody ever wanted what was in my lunch box—apples, sliced carrots, cooked liver, or soggy baked bean sandwiches. My mother had quite a rotation of healthy foods that I tried to keep hidden and wouldn't dream of trying to share with my schoolmates.

We were even exposed to chiropractic treatments, and I became very comfortable at a young age with a practitioner doing adjustments to my neck, torso, lower back, or any other part of my body. Having my neck adjusted never fazed me at the time. I could completely relax and allow the chiropractor to do the proper adjustment. Given my injury, having a neck or any other kind of "thrusting" chiropractic spinal adjustment close to that area is out of the question now.

While there were some false starts with Mother's ideas, there were many that today are very much mainstream. These experiences opened my eyes and instilled an openness and willingness (with a little better vetting) to try alternative treatments.

Acupuncture

I have to give a lot of credit to acupuncture treatments I have had through David Kerbs, doctor of acupuncture and oriental medicine. He made many visits while I was in inpatient rehab at HMC and spent a lot of time working on my arms, wrists, hands, and fingers. My top priority for recovery was to regain as much fine motor function as possible, and there is no doubt in my mind that his treatments were crucial to the hand function I have today.

He made incredible personal sacrifice to see me while I was hospitalized. He had a family life, an active practice, and was going to Bastyr University in Kenmore, Washington, for advanced studies. Layered on top of this were at least a dozen visits, probably more, to see me that required at least a thirty-minute commute each way. I will always be grateful for the sacrifice Dr. David made to treat me. It was exceptional.

I am completely independent and have use of my hands and all my fingers, which is atypical for an incomplete SCI. Dr. David and I have continued to work together, albeit not as much as we did in the early post-injury years. Acupuncture has also been helpful with muscle contractures, spasticity, and pain management.

Cranial-Sacral Therapy

I recently tried a treatment approach called cranial-sacral therapy. I had actually tried this once before in 1997 at a health center in Tucson, Arizona, mostly as an experiment to find out what it was. It is a very benign treatment with no bending, no manipulation, nothing oral—just hands touching your body. It isn't massage either.

As I understand it, around the spinal cord, there is space called the subarachnoid space that contains cerebrospinal fluid. The subarachnoid space extends into the base of brain where the body is constantly making and reabsorbing cerebrospinal fluid, ensuring a careful balance is maintained.

The fluid serves multiple purposes, from flushing metabolic waste, to acting as a lubricant of the spinal cord itself. A practitioner told me that this fluid has its own pulse, separate from the pulse of your cardiovascular system. Trained practitioners can feel this pulse by simply holding their hands under your spine, head, and sacrum. With gentle hand movements, a practitioner can actually manipulate fluid movement to remove blockages and allow the body to restore itself.

The first time I tried cranial-sacral therapy in Tucson, I was totally relaxed, light-headed, and even a little dizzy afterward. I walked back to my room, lay down, and slept nonstop for ten hours. Sleeping nonstop never happens for me.

My good friend Bob recently recommended a practitioner in the north Seattle area, a terrific man named Ko. We worked together once every two weeks for six sessions, but I wasn't feeling any different and as a result discontinued the sessions. I think there is definitely merit in the treatment. It is completely safe and most likely there were changes occurring at a more subtle level, where I couldn't feel them. Dr. Ko said he could feel changes.

I think for the therapy's efficacy to shine, I needed to see him a couple of times a week consistently for a couple of months to fully evaluate its benefit. At that point, however, it wasn't economically feasible, and I decided to put further treatments on hold.

Pilates

My good friend, Bob, has been on me for years, at least ten, probably longer, to try a fitness modality called Pilates. Bob had been doing it for years and constantly sang the praises of its benefits. Pilates is a set of exercises developed to emphasize breathing, body alignment, core strength, and improved coordination and balance.

As a member of the SAC, I have access to a Pilates center staffed with best-in-class instructors. A lady named Danielle manages the team. I got partnered with Danielle in early 2015, and we worked together for about eighteen months. She came highly recommended and did not disappoint.

When we first met, I explained the details of my condition, residual deficits, and limitations. I said I had two goals for working together—better posture and improved gait. I said I have plenty of motivation to do exercises on my own; what I needed most were the right exercises, technique, and frequency.

She seemed happy to adopt me as a "project" and off we went. I have learned many helpful exercises, none more so than concentrating on my feet and glutes, harnessing all my visual energy on those two areas.

We started modestly on a flat bench working on core muscle groups. Coupled with that were exercises that involved—interestingly enough—ballet movements called the plié and relevé that helped me stretch my ankles. A ballerina I am not, but seemingly innocuous exercises challenged several of my weaknesses in terms of posture, ankle flexion, balance, core strength, and foot position. This was just the beginning.

Over the months, we have added several new exercises, each one emphasizing half a dozen different motions simultaneously. One seemingly simple exercise involved lying flat on my back on a padded bench with my arms by my sides. Danielle placed a two-pound weight in each of my hands.

An objective of this exercise is to elongate tight muscles while helping improve postural strength. To do this I had to activate multiple muscle groups concurrently, a big challenge for a damaged neurological system. With weights in hand, I fully extended my arms straight up in the air, slowly sat up, and leaned forward, bringing my arms down and reaching forward to try to touch my toes (I couldn't actually touch them but got within a few inches).

Following that, I slowly reclined my body back down to a flat position while rotating my straightened arms and hands directly over and behind my head as far as they would stretch. I repeated this motion several times. It was a semicircular kind of motion.

While doing this simple sit up and lie down motion, Danielle had me activating several other muscle groups at the same time: flexing my ankles, tightening my quads and glutes, pulling my back flat into the bench, and pinching my shoulder blades together.

We have added many other exercises to the arsenal, all of which challenge me in similar ways. There's one thing I appreciate about Danielle and the Pilates approach—it requires activating multiple muscles at the same time, and using precision in the way an exercise is carried out. These exercises are very different from some of the intensive weight and machine lifting I have done but similar in challenging multiple muscle groups at the same time.

Massage

I have had massage appointments in the past, but not on a regular basis, partly for economic reasons and partly because my stretch routine does a similar thing. It involves doing "deep tissue" massage using a foam roller. With this roller, I can place my body weight on it in many different positions and use it to roll across my thighs, legs, and even from my buttocks to the base of my neck. These movements massage my iliotibial bands (IT bands) on the sides of my legs, and my hamstrings on the back of my legs. I can also use it to massage the interior band in my leg called the adductor.

I can do more aggressive deep tissue massage on my own utilizing an eight-pound weighted ball. These balls are sturdy and about ten inches in diameter. I find a stretch mat and, along with the weighted ball, use a variety of body positions to lean on the ball. For example, I get on my hands and knees, place the ball below one of my shoulders, and then bend down far enough to lean one of my shoulders onto the ball. I move my shoulders around on the ball, massaging my rotator cuff, deltoid, and pectoral muscles to work out kinks and soreness and to increase blood flow.

The depth and intensity of the massage depends on how much body weight I allow to lean into the ball. This is very effective. I use multiple variants, placing my body weight on the weighted ball to massage upper and lower back, shoulders, buttocks, quads, hamstrings, legs—whatever part I want to focus on.

This has been especially helpful for my shoulders, which tend to take a lot of stress from certain strengthening exercises. When I have had a massage appointment with a therapist, most of the time it has been focused on a particular area, which has been helpful.

Recently I had a session with one of my favorite therapists, Julie, and worked on an issue with my left shoulder. It had been bothering me for a couple of months and she performed some wizardry on it. The results have been great.

Massage is a very helpful modality. Many times, it can be topical in terms of pain relief. Most of the time, I do massage the "poor man's" way, because I can do it now without assistance. I only seek out paid services when I have a particular area that needs attention beyond what I can do on my own.

Reflexology

One of the consequences of this injury is significantly reduced sensation in my feet. Often I don't feel them, or they feel like tree stumps with no roots to anchor me. This is one of the main reasons I struggle with balance, because the feet send all kinds of sensory input to the brain to tell us where we are in space, which is known as proprioperception.

This input automatically helps us balance without conscious thought. Without that input, as in my case, my brain is grasping for any kind of sensory input available. My heels are most compromised, meaning they feel the least. A modality called reflexology has been especially helpful for me in trying to stimulate those senses and wake them up.

When a skilled practitioner performs this reflexology, after a little while, my feet start to "wake up" and feel pressure and some of the practitioner's touch. It is a great feeling, although it is short-lived. For a few minutes I regain some sensation and my balance improves. After I get off the table, it is nice to stand and actually feel parts of my feet and toes.

Since starting Pilates a few months ago, I was introduced to a small metal device called the foot corrector. It sits on the floor, and I place one foot at a time on it, using different foot positions, angles, and resistance. It, too, is helpful in bringing my foot sensation out of its dormant stage and for a few minutes helps me experience a slightly awakened foot. I practice on it frequently.

Although always wary of foot infections, I walk around the house in socks rather than shoes, hoping to activate the senses of my feet. Having better foot sensation will improve balance and gait and require less visual cues and neck bending to see what my feet are doing when I do walk.

Medical Marijuana

I am an authorized medical marijuana patient. Although the rules in Washington State are changing in terms of medical versus recreational marijuana use, I was authorized a few years ago to use it to manage spasticity. Dr. Tom Curtis, whom I came across at a holiday party, introduced the idea to me five years ago.

Dr. Tom had been my physiatrist years before I suffered this SCI. In the course of conversation, he asked if I had ever considered medical marijuana. I told him no, I hadn't. He said there was some very interesting research going on in Canada, specifically with a compound call Sativex.

The study was sponsored by one of the major pharmaceuticals and was researching Sativex efficacy in the treatment of multiple sclerosis (MS) and the resulting neurological deficits, spasticity in particular, that

these patients face. A unique method for dispensing it was being exper-
imented that involved a spray, akin to something like a Chloroseptic
spray, if you've ever used it for a sore throat. Sativex would be dispensed
in a similar spray form and be quickly absorbed.

Some of the early tests showed promise. It is still research in progress.
Because it was 2010 and Sativex was only available by MD authorization
in Canada, it was inaccessible in the States. I was aware of it, but at the
time there was nothing I could do. I was intrigued.

Now in 2016, considerable amounts of research are in progress, both
anecdotal and controlled. It has become more widely known that cannabis consists of a psychotropic or hallucinogenic compound, tetrahy-
drocannabinol (THC) and a non-psychotropic component, cannabidiol
(CBD). Typical cannabis strains of the past had very high percentages of
THC and very low CBD, although the two work synergistically together.

The THC gives you the "high." CBD however, does not, and this is
where cannabis is getting a lot of attention in terms of medicinal benefit.
While there are lots of anecdotal reports about the benefits of THC (pain
relief, nausea control, mood enhancer, stress relief, sleep aid, relaxation) the
evidence is mounting quickly that there is an indisputable benefit in using
high CBD cannabis for patients with epilepsy and seizure control issues.

I have a very good friend who suffered brain trauma from an accident
about the same time I was injured. High CBD marijuana in many ways
helped save her life, because she was suffering hundreds of grand mal seizures a month. There are many stories out there like hers, and the medical
establishment and pharmaceutical companies, like GW Pharmaceuticals,
are spending time and resources studying cannabis very closely.

My friend and I had dinner a few years ago. She talked about medical marijuana, CBD, and the research that was currently happening,
not just related to the treatment of epileptic seizures and MS but also
for patients like me, suffering from neurologically induced spasticity.
My ears perked up.

She told me about the transformation in her life that high CBD cannabis was allowing her to experience and some very new, cool ways that

cannabis could be taken, besides the traditional method of smoking. These new methods included edibles, drinks, capsules, tinctures, vapors, and more. I had never heard of vaporizing, and she asked if I had ever heard of e-cigarettes. I said no.

She explained that with a "vape" device you have a vial of cannabis distilled into an oil form, attached to a rechargeable heating device, and you simply put the device up to your mouth and breathe in. The device heats the cannabis oil in the cartridge and voila—vapor. You breathe it in, hold it for a few seconds, and breathe out the remaining vapor. It is the cannabis version of an e-cigarette.

There's no smoke, little to no smell, no burning, no tar or other untoward chemicals in your lungs, no matches, no ashes, no buds—just vapor. I said I would like to try it, but only in the high CBD form because I was not interested in getting high. I suffer from severe spasticity and take several prescription muscle relaxants for it, so I was anxious to give high CBD cannabis a try.

After getting authorization from my practitioner at HMC, I made my first visit to a medical marijuana dispensary. This was in 2013. It took some time to get educated about all the offerings, and I was most interested in the vapor option. The cost for the device and oil vials were prohibitive at that time, so I took a couple of baby steps and bought a few high CBD capsules instead. I took the pills at night and noticed little change.

Perhaps I needed to take more, or the capsules weren't high enough in CBD content. I didn't know, but this led me on a three-year journey since that dinner to become more educated on devices, quality control, customer experiences, manufacturer protocols, and trial and error to find the right concentration and delivery mechanism. I use a vape device today with cannabis oil, only at night, when I'm in bed ready to go to sleep. It is still a work in progress, as is the entire cannabis industry in Washington State.

I do believe there is a medical benefit to this alternative, and it won't be long before I discover the right combination and approach to using it that will materially relieve spasticity symptoms at night. If I can get a substantial reduction in nighttime extensor cramps, I'll consider using it during the day—the high CBD component only. I have no interest in being high. My ultimate goal would be to replace my prescription muscle relaxants with high CBD cannabis. I believe there is huge promise here and it won't be long before the federal government gets out of the way and declassifies cannabis as a schedule 1 controlled substance.

A Quiver Full of Possibilities

There are other modalities in my "quiver" of things to try. A few I have tried on a limited basis, and I believe all are viable options to consider. Yoga is an exercise I have considered doing for some time. A good friend of mine, Tanya at the SAC, has been encouraging me to participate in a yoga class. I did yoga before the injury and know there are many types.

My flexibility and balance challenges would limit me in being able to do many yoga exercises, and I would only do what I could do, perhaps even use a grab bar for support. One thing that intrigues me about yoga is the emphasis on breathing. When I become highly spastic, I know that taking several breaths helps me release the "emergency brake" and can reduce some of the severe seizing, if only for a few moments.

I did my first post-injury yoga session on Thanksgiving Day 2015 with Diane and Alana. They had invited me to their "hot" yoga class. Though very challenging, I had a good experience and am interested in trying again.

Stretching is helpful, but I do experience rebound effects. I stretch and stretch, and a few moments later, it's like I never stretched at all because I get this counterpunch effect where my stretched muscles reverberate and seize again. I will try yoga again in the future and, like any new modality, search for the right balance to get a good result.

Hypnosis

Hypnosis is another possibility. I tried it once around the time I had my severe setback in November 2007. I don't recall getting much if any benefit, but in retrospect, my frame of mind was not in a receptive place. There are reports from SCI research that hypnosis can be helpful for pain management, and from that perspective, I would consider it. It's not my first choice of modalities, which is why I haven't gone back to it, and also for economic reasons because insurance does not cover it. I also have questions about whether my mind would permit me to relinquish control to someone else. After all, there is a part of me that likes control. I haven't ruled out hypnosis, and it remains an option.

Feldenkrais

Feldenkrais is a modality that teaches new movement patterns to replace old ones that are strained and inefficient. The goal is to effect these changes through slow, gentle, and repeated movements. Back in the 1980s I used a massage therapist named Annie for several years. She eventually replaced her massage practice with one committed to Feldenkrais. She became a certified practitioner and has gone on over the years to build a substantial practice.

I haven't seen her in over thirty years but do know she has built a very successful business called Sensing Vitality. Of all the modalities I have yet to try, this one intrigues me the most. The concept is about awareness through movement. One of the biggest things I struggle with and want to improve upon is movement.

Biofeedback

Biofeedback is another option to consider. Using different types of instrumentation, biofeedback can provide the body with input about its physiological functions. This feedback is useful in learning to manage those physiological functions at will.

I relate this to having my blood pressure taken with an electronic monitor, which I do on a regular basis. When I get a reading, and it is higher than I would like, I will sit still and try to relax. I take deep breaths. I visualize a peaceful location. I still my mind, close my eyes, or recline in a chair.

After a few minutes, I take my blood pressure again, and almost every time, the reading will be lower. The blood pressure monitor has provided physiological information, and I have used it to manage my blood pressure effectively. My interest in this modality is how it could be used to better manage pain. While I have used various approaches to managing pain, I haven't done it in a way that provides usable data (unlike the BP machine) after performing an activity.

For example, it would be very interesting to see if my pain level could be quantitatively measured when I stand. Once I had a baseline reading, I could try a pain relieving technique, perhaps breathing or meditation, and measure my pain reading after to see if it changed. This modality hasn't risen to the top of options I'll try, but for many SCI patients I do know it has been helpful.

Meditation

Another modality in my quiver (other new ones may come along) I'll call meditation. I suppose a number of variants could fall under this umbrella—Zen, mindfulness, intention, breathing, relaxation—essentially using the power of the mind, its unique energy, and its plasticity to effect positive change. I do believe in the brain's plasticity, as well as a universal energy force, and perhaps there is some confluence of these beliefs that may lead me down another road of healing and recovery.

Exoskeletal Robot Suit

I recently attended a spinal medical conference in May 2016 held at the Seattle Science Foundation in Seattle, Washington. One of the speakers was Dr. Thomas Schildhauer, Medical Director, Professor, and Chairman of Department of General and Trauma Surgery at BG University Hospital Bergmannsheil, Bochum, Germany. He presented a fascinating speech on exoskeletal robotic systems that can be attached to patients with spinal cord injury, both complete and incomplete. He focused primarily on a robot suit that originated in Japan. In basic terms, when the suit is attached to a patient, a closed-loop system is activated whereby neurologic signals in the brain can be detected and communicated to the robotic suit, which then triggers a muscle response in the impaired area, such as a hand, calf, or quadriceps. The activated muscles respond and allow the patient to generate movement in areas that had previously been dormant.

His research and findings have been nothing short of groundbreaking, in my opinion. He profiled a complete SCI patient who had been wheelchair bound for seven years. After several months of therapy using the exoskeletal robot system, the patient was able to perform walking movements with the aid of a walker. This is nothing short of miraculous, and I believe validates points I have been making about the brain's plasticity and ability to reorganize itself. These findings are particularly exciting because previous thinking was that SCI patients who were considered complete (i.e., no function below the level of injury) now have a mechanism for regaining some amount of function. Previous thinking was that SCI completes could never regain function below their level of injury.

I am keenly interested in following up on this modality and may consider a trip to Bochum, Germany, to perhaps participate in his research. I'd be particularly interested in learning if it could help with some of my residual deficits, especially pain and spasticity, and if it could help "wake up" many of my impaired waist-level functions.

Intrathecal Baclofen Pump

This is a medical device that looks like a hockey puck with a catheter attached to it. It is surgically implanted in the lower abdomen just below the skin layer. The catheter is carefully extended to the spine, and the end is placed in the subarachnoid space that contains the cerebrospinal fluid surrounding the spinal cord. The device itself contains a liquid form of baclofen. It can also be used to dispense other liquid medications. It is a smart device in that it can be programmed by an external device to dose medication depending on time of day, or it can be manually controlled depending on how you are feeling.

Instead of taking baclofen orally, in which some of the medication's efficacy is lost because it has to travel through your digestive system, this device dispenses the medicine directly to the area where it is needed. The device is refilled by injection at a frequency of three to six months depending on dosing.

I considered taking an experimental dose in which a medical specialist injects liquid baclofen into the subarachnoid space. The purpose is to see how your body responds to the medication and to determine whether you would be a good candidate for the device.

At this time, I decided to forgo the test. Given the amount of activity I do, especially in the gym, I thought the size of the device in my abdomen would be an exercise impediment. In addition, I have had a couple of bad infections, including MRSA, and wasn't ready to assume that risk. There may be a time in the future when I will reconsider this option. I am aware that for many SCI patients suffering from severe spasticity, the baclofen pump has provided significant improvement in quality of life.

Stem Cell Research

One last word on the science of medical research for SCI: I do know there are limited, highly controlled stem cell trials in progress that are looking at the efficacy of injecting stem cells in patients within two weeks of having experienced spinal cord injury. The candidate patients have to be "completes," meaning there is no movement below the level of injury with little to no hope of functional recovery.

My opinion about stem cells is that there is no breakthrough on the horizon. I certainly could be wrong, and I hope I am, but I believe the real breakthrough in finding a way to heal SCI lies in the power of the brain's plasticity and unlocking that door in a way that allows the body to do what it does best—heal itself.

. . .

I am open to new ideas and will always vet them to ensure that it isn't some charlatan preying on and hurting people in trying to find a remedy or cure. These con artists are out there, and given the gravity of my injury, I think it is best to be conservative. I've fought with every ounce of my being to recover and will never put that progress at risk by trying something that could permanently set me back.

CHAPTER 19

Rediscovering Jamie

For my entire professional life, all thirty-three years of it, I have been known as **Jim**. My given name is James. Growing up, through high school and college, I had the usual parade of name variants. My most common and preferred, used by family, was Jamie. Like anyone, I had my share of nicknames, some I liked better than others, and a few were downright derogatory.

Ozzie, or Oz, is the nickname that has been most durable and dates back to my high school days at Avon Old Farms School. Ozzie is the nickname I liked the most.

There are many nicknames that I didn't care for and that left an imprint on me. I think they also left an imprint on others.

Mortel, the Friendly Grelb was coined by my father in my youth. He was a creative type who anointed me with this name as a consequence of my being crabby at times, especially on family outings, playing tennis, or other situations when I displayed a poor attitude.

Bot, short for Botticelli, came from my two older brothers. They called me that just to annoy me, and the more they used it, the more it annoyed me. They loved calling me this because it always got under my skin and my poor, sulky attitude didn't know how to deal with it. It was a unique selection given that Sandro Botticelli was an Italian painter, and I know nothing about art.

James Henderson, Lord Airborne, a reference to being spacey or a bit of an airhead, takes the cake as being the most belittling. Its origin was from a guy I worked with at a summer internship at Waltham Hospital in Waltham, Massachusetts, after my junior year in college. I never cared for the guy because he enjoyed putting people down. I thought he was kind of insecure and a bully. This name also had a short shelf life.

Flash, which never really stuck, was an attempted label by a camp counselor from when I attended NOLS (National Outdoor Leadership School). One night he observed my camera flashing when I was taking nighttime shots. This same counselor, writing my evaluation after the thirty-five-day expedition, expressed that I "often had a poor attitude."

. . .

Many of these monikers were assigned to me based on what other people thought about my attitude and aloofness, which in my youth and young adult years was nothing to be admired. I often struggled with seeing the downside rather than the upside of things. One friend referred to me as a "defeatist."

I'm not sure why I had attitude challenges, but as I grew a bit older, I gained a better understanding of where they came from—me. My bad attitude didn't originate with anyone else and wasn't caused by anyone else. I remember one time hearing the words "the person who talks most to you is . . . you."

These nicknames did have an effect on me. These labels of poor attitude and aloofness left an imprint that I compensated for in a protective way. I began to insulate myself and became guarded and cautious. As I entered the workforce, I knew I wasn't going to be successful with a poor attitude and aloofness. Rather than deal with it, I chose to suppress it when I was at work.

My work name, Jim, which I'll explain in a moment, became a "shield" of protection, a way of creating an alternate me. This is how I was able to build a successful professional career, but at the same time it came with some unintended consequences. I became more distant from people, except in some select cases, and developed an intimidating, "hard-ass" demeanor, which many of my work colleagues found mostly acceptable but not particularly approachable.

I built a good reputation, accomplished a lot of great things, but many colleagues found me distant, uninterested, and unengaging. Toward the end of my time as an IT director in June 2007, it had become clear to me that many in the IT organization didn't really care for me. I had been working on trying to improve my persona and people skills just as the accident happened.

In early 2007, I began to better understand the unconscious mind and the influence of self-talk and thought control. I realized that I was the one in control and needed to step up and take charge. I made the decision to do exactly that. It wasn't an overnight thing, and my attitude journey continues today. Attitude has been front and center in my recovery, and I have used its power to help deal with this injury.

So who am I today? This topic of multiple identities really confronted me in early 2006 when Diane and I attended a work event. One of my work colleagues, Carla, was in attendance and overheard Diane refer to me as Jamie. Her ears perked up because she hadn't heard the name before, and she was amused—to think that the Jim she had known for the past twelve years was actually known by a different name.

She asked me what she should call me. I told her to stick with Jim for the time being, until I could figure out what I actually wanted to do about it in the workplace. In the meantime, the Jim/Jamie identity spoof spread rapidly around the company, generating a lot a buzz and amusement.

Jim came about less by intent and more through my own acquiescence. When I first started out in the working world in 1979, working at my second summer internship for a software company, I would introduce myself as Jamie, but people would consistently default to Jim. So I kind of caved in and rolled with it. At least that is what I thought at the time. It became apparent over time that the name "Jim" served other purposes in terms of suppressing some of my character issues, especially attitude.

I eventually found myself living a life of multiple identities, at least as far as my name was concerned. Most of my work colleagues knew me as Jim, and most friends and relatives outside of work knew me as Jamie. There were a couple of non-work friends who knew me as Jim. At times, I found myself in this conundrum of trying to figure out which name the person I was talking with knew me by.

I suppose it became kind of a game, and it had worked well, until the point that Carla discovered "Jamie." That's when I had to decide what name to use with my work colleagues. What name do I go by? How will people I know adjust to knowing me as Jamie instead of Jim?

In the fall of 2006, I applied for an officer-level position at the company I was working for. I served as a director in the IT department and had done so for the prior seven years. When my boss, the VP of IT, made a move to another department, his position opened, and I took the opportunity to apply. I was one of a handful of finalists and felt I had a good shot at getting it.

During an interview with the CFO, to whom the VP position reported, I learned that he had convened a number of small focus group sessions with members of the IT department. He went on to say that during these focus group sessions there wasn't very much advocacy for me, and he wanted to know what I made of it. It was a difficult question, a bit surprising, and I found myself in an awkward position, trying to put myself in the shoes of the IT staff and imagine what they thought of me.

To be honest, I felt that people might have considered me distant, not personable, and unengaged in the details of their work, as well as their personal lives. I was not a management-by-walking-around (MBWA) manager. My office, where I spent a lot of my time doing work, conducting meetings, etc., was in a corner of the building, away from the staff cubicles. Others may have thought I was a bit of a hard-ass—stiff, firm, and cardboard-like.

In fact, I had heard these types of comments about me, some of it directly and some of it through others. It didn't feel good to hear these remarks.

I shared this with the CFO. He told me what I said was pretty close to the feedback he had heard and that this appeared to be a development opportunity for me. I knew at that point I was out of the running. It was a tough reality check.

Later that fall in 2006, the results of the annual employment survey were delivered. My employer performed this survey every year to get detailed feedback from all employees on a wide range of subjects, including feedback on management, supervision, and leadership. My scores were generally good, except in the area of people development. The results of the survey confirmed what I had heard from the CFO. I had a blind spot—a significant development opportunity—in an area that had never surfaced before in any of my feedback or performance reviews.

The company gave me the opportunity to work with a leadership coach, a person who generally only worked with officer-level executives. The company was going to make her available to me, so I jumped at the chance. One of the first things I did was identify six employees who knew me well and who would be willing to give me open, honest, and direct feedback.

I met with each one and learned a lot about this people development opportunity and what I could do to improve things. The feedback was tough to hear, even though I had prepped myself in advance. At that time, I was feeling pretty low.

This development opportunity was a gap in my job performance that I needed to address. "People development" was a skill expectation of me as a person holding a director-level management position. I was expected to be engaged with all the members of my team, to interact with them regularly, and especially to help all of them understand, pursue, and achieve their own professional goals. As a leader, I could help team members accomplish this by providing coaching, training, challenging assignments, feedback, and other resources for their own growth. Part of my job was to partner with each person in his or her personal and professional development as a coach, advisor, or mentor. I needed to be more involved in their professional lives and to help them grow.

The leadership coach, Sherryl, and I developed a close working relationship over the next six months. We met on a regular basis to work on my people development opportunity. She recommended a couple of books, which I read and we discussed. One of the crucial moments for me was recognizing that I was managing with my head and not my heart. We discussed how to blend both in leading people, engaging staff, and helping grow and develop them. We also spent time discussing the Jim/Jamie conundrum and the fact that I wanted to fix it.

I wanted to discard Jim, the stiff, firm, cardboard-like manager, and make a switch to Jamie, an engaging, people-oriented, blended head-heart leader. I wanted to be authentic, real, and approachable, someone people would be comfortable communicating with, no longer a stranger, but interested in the lives of others, out and about visiting with the team. I realized the working Jim wasn't the real Jamie, and that I needed to make the transition from Jim to Jamie.

And then . . . the accident happened. It happened just a few hours after Sherryl and I had met that morning.

So began a multiyear odyssey to put myself back together. The accident shattered me in so many ways. Physically I was a mess—paralyzed, motionless, and in a lot of pain. Emotionally I was scared, very scared. The future was unknowable. I was depressed, anxious, and lost.

Spiritually, I was disconnected. I couldn't believe the God to whom I had professed my faith had allowed this terrible tragedy to happen to me. Where was he to protect me? The church I belonged to at the time abandoned me. I had so many questions and no answers.

The identity part of recovering from this catastrophic injury has been one of the most difficult. The work Sherryl and I were doing was derailed and never resumed. I was, however, determined to make the shift to Jamie. Jamie is who I am.

Now, when I meet new people, I generally introduce myself as Jamie. Occasionally I will use James. Many former colleagues and long-standing friends who have known me as Jim continue to call me Jim. I can live with that, but I know now who I am—Jamie is the real me.

"Jim" worked in the professional world, but when I was Jim, I wasn't being authentic. I didn't allow the complete me to be revealed; I suppressed him, I suppose, to keep from exposing my vulnerabilities. I had wanted to convey confidence, strength, and stature and had cared more about being respected and less about being liked. I had wanted the people I worked with to know the professional me and not the real Jamie.

Jim was the "head" that Sherryl and I discussed. Jamie was the "heart" that was missing in my leadership style. It's unfortunate that when I returned to work in 2008, I wasn't able to manage a team any longer and only worked as a part-time individual contributor for the next four years.

The good news is that my transition from Jim to Jamie was an important component of my recovery and finding my real identity. I do have a heart and just need to make that more visible and not hide it any longer.

There are many things revealed in these pages that I would never have talked about twenty years ago, let alone memorialized in a book. That was the old me—hidden, shielded, protected behind Jim. I was living a work life for most of my adult years that was productive, useful, fun at times, adventurous, aspiring, and competitive but with protective walls blocking true interaction with others. In a way it was an alternate life—not a lie, but not truly authentic either. My work persona was only one part of me—my intellect, my brains, my logic, and rationale. The whole me was there, sometimes exposed, but most of the time reserved in the background, tucked away and visible to only a trusted few.

As I have processed things over the past nine years, this idea has become very important: to be me, the whole me with head and heart connected as one. Jamie is the catalyst for this change. Perhaps it is a "coming out" of sorts, coming out of my shell, my protected cocoon. Jamie is authentic, real, open, and vulnerable. Jamie doesn't need the protection of Jim any longer. I'm at a point in my life where it is okay to be open and honest with everyone around me and with myself.

When a life is completely shattered in an instant, the process of rebuilding begins. That is what happened to me on that fateful day in June 2007. Part of choosing to win wasn't just rebuilding my physicality;

it was rebuilding Jamie. I didn't want to re-create my old Jim workplace persona, the one who kept people at a distance, who was viewed as a "hard-ass" by coworkers and was, by many accounts, considered intimidating or unapproachable.

An accident such as this strips you down. It breaks down your pride. It breaks down your ego. It breaks down your walls. It breaks down all your protective behaviors. It distills you into your raw self. You are naked, exposed, and vulnerable. In these pages I am "exposing" my heart. I'm okay with it, because I now know how important it is to be real, authentic, and genuine, regardless of the setting, relationship, or situation.

I don't have to be one person at work and another person at home. I can just be me, true to myself, accepting of myself. This meeting of head and heart, being Jamie again, has been just as instrumental in my overall recovery as working out at the gym and getting physically stronger.

Choosing Jamie was a choice to win.

CHAPTER 20

Lessons I Didn't Expect to Learn

Accept that Life Isn't Fair

Life isn't fair. There were no promises when I came into this world that life would be fair. There are no guarantees made to any of us. Everyone has or is currently dealing with some kind of difficulty or, at a minimum, knows someone who is. None of us are insulated from the curveballs life throws at us.

Wouldn't it be incredible if life were peaceful and smooth, with no hardships, no bad things, no accidents, no disease, no conflict, and no adversity? It is a given that we will all face something in our lives, something out of left field, something we never saw coming. This is a life certainty. How we cope with these "curveballs" can define us, or we can take control and define it—"it" being the event, or circumstance.

When I think of my childhood, adult life, married life, "daddy" life, and professional life, I can think of many difficulties I encountered. In terms of being a father and raising a family, one of the hardest challenges was discovering Kevin's anaphylactic allergies to nuts—of any kind—and learning to manage his sensitivities.

We first discovered his allergies when he was a toddler and we were feeding him baby food. He ate something that had a nut ingredient, and we noticed his front lip start to swell. We had no idea what was happening but called the doctor and were advised to seek medical attention immediately. At the ER, he received an epinephrine shot, which quickly suppressed the reaction. He went through a battery of tests, which confirmed his allergy. Epinephrine kits, aka EpiPens, became a staple of our household and everyone was instructed in how to use them.

Over the years (he is now twenty-eight), Kevin has had countless anaphylactic reactions, and with most he was able to readily get medical attention, but there were a few times where we came very close to losing him. The most serious happened about ten years ago, on a ski trip to Whistler Blackcomb in British Columbia.

We had stopped for lunch at an on-mountain lodge on Blackcomb called the Glacier Creek Lodge. We had eaten there many times without any issues. On this day, Kevin forgot to carry his EpiPen kit with him, but we figured the risk was very, very low given how many years and times we had eaten at the lodge without incident. As bad luck would have it, Kevin had a severe reaction to something he ate. Without an EpiPen, we quickly sought out the ski patrol in the building.

Unfortunately, they were nowhere to be found. The patrols were all on-mountain. We were in a terrible panic. Kevin was placed in the first-aid room, but there was nothing we could do for him without an EpiPen. His breathing passages were swelling up and closing, and he was beginning to turn blue. Diane sobbed uncontrollably, afraid we were going to lose him.

At last a staff member was able to reach the ski patrol, which by sheer luck happened to be skiing in the direction of the lodge. Frantic, I went outside, flagged the patrol down, and thankfully, they happened to have an EpiPen kit with them and quickly gave Kevin an injection to curtail the reaction. He was then airlifted off the mountain to the closest ER. In four hours he was discharged, back at our unit, and enjoying dinner. It was a good ending to the story but one that was very close.

Alana has also had an unfair share of medical issues that have required a considerable number of ER visits, doctor and therapy appointments, and surgeries. Diane has had her share, too, not to mention my own, unrelated to my current quadriplegic condition. I remember hearing one friend of

Alana's once say, "You guys just never get a break." One of my friends has referred to our many challenges as the "ongoing Osborne tragedy."

We certainly don't have a monopoly on injury, disease, or misfortune; however, the cumulative aspect of all these events in our lives has taken its toll. I keep wondering when the next shoe is going to drop. We do yearn for some smooth sailing and peace of mind, but at the same time, I've realized, as a consequence of my injury, not to dwell so much on what happens next.

I have come to accept that in all likelihood something else will happen, but I can't live my life worrying about it. If I did, I might not do anything at all. Having these events happen, from the least to the most severe, is unfortunately part of life's unscripted script. Sometimes it is difficult to keep our heads up and press on, but we continue to try.

Make the Best of It

My mother-in-law, Muriel Kendall Bessemer Lord Walton—that is quite a mouthful and is indicative of her advanced age of ninety-one and having outlived three husbands—is a remarkable woman. She is unfortunately dealing with dementia and the dreaded Alzheimer's. She is not the same strong, independent, vibrant, professional woman I once knew, but her memories and keen insights will stay with me forever. She, too, has faced life's unfairness in many ways.

On one occasion in the mid 1980s, she and her second husband, Fred Lord, were on vacation near Durban, South Africa, traveling with another couple. They were driving on a two-lane highway and were victims of a head-on collision with a bus. Fred and Muriel were critically injured, with Fred being the worse off of the two. The other couple escaped with minor injuries. After convalescing in South Africa, Muriel and Fred came back to the states to continue rehab.

Muriel made a strong recovery but had some residual deficits. Unfortunately, Fred had suffered brain damage. As one of the premier scholars of the Educational Testing Service in Princeton, New Jersey, and one of the noted quantitative researchers for the SAT exam, Fred's intellect had been beyond superior.

After the injury, however, his brain function was severely impaired and so were many of his physical capabilities. Muriel committed over fifteen years of her life to taking care of Fred while they lived in Naples, Florida, until Fred passed away. I always admired Muriel for dedicating her life to Fred's care, for keeping him at home and not in a long-term care facility.

Her constant refrain to me was, **"Jamie, I just make the best of it."**

In addition to her caregiving responsibilities, she went on to found a Woman's League in the Naples area, which has grown today to be a premier women's organization with several thousand members. I've always had great respect and admiration for her. Her simple life lesson of "making the best of it" left a deep impression on me, and later I was able to apply her courageous motto to my own life. If I ever go to a place of feeling sorry for myself, I think of Muriel and the simple life truth she taught me.

Play the Hand You're Dealt

I have been a rabid professional football fan my entire life. Having grown up in New England, and living in the area through my college years, I always rooted for the New England Patriots (at the time known as the Boston Patriots). When Diane and I switched coasts and moved to the Seattle area in 1981, it wasn't long before my allegiance shifted to the Seattle Seahawks. In the 1980s, the Seahawks' head coach was a man named Chuck Knox. Coach Knox was fond of many different phrases, but the one he repeated that resonated with me the most was **"Play the hand you're dealt."**

I can't think of a more appropriate phrase in terms of coping with my injury. Yes, I got dealt a bad hand, but that doesn't mean there aren't many more good hands to play. This terrible accident has dealt a significant blow to my psyche, physicality, relationships, career, friendships, and goals. This is my hand, using the card game analogy. How am I going to play it? Fold and go home? Play on?

I choose to play on and am confident that the new hands I'll get will reveal more new and exciting things than I could have ever imagined. Do I get discouraged and want to fold sometimes? Sure. The difference is that I don't dwell on the worry. I let the discouraged thoughts happen, acknowledge them, and send them on their way out of my mind and let them disappear. I simply keep playing.

Focus on the Things You Can Do

It would be very easy to dwell on the things I can't do. Because of the hard work I've put into rehabilitation, I can do many activities today, but there are still many things I can't do. I can't run, jump, dance, do high cadence exercises, drive a stick shift, or walk without fear of falling. It's hard to stand in place for long without experiencing severe spasticity. I can't be sure I will ever be medication-free, be fully in control of all my waist-level functions, or not feel depressed at times. I can't live without pain—at least for now. What I wouldn't give to go a day without pain! These are things I can't do, but through this journey I've learned **to focus on the things I can do, and build on them.**

From the early post-injury days, when I had no hand or finger control, to today, when there is almost nothing I can't do with my hands—gripping hand weights, touching my thumb to all my fingers, using chopsticks, keyboarding, writing, teeth flossing, dressing, taking a shower and standing up, dressing myself, buttoning a shirt or folding laundry—I have come a long, long way. Rather than using the things I can't do as a boat anchor to tie me down, I use the things I can do as the wind under my sails that allows me to reach and achieve new goals.

It would be easy to feel frustrated about the things I can't do, but like everything, it comes down to choice and attitude. I choose to focus on the things I can do and take a lot of satisfaction in breaking new ground. As Muriel would often remind me, "Jamie, keep your head up."

Practice Overcoming

While living in Arizona for a few years, from 2012 to 2015, when Alana attended Arizona State University (ASU), I joined an LA Fitness club not far from our home. I was a regular there four to five times a week. I primarily worked out on my own. While I was there, I had the good fortune to meet a man about my age, perhaps a little older, named Paul. We introduced ourselves one afternoon on the stretch mat and soon were sharing our stories.

Paul was raising three sons and spent time with them in the outdoors hunting, camping, and mountaineering. He was amazingly fit and took the time to take me under his wing and teach me a lot of new exercises, many of which I use today. He seemed like a man who had everything—until he told me about the tragedy in his own life.

Several years earlier, he had lost one of his sons in an auto accident, which had happened only a short distance from the LA Fitness club. For reasons unclear to me, his son drove his pickup truck into a telephone pole, causing it to catch fire and explode. His son never had a chance.

I can't begin to fathom the loss of a child, especially in such a horrific way. He told me about the initial years of grieving that followed such a tragic loss; how extraordinarily difficult it was to try to make sense of his loss and find a way forward. He said one of the ways he'd found that helped him was to introduce himself to people at the gym, not just any and every person, but those he felt drawn to, those he felt were, perhaps, kindred spirits, dealing with some kind of life difficulty.

His story brought tears to my eyes. I could feel his shared emotion when I told him my story. He went on to tell me what brings him the most solace when he looks back on the tragedy of his son's death.

"Jamie," he said, "what I am most proud of since my son died has been **overcoming—overcoming the loss, anger, depression—overcoming— that is what means the most to me.**"

He asked what has meant the most to me since I was injured. I said, "Paul, I suppose it is exactly what you are talking about, but I had never thought about it in those terms. I've thought about how hard I've worked, some of the really cool things I've been able to accomplish, and also . . . surviving. But I think the word you used, 'overcoming,' is exactly what I am talking about. Overcoming the loss, anger, depression—all of it. I can't really say I've overcome, because it is a process, a lifelong process. I believe that I'll always be overcoming."

Seek Mental Health Intervention

As I have mentioned in other places in this book, one of the things I underestimated most after the accident was the toll this event would take on my mental health. In the hospital, I thought I had my mental act together, and I underestimated the need to seek professional counseling. *So, a word to the wise—if you experience a tragedy in your life,* **seek mental health intervention** *asap*. Grieving is a necessary process for recovery, and having a trusted professional resource is very important.

For my whole life, up to the time of my injury, I had been conditioned to fight these things on my own. Seeking professional help felt like I was being weak. Even after the severe setback I experienced in November 2007, I still thought I could grind it out on my own, but to no avail. One reason I tried to soldier on by myself was that I had never been depressed before in my life. I looked at this mental downturn as a transient event that would pass in short order. I kept finding excuses not to do it but never being real with myself that I needed help.

I think what I struggled with most was the thought of being vulnerable, revealing myself, and feeling exposed. After my setback, it took another six months before I got off the sidelines and took action. There is no doubt in my mind that if I had I engaged professional help shortly after being discharged from HMC, I might have avoided the severe setback I experienced. At a minimum, I think I would have been able to understand the complex feelings of loss that were dragging me down.

Pace Yourself

Pacing myself was one of the hardest things I had to learn. When I began rehab, I created an artificial sense of urgency in my mind, similar to cramming for a final exam. In my case, I felt I had six months post injury to regain as much function as possible while there was still time. After all, Dr. Barry had told me that most of my progress would be made in these important first six months.

I had it locked in my head that I had to be back to work within that time frame, by December 2007. It was extremely important to me not to endure what I perceived to be the embarrassment of going on long-term disability. I had established a misplaced mind-set. I believe this self-inflicted pressure was too much for my mind and body to handle during my yearlong period of spinal shock.

Dr. Jens had also told me that it was very important to my recovery for me to get back to work. I had a six-month checkup with Dr. Jens in January 2008. He reviewed the results of a CT myelogram, examining in detail the healing progress of my spinal cord, and the results looked good, so good that he remarked, "Jamie, it is unusual for a surgeon to say this, but you will not require surgery. The cyst inside your cord has healed, the supporting ligaments for your cervical spine have healed, and your vertebrae are in good alignment."

I was, of course, very pleased to hear this.

He continued, "If your symptoms change, come back and see me, but at this point you can move forward with normal activities. By the way, are you working yet?" I said no, I was not, because Dr. Barry thought I needed more time. Dr. Jens said, "**Jamie, it is very important in your recovery to get back to work,** to get into the flow of being productive, being around your colleagues, and having a schedule every day." He was absolutely right.

By the time I had this conversation in January 2008, my setback had already occurred, and I was in the beginning stages of my "climb out." I took his statement as one of encouragement, meaning that he thought my faculties were stable enough to consider going back to work. I had been quite anxious about seeing him, though, because this was our first visit since my second crash in November 2007. I was worried he would feel disappointed after being so bullish about my making a rapid recovery in the first few months post injury. He wasn't at all. Instead, I felt reassured, not pressured, by his words.

I remember having a conversation with one of the HMC OTs, Susan, in fall 2007. She asked if I was back to work yet. I interpreted that comment to mean she expected that I would already have done so, presumably based on the trajectory of recovery I had made up to that point. That conversation never left my head and orbited there for months as I continued to push harder and harder. "Gosh," I would think, "I don't want to let her down."

I realize now this was really a projection of not wanting to let myself down. My second crash came in the form of a mental crash, so work was put off for a time.

It took another seven months to get things worked out with the company, and eventually I was able to return to work in July 2008 in a part-time role. Working again did matter, and it was a very important element of my recovery. Although the position I came back to was very different from what I had been doing prior to my injury, I was working.

Until I had returned to it, I didn't realize at the time how important working again was to my recovery. It refocused my attention on something besides my impairments and the various therapies I was doing several times a week. Also, by then I was working with a mental health therapist, and this time I became very proficient at pacing.

Take Time to Reward Yourself

Doing a day with spinal cord injury is difficult. There is never an easy day. Each one takes considerable energy, concentration, and determination. I remember a conversation with Dr. Barry, who said, "Remember, Jamie, the energy, focus, and time you expend to do anything is considerably greater than before, and **take time each day to reward yourself—in a way that is meaningful for you."**

I thought this was terrific advice, so I applied it then and continue to do so nine years later. I reward myself in a variety of ways. Sometimes I say a prayer before I go to bed, just thanking the "force" for providing me with the energy and stamina to do the day. Sometimes I read a book. Other times I take thirty minutes on the stretch mat after exercise when my endorphins are circulating and I have my headphones on, listening to a favorite playlist. Other times I have a cocktail or dinner out with a friend. Whatever day it is, wherever I am, I make it a point to reward myself with something—kind words, a social visit, or just some quiet moments in meditation, relaxing, or journaling.

Celebrate Victories

Victories come in all shapes and sizes. Some of my early victories were small, pedestrian activities like being able to touch my thumb to my forefinger. Another was being able to hold a utensil. There was the first time I was able to button a dress shirt. I was really proud when I was able to dress myself standing up, without having to sit down in a chair.

Other victories would come later. One was being able to walk, gingerly and with helpers, around the perimeter of HMC just prior to being discharged. Another was the first time I walked around our neighborhood block, a distance of one kilometer. I remember the first time I was able to shuffle a deck of cards using both hands. I was so excited when I was first able to walk up a flight of stairs without holding the railings.

There have been numerous victories I have accomplished in the gym, like doing my first push-up. I remember with a big smile the first time I was able to hang from a pull-up bar, arms fully extended, and without swinging my legs do a legit pull-up, chin just cresting the bar. There was the first time I was able to bench press 135 pounds, not an enormous feat by weight-lifting standards, but for me an epic accomplishment.

Each time I achieved a victory, regardless of size or perceived difficulty, I shared it with someone. Often it was with Diane. Many times it was with my brother Tom, or sister Allyson, or another family member.

Sometimes it was a close friend, medical practitioner, or workout mate. I'm sure there were others. I always made it a point to share it with someone, and to see or hear him or her lifted up, inspired, and as excited about the achievement as I was. Their excitement fueled my fire to keep working as hard as I could to achieve the next victory.

Visualize Healing

In the first few years post injury, my good friend Peter from West Seattle would come over to the house for a couple of hours. Early on his visits were a couple of times a week and then they settled to once a week as his schedule permitted. We would first go out for a walk in the neighborhood and then come back to my bedroom, where he would read to me while I lay on the carpeted floor and did a stretch routine. During those stretch routines, and at other times when he wasn't with me, I would visualize healing.

The picture I always imagined was a beam of light coming from the heavens, shining in a straight line right on my spine, illuminating my body, and bringing healing energy to the exact location in my spinal cord where the damage was. I had a clear recollection of the MRI film study where the "cloud" of damage in the C5–C7 area was visible. I visualized the light beam filled with healing energy, breaking up the cloud of damage in my spinal cord just as the rising sun might burn off and dissipate morning fog.

I believe with all my being that **visualization is a powerful force** that can tap into parts of the universe that science has no explanation for, whose answers are locked away in the brain's plasticity. All the significant goals I've achieved have occurred as a direct consequence of visualization.

I listened to a lecture once where the speaker asked the audience, "Can you improve your golf game without actually playing?"

Someone answered, "No way, you have to pay your dues on the driving range and play a lot if you are going to improve."

The speaker responded, "Well, there is actually evidence that you can improve your golf game by picturing it, envisioning what your swing is doing, contemplating body mechanics, and seeing the ball fly straight and long down the fairway. **Play the movie over and over in your head, make the necessary adjustments, and you will find that your game will improve."**

He provided several examples in his answer, which I found fascinating and believable. My takeaway was that visualization is an incredible force.

Tap into the Universal Force

I do believe there is some kind of **universal force**; whether it exists in us, all around us, or both, it is there and I can tap into it. I have no doubt that anyone can, if they focus and visualize it, and allow themselves to be guided by it. For me, thinking about the God force in this way brings clarity to what has been muddled in my head for so many years. Raised as a simple Protestant, exposed to cults, betrayed by conservative Christianity, I am now a "believer" in the universal force in which we are all immersed. I believe there is a spiritual life in some realm, and the power of the mind tapping into this force is possible. I believe that tapping into this energy source has been an important element of my recovery.

Stay Socially Involved

By nature I am an introvert. I can be an extrovert, but it takes energy and is tiring. Being an extrovert does not energize me. Coupled with my injury, I have a constant pull to withdraw, be alone, by myself, even be a bit of a hermit, but I know how important relationships are in normal life, and even more so when dealing with catastrophic injury.

Even with the headwinds that continue to push against me, I make it a point to get out at least once a day, whether it is to spend time at the SAC, have dinner with a friend, enjoy an outing on a boat, or host friends at home. I don't host often, because it is exhausting, but it can't be understated how important **remaining socially engaged** is when you are living with impairments.

We are all social beings and need a sense of belonging and being supported and loved. I could easily spend my time alone and live in my own world, but I know that isn't healthy and ultimately will prevent me from finding the joy, fulfillment, purpose, and value that I yearn for in this "new normal."

Advocate for Yourself

Medicine is not always precise. As much as we want to view our medical experts as being the final word on various medical matters, the fact is they are not always right. I am the beneficiary of what I consider the best medical care in the country if not the world. The best orthopedic and physical medicine specialists you can hope to find treated me.

I was also told shortly after I was injured that the steepest recovery trajectory would be the first six months. After that, the trajectory would flatten out, and my maximum recovery would be reached after one to two years. I can say unequivocally that I have had considerably more recovery in the past six years than I did in the first three. In my experience, if you consistently work at it, things can continue to improve.

I have never felt like I hit a plateau or was "redlined." Progress is hard fought and takes time, but it will come. Educate yourself. Plug in to support groups either online or in person. Be your own advocate. The most unexpected thing for me is to learn that **recovery can continue**. This is proof that we as patients should not equate ourselves with the norm and call it good. Population studies do not predict your outcome.

This is not a criticism of anyone involved in my medical care over the years. The point is I had to learn to **take control of my own care**, and I urge others to do the same. Be your own advocate, or engage someone to be an advocate partner with you. It is important to ask questions, get clarification, understand the "why" behind how your care is directed, educate yourself, and not be afraid to explore second opinions or even alternate treatments, so long as the care is coordinated. I think the most important lesson I learned was to not be passive about my care and not to blindly accept everything I was told.

For instance, I am keenly interested in tracking my blood work, understanding and monitoring numbers that are critical to my long-term health. I make sure I have an annual physical. I also have had a history of abnormal mole growths—none cancerous, thankfully—and make sure I see a dermatologist annually.

Several years ago, as part of my annual physical, I requested a couple of blood tests. One in particular was to check my levels of reactive protein, or CRP as it is called. This specific test is called a high-sensitivity CRP test that checks for internal vascular inflammation. I learned about this test from a book I read called *UltraPrevention*, by MDs Mark Hyman and Mark Liponis, a book about taking proactive control of your health.

My internist asked me why I wanted the test, because it wasn't part of the routine blood work done for a physical. I said my understanding is that internal vascular inflammation and my lipid profile (cholesterol, triglycerides) were important markers of cardiovascular health. High cholesterol coupled with high internal inflammation is a bad combination and places you in a high-risk category for a cardiac event. My doctor tried to downplay the correlation, but I insisted on the test, even if I had to pay for it myself. Fortunately all the numbers came back good.

Set Goals and Build on Them

I have always been ambitious, have had aspirations and goals of what I wanted to achieve professionally—the kind of parent and spouse I wanted to be, the retirement I wanted to have, the values I wanted to impart to my children, and the legacy I wanted to leave behind. After my accident, these goals were turned upside down. The cards were reshuffled, and I was dealt an entirely new hand, which left me asking, *How am I going to play this new hand in my life?* The unexpected lesson was to **recalibrate previous goals into new ones**, basically hitting the refresh button and starting over.

Physical restrictions allowed me to expand my personal vision and clarify my priorities. Instead of a professional ambition to be a senior leader with a large organization, my new goals were seemingly pedestrian, but they were incredibly important at the time. I wanted my hands and fingers to work again. I wanted to be able to hold a utensil and feed myself. I wanted to be able to type an email, drive, hold clippers to clip my nails, and floss my teeth. I wanted to be able to stand and move my feet, to do the activities of daily living without being assisted. I wanted to be able to work out, get my heart rate up, and generate a sweat.

You wouldn't believe how important generating a sweat from a workout was to me. It took me three years to get that point, but I was undaunted in pursuit of that goal. Goals, aspiration, and perseverance have been the tenets of my recovery, along with my unwavering belief that these goals were possible and that I must never let go of those dreams.

I resolved to stick with it and never give up; no matter the obstacle, never quit. I hate the notion of quitting or folding my hand and throwing in my cards. The thought of quitting makes my stomach churn. If one approach didn't work, I tried another, and another, until I was able to do what I was striving for.

I remember in inpatient rehab working on my finger strength and coordination. The therapist had me trying to pinch clothespins. They were color coded, and each color represented different levels of difficulty. It was frustrating at first because I couldn't get my fingers to even hold the clothespin, let alone apply any pressure to pinch it so I could fasten it to a line. But I didn't give up.

I pressed on for weeks until I could finally grip the clothespin, squeeze it, and fasten it to the line. I started with the easiest one, and after five weeks was able to do the same thing with the most difficult one. This process played itself out with countless exercises; I started at ground zero and worked my way back slowly. As a result, new nerve circuits were built around the damaged area in my spinal cord, the nerve impulse highway, and these circuits began telling my fingers what they used to do without thinking. **Have goals and keep reaching for them with belief, hope, and faith**, and you will get there. I promise your goals will come and they will allow you to reach your potential.

Engage in Community

For most of my life, I have been a taker. Unlike my father and older brother, who unselfishly have given so much to others, I have exhibited more of the narcissistic tendencies of my mother. I have provided financial support to my alma maters and other charities, and even today continue to provide financial support to a young child in Indonesia as part of a Christian organization. But overall in my life I have largely been focused on my well-being and myself.

With the exception of a brief period participating on a neighborhood club board I have never served on any company boards, or volunteered meaningful time to nongovernmental organizations (NGOs). I am a quadriplegic. I am part of the SCI community. There are several organizations that provide support services for people like myself who are afflicted with this unimaginable injury. I have never offered my time to help these organizations. There is a very prominent one here in the Pacific Northwest called the Northwest Regional Spinal Cord Injury System. It would be very easy to just pick up the phone and talk to someone about how I could help. Why haven't I?

In one word—denial. I hate thinking of myself as quadriplegic, disabled, or impaired. When my body betrays me—when I have a bladder accident, or fall down because I lose balance, or have involuntary tremors—I am harshly reminded of what I'm struggling to deny. I am quadriplegic, bottom line. The unexpected lesson is coming to grips and accepting that **I am part of a community that I didn't plan on joining**. This isn't easy for me, because it goes against the grain of how I want to see myself: independent, capable, durable, resilient, and unimpaired.

Give Back

This leads us to the next lesson, which is giving back, or as my mother would say, **"putting back in the bucket of life."** I have given a lot of thought to this, nine years of thought, and I know that my plans to "come out," so to speak, with this writing, with my story, is the right step in the next chapter of my life.

I didn't reach this decision easily, because there have been so many conflicting forces at work. When I step back and try to examine the rest of my life, however much time the Divine has in store for me, I know now that there is a larger purpose and it is important to grab hold and go with it. The messages I have been receiving from the universe to do this are clear. They have come from many sources and the message is always consistent: "Tell your story, Jamie. There are people who need to hear your story and may possibly benefit. Get out there and do it."

Take Control of Your Life

I wouldn't describe myself as a control freak, but I do like to be in charge. When it comes to this injury, it would be very easy to succumb. It's a cruel and relentless injury. I only have to think about last night to be reminded. I was in bed for seven hours and woke up five times, each time groaning in pain, modulating my every movement carefully so as not to trigger the dreaded extensor cramp. I would slowly rotate my body to my right side, swing both legs out of bed, rock back and forth to elongate my calf muscles while sitting on the side of bed, and then slowly stand to use the urine bottle.

I think I slept in increments of sixty to ninety minutes before repeating the process. Even with this type of fitful sleep, I got up, had my morning round of medications, and started the day. The lesson I didn't expect was how important it was to **use my control tendencies to take charge of my life and exert control over this injury**.

It would be easy for this injury to take control of what I do. It could easily confine me to a wheelchair if I let it. It could easily make me dependent for help on anything—walking, eating, and driving. Instead, I chose to take control of it, and live life on my terms. One of my terms is that I will not be enabled. My terms include being capably independent, not dependent on assistive devices, or helping hands, or government assistance.

When I think of taking control, I hear my mantra, "Choose to win." Winning doesn't mean there is a winner and a loser per se; it means living my life on my terms, not on the terms of the injury. The injury would prefer I didn't do anything. Chronic pain, severe spasticity, poor sleep, and fatiguing medications that make me drowsy would collectively justify not exercising and staying home to take a nap.

But I say no.

I tell my injury I am in charge, and that regardless of how hard it tries to discourage me from doing what I want to do, it will not prevail. I have a competitive mentality, and I harness my inner determination to fight the good fight. This fight is on my terms; I am winning and will continue to do so.

Keep Hope Alive

I have been able to accomplish a lot of really cool things over the past nine years. But I will not stop there. I have some new goals, which primarily center on physicality. What I didn't expect early on was that I would ever get to the point of **taking on the level of goals I am contemplating now**.

One goal is to go ice-skating. When I was an adolescent, my mother introduced me to figure skating in the next town over, Wellesley, Massachusetts. She took me to a local indoor rink for lessons, and soon the class put together a skating show. We performed several shows in the Boston area.

When I attended high school at Avon Old Farms School, an all-boys boarding school, they had a newly built rink, and I learned how to play hockey. Hockey skates are a little different from figure skates, but I had spent several years on ice and was able to quickly pick up the sport. By senior year, I was a third stringer on the varsity team and had a chance to play in several games. I loved being on ice.

I am going to ice-skate again. I've visualized this in great detail. I'll be dressed warmly, rent skates, wear a helmet and knee and wrist pads, and start first by holding the railings and having someone on my other side. I have another similar goal to go rollerblading. I've rollerbladed before and would wear similar protective gear. Our old neighborhood was situated on a one-kilometer flat loop with limited traffic, which would have been a perfect venue for the attempt.

Skate skiing involves similar motions and is another goal. I've never tried skate skiing. I hear that it is an awesome aerobic workout and involves similar leg movements as ice-skating and rollerblading.

Other goals include renting cross-country skis and trying them out on flat, groomed runs. I have done cross-country skiing before, and it is probably the least risky of these activities because it is on snow, on flat surfaces, and I would use poles to maintain balance. I'd probably have someone tote along a portable camping chair so that I could stop and rest my legs along the way. I plan to do this at Snoqualmie Pass, which has a Nordic center.

I have a couple of cycling goals. I want to travel to Lake Annecy in France and cycle around it. The ride is about thirty miles and has been a stop on the Tour de France, recently used for one stage as a time trial.

It is in an opulent location and was where I have dreamed in the past of building a retirement home. Perhaps at the same time, I'd like to travel to southern France, Provence, and tackle again the famed climb of Le Mont Ventoux, which I have done once and would love to do again, this time starting at one of the other ascent points from the small town of Bédoin (pronounced bed-win).

I also have a number of goals in the gym that I want to accomplish. One that has been on my mind the most is to do ten pull-ups, legit ones—arms fully extended in a hanging position, pulling my body up with chin over the bar, back down, ten times—with no leg swings or other ways of cheating. I have many other goals in mind and will apply the same focus and determination to see them through. I am keenly interested in zip-lining or trying to do an outdoor adventure course.

I am anxious to be able to take on these challenges, the ones that are next in line on my list. Accomplishing these goals, though ambitious, will continue to demonstrate that they are possible with a commitment to prevail and a choice to win. I can't wait to be able to share these stories.

Apply Effort

All the goals, aspirations, and desires I have will require considerable training and effort. Nothing about this injury is easy. Nothing is handed to me. No achievement happens without some price to pay. It is all daunting, painful, and uncomfortable. It requires commitment, determination, and hard work.

You have to want it, whatever it is. You have to need it, whatever it is. Perhaps it is a stronger physical or mental constitution. Maybe you want to heal broken relationships. You may be ready for a healthier lifestyle. It may be time to reinvent yourself with a positive mental outlook. Life may have thrown a terrible curveball at you with a disease or injury. The recipe is what you want to achieve, the need, and the thing you have to have. The ingredients are desire, belief, hope, and faith. The finished product is a direct consequence of the effort you apply to mixing all the ingredients, preparing yourself with a clear, visualized outcome, and then following the instructions (the recipe) you have developed and seeing your hard work take shape in terms of the outcome you want to achieve. Absent effort, nothing happens. The recipe remains a recipe, and the ingredients sit idle. Mix your effort with determination and resilience, and you will make your dream come true.

. . .

To summarize, there were many things I discovered the hard way, lessons I believe can be helpful to anyone facing this unimaginable injury, or any other physical affliction, disease, or challenging life event. Here's a pocket list:

1. Accept that life isn't fair.

2. Make the best of it.

3. Play the hand you're dealt.

4. Focus on the things you can do.

5. Practice overcoming.

6. Seek mental health intervention.

7. Pace yourself.

8. Take time to reward yourself.

9. Celebrate victories.

10. Visualize healing.

11. Tap into the universal force.

12. Stay socially involved.

13. Advocate for yourself.

14. Set goals and build on them.

15. Engage in community.

16. Give back.

17. Take control of your life.

18. Keep hope alive.

19. Apply effort.

CHAPTER 21

A Day in the Life

When I first returned to the SAC in 2010, three years after my accident, it took several months before I understood the transition process my body was going through at the start of a workout. For three years prior to rejoining the SAC, I never approached the idea of pushing through exercise pain so that it could merge with my neurological pain. The neurological pain was like a governor, restricting me from even reaching the point of getting warm and generating a sweat. A second governor was fear. I was scared of doing anything that might set me back. I was very concerned about going backward, regressing, and losing hard-won gains. My approach had been to approach things with an overabundance of caution. Over time, in 2010 and beyond, my fear was slowly replaced with trust and confidence.

In the past year, I have become much more of a morning person. I always thought early morning workouts would be too difficult because my body was so stiff, seizing, and spastic when I got out of bed. It didn't start out that way. Up until last year my workouts used to always be in the afternoons after 3 p.m., when the afternoon dose of medications was in my system and my body was more limber from just moving around during the day. Doing anything early in the day was out of the question. My body was too stiff, and I didn't have the courage to try something different. I was too afraid I might injure myself. As time has passed and I have regained more strength and confidence, I've been willing to try things I thought were out of reach, such as morning workouts.

Mornings are now my favorite time of day, and it is always a good feeling to have my workouts done before 9 a.m. and then have the whole day in front of me. I enjoy morning workouts much more now, because it is a great way to launch the day with a clear head and an energy afterglow. After exercise, I always ice my back and hips for one to two hours while taking 400 to 600 mg of ibuprofen to control my body's inflammation response and pain.

In the past year, I've trained myself to work out in the early morning. Four days during the week—Mondays, Tuesdays, Wednesdays, and Fridays—I'm up at 3:45 a.m., shuffle to the bathroom, get into my exercise clothes, take morning medications, read Internet news, and make my way to the car by 4:20 a.m. for the fifteen-minute drive to the SAC, which opens at 5 a.m. on weekdays.

On Sundays I'm at the club when it opens at 7 a.m. Thursdays and Saturdays are typically non-gym days, although I never sleep in. It's too uncomfortable to stay in bed for longer than seven hours. It just makes the pain and spasticity worse, and I do better once I'm up and moving around.

Gym workouts in the early morning are both the hardest and best time of my day. I feel awful when I first start. When I park my car at the SAC and make the short walk to the gym door, my legs are barely moving, just shuffling. At this stage in my day, I am doing everything to be mindful of every step simply to ensure I don't fall. I probably should use my trekking poles, but I don't. My practitioners would prefer that I did. I make it a point not to use anything assistive for walking unless I am outside walking a long distance. Otherwise I assume the risk, feeling that every movement I make on my own is in some way training my body, helping to rebuild new circuits that will enable me to function better. I'll never learn to be independent if I am dependent. That's one big way I challenge myself.

Once in the gym, moving gingerly, I make my way to the cardio room to get warmed up on a cardio machine. My hundred-foot walk from the locker room to the cardio room is labored, and I concentrate on every step. When I fall, it is like a tree falling. My body goes completely rigid. It is very unnerving, because once my body seizes I've lost control. I can't make any adjustments to catch myself and regain balance. The fall happens in slow motion. When I hit the ground, I accept that the full force of my weight landing on the surface is going to traumatize some part(s) of my body. I have had at least two dozen falls and countless other close calls.

My elapsed time in the gym can range from two to five hours, depending on the day of the week. As I now work out alone for the most part, my exercise regimen varies. I've learned a lot over the years from my gym mentors and from observations and tips from friends.

When I'm at the gym, a transformation occurs as I press through the pain of my injury. Once I get moving on the elliptical or recumbent stationary bike, where I typically warm up, the transition takes about thirty minutes. The unproductive pain of the injury merges with the productive pain of the workout, and they become one.

I try to do creative workouts that emphasize different areas of the body, including chest, shoulders, back, arms, core, waist, legs, and ankles. I also try not to be too repetitive from week to week, although there are some rituals I like to keep, including using the sled and doing push-ups. My friend Kevin and I use the sled twice a week, once doing pushing exercises and then reversing direction and doing pulling exercises with a thick rope attached. I try to take advantage of all the different types of equipment and exercise devices such as bands, balls, kettlebells, TRX straps, hand weights, weighted balls, BOSU balls, and others. As I have said, I have a circuitry disconnect between the upper and lower half of my body, so I work extra hard on trying to strengthen my lower core, down below my belly button. This is a hard area to isolate and for me an important focus area. All in all, exercise has been the equivalent of a part-time job, and I envision it remaining that way for the foreseeable future.

While at the gym, I need to keep moving. If I stop for even a few minutes and stand in place to talk to someone, the rebound effect kicks in. My muscles seize, and the longer I stand in place the harder it is for me to resume walking because of muscle "tone"—also known as "neurological spasticity."

I always start and finish my exercise programs with stretching. At the end of a workout, I usually have a soaked shirt and the endorphins are plentiful. My physical pain is at its lowest when I am stretching on the mat post workout. I feel good about myself. It feels good to have done something productive. My body is warm, blood is circulating, and for a few minutes I quietly relax on the stretch mat.

Once I'm done stretching, I experience what I call the rebound effect. The four- to six-hour exercise window that the medications provide begins to wear off. I'm cooling down. All the stretching I just completed produces a counterreaction. I can almost hear my muscles groaning—"You gonna stretch me? If you do *that* I'm going to counter with seizing until those muscles are as rigid as when you started to work out." Like clockwork, my body begins to seize, constrict, and quickly become rigid. It is a strange neurological reaction. I would think all the stretching and exercise would make me more limber.

When I am in continual motion, my mobility is generally better. When I slow down, cool down, or stop, my muscles seize. Walking becomes very labored. I move slowly, like an inchworm, back to the men's locker room. When I get to my locker, my body is starting to become more mobile again, enough so that I can shower, shave, get dressed, climb up the stairs to the lobby, return the locker key, pick up my club access card, and make the short trek outside to my car. The warmth of exercise and the medications' effectiveness have dissipated.

I have to meter my time very carefully when I leave the gym. I always make a brief pit stop in the upstairs bathroom before I leave, to empty my bladder. That gives me about fifteen to twenty minutes to make it home before my bladder comes calling again. This frequency is not typical for the rest of the day, but I tend to push a lot of fluids while I'm working out. If I get stopped in the club lobby or outside before reaching my car, I can't talk for too long while standing in place or I will likely pay a price in terms of a bladder accident before I reach home. There have been a few instances when I didn't make it, and because of my compromised waist-level functions I either spotted or had a full-blown bladder accident. It is very frustrating when this happens. Nothing makes me feel more impaired than when I can't control certain bodily functions. I know there is a reason for it, but that doesn't make it any easier to process. I've had to work hard to forgive myself when these kinds of "accidents" happen.

On Fridays and weekends, when I am not working at the college, I catch up on a variety of projects, which generally keep me close to a desk, chair, and personal laptop. Besides writing this book, which is very exciting, I'm pursuing speaking engagements, building a website, and launching a foundation. I also reserve these days for medical appointments and getting caught up on other things that accumulate during the week.

Other things may include taking care of typical family business matters or doing some long overdue projects. One big project I finally completed was organizing our estate planning documents, especially general and medical advance directives, given my injury. I'm also working on digitizing and cataloging boxes of family photographs. Pedestrian, sure, but great for posterity.

On my non-work days, I usually fix my own breakfast, which is tolerable, because the endorphins haven't completely worn off yet after I've exercised. On workdays, Diane is kind enough to create a combined breakfast/lunch bag, which I take to the office after exercise and "graze" pretty much all day long. I understand doing that is better for your digestion rather than eating a few large meals.

Besides working on this book, I spend a lot of time writing on other projects. I keep a journal. I keep "to do" lists. I especially enjoy writing letters to my wife and children for special occasions, which include holidays, birthdays, graduations, and weddings. They all enjoy the letters, and I take great pride in seeing their reactions.

Several years ago we decided that for the Christmas holiday we would forgo material gifts and replace them with "letters of love." This is a tradition that has taken hold and even the kids enjoy writing their own "letters of love" to each other, and to Diane and me.

Here is a letter I wrote to Kevin and his wife Viki for their recent wedding, a letter to Alana that was a graduation gift, and a recent Happy Mother's Day letter to Diane.

November 14, 2015

Dear Viki and Kevin,

On this most special day, your mom, Alana, and I want to congratulate you both on your marriage. We are so happy that you have decided to join together in marriage and commit your lives to one another. It is an awesome statement about your love for each other.

To Viki, we are honored to have you join our extended family! Since the day we first met you at the airport in Honolulu in December 2013 we could sense you were a special person—gifted with a gentle, kind, caring, and confident and loving spirit. Sometimes you can just sense a person's spirit, and we felt that way when we first met you. This is a very memorable time in your life, and we have complete trust that you will care for and love Kevin with all your heart. You have had a few years to get to know Kevin, his character, his personality, his goals, strengths and weaknesses, and to know that you will build a life together where you can treasure every moment and be thankful for every day.

We admire you, Viki—your intellect, professionalism, and steady and even-tempered demeanor. Our collective wish for you is that life with Kevin will bring you joy, happiness, and fulfillment, and most importantly unshakeable love. Love transcends all and will allow you to cherish the good times and work through the difficult ones. Please know that as Kevin's parents we are always here to support and love you!

To Kevin, we are happy beyond words that you and Viki first met at a local restaurant and have come to this time several years later to be married. You have built your relationship over the past few years, gotten to know each other, learned about each other's goals and dreams, personality and character. It was a very special moment for your mother and me to be there at your Shanghai apartment in October 2014 with Viki's parents and relatives when you first proposed. You have had an amazing life journey from the time we first welcomed you into this world in 1988 to today.

We are proud of you and amazed at the courage you have displayed in overcoming so much adversity, traveling to a foreign country on your own, learning a new language, finding work, and meeting your future wife in Viki. You, too, have had time to get to know Viki, her parents, some of her relatives and friends (and many more today!!), and discover what an amazing lady she is, and how proud we are that you decided to join your lives together in marriage. This really goes without saying that we will always be here to support and love you!

To Viki and Kevin, you are one beautiful couple!! The pictures you sent are incredible! They are some of the most beautiful pictures we have ever seen. They should be in a magazine! The smiles on your faces tell it all in terms of your love for each other. Our wish for both of you is that the love and support you feel for each other and that surrounds you both with family and friends will always be there to support you, love you, and lift you up during those times when it's needed. May you treasure every day together, and do the little things that remind one another of your commitment and love for each other. Maybe it is a special card, bouquet of flowers, a gentle touch, a hug, or kind word to reinforce the bonds of your amazing relationship. Respect one another, care for one another, do fun things together, laugh together, and prosper together. The most important word here is together. Grow together. Lift each other up. Make awesome memories together. Live the lives you want, together, not what others want for you. Make it your own, and give thanks, every day, that you have each other in your lives.

Your marriage, your relationship, is more important than any job, any amount of money, any ambition, or any material thing. Marriage takes work. There is no script. It takes good communication, good attitude, and compromise. Be willing to adapt. Be open to change. Most importantly, you are a couple; move forward in your lives, together, as one and make it the best life it can be. You have an awesome future ahead of you—together!!

To Viki's parents, we are so proud to know you and to have had a chance to meet some of your extended family. We are very sorry we could not attend in person but do look forward to a time in the future when we can visit your home and experience some of your lives in China. We feel especially fortunate to have met you in person over a year ago in Shanghai, where we got to be together, and cry together, when Kevin and Viki got engaged. We could feel the love in your hearts, your kind spirits, and your support for Kevin. We are now related, and that makes us feel very special and proud. You have raised an amazing daughter in Viki, and we are so happy that she will be Kevin's wife. We think the world of her and admire her character, personality, and values. You must be very proud of her. She is a reflection of the two of you, and we couldn't be more honored to have her as part of our extended family, just as Kevin is part of your extended family.

We look forward to the day when we may welcome you to the United States for a visit, show you around, and perhaps take a fishing trip! We think it is fantastic that you raised your family with a love and appreciation for the outdoors. It is very similar to how we raised our children, doing many activities in the outdoors like skiing, camping, boating, cycling, and hiking. The outdoors is very special to us. It is a place to appreciate the wonders of nature and to rejuvenate our mind, body, and soul. It is a place where we can find peace and quiet, and it connects us.

I would like to end this letter with a very big thank you! Thank you for loving and supporting our son, Kevin. Thank you for the extraordinary amount of planning, logistics, and expense that went into having this wedding at your home with so many guests. We are in complete awe of how you have been able to do this, and make it such a memorable day for Viki and Kevin. Thank you most for granting your permission for Kevin to propose and marry your beautiful daughter, Viki. We are thrilled!

Our very best to you, Kevin, Viki, extended family and friends for this day that I know Kevin and Viki will cherish for the rest of their lives.

With much love,
Jamie, Diane, and Alana Osborne

• • •

Graduation—ASU Cronkite School of
Mass Communications & Journalism
May 12, 2015

Dear Alana,

It is with enormous pride that your mother and I applaud
you for this incredible achievement. You have graduated
with an undergraduate degree, a master's degree, completed an advanced curriculum of the Barrett's Honors
Program, and if that wasn't enough you did so with top
academic credentials—summa cum laude. Further, you've
complemented your academic achievements with numerous areas of real-life professional experience by working
at Eight, Arizona PBS, Right This Minute, ASU News
Watch, Public Insight Network, as well as completed
an entrepreneurial project to launch your own business,
Story Sisters.

It is not lost on any of us that all of these achievements
were done during multiple years of persistent, frustrating
health issues with a diagnosis that took years to finally
determine. You've had to adapt to all the life changes that
accompanied these findings, and you've done all of this
before even turning the age of twenty-one.

This doesn't happen by accident. It doesn't happen by
being lucky. It doesn't happen by taking the easy route.
It doesn't happen by being in the right place at the right
time. It doesn't happen without some setbacks. It isn't
easy. It happens because you had clear goals. It happens
because you were committed, ambitious, focused, determined, resilient, and hardworking. The college experience provides numerous opportunities and obstacles, and

you've managed with moxie and gravitas to work your way through all to reach this momentous occasion.

You will look back at this moment in the years to come and be reminded of all that you've accomplished and the enormous potential you have to make a meaningful difference in this world. Our world is broken, divided, and angry. There is much tension in many places. You are needed. Your gifts, character, and morals are needed to touch lives and remind those less fortunate and suffering that there is opportunity for a better life, and to find ways to provide people opportunities in the same way opportunities have been provided to you.

There are myriad ways to take your life's journey, and no doubt there will be twists, turns, achievements, setbacks, wins, losses, highs, lows, successes, failures, and everything in between. Always remember that life is a journey, filled with happiness, laughter, opportunities, and uncertainty. Life is not fair. Life, for as long as the divine allows us to be here, boils down to this simple truth—love and be loved. Like so many it is easy to get caught up in the race to be more, build your resume, check off more accomplishments, get caught up in the narcissistic force of it's-all-about-me.

There is nothing implicitly wrong with pursuing your ambition, having goals, gaining credentials, or building a resume. It's just not the endgame. Life is about how you use the amazing gifts you have to better the lives of others, in some way, every day. It may be a creative idea, a completed project, a touching presentation, a special smile, or kind, empathetic words for someone in time of need. Use your bountiful gifts, my dear, to build a better world, in some way, your way that brings you joy and fulfillment.

As you move into this next chapter of your life, understand that it will be different, but in many ways the same, just with a different focus and greater reliance and trust in yourself. You are plenty capable of building your life the way you want it, with your goals and your aspirations. You can trust yourself. Believe in yourself. Have faith in yourself. Persevere and always be hopeful. Stay positive. No matter what the struggle, no matter what mountain stands in the way, you have the skills to climb, conquer, and enjoy the view. Be patient with yourself. Perfection isn't the goal. Giving your best effort and doing your best life's work is the goal. Be good enough for you, not anyone else. Live your dream, not anyone else's.

There will always be naysayers—people who say this won't work or you can't do this. Use all of that as motivation and stay true to your dreams. As a famous football player once said, "Dreams don't come true, dreams are **made** true." You reap what you sow; in other words, what you accomplish in life is a consequence of your effort. Things aren't given to you. You have to go out and earn it, and you will. You have all the ingredients. You have the character. You have the skills. You have the belief system. Go forward with your shoulders back, head held high, confidence in your voice, and good eye contact. Listen to understand. You will always be regarded as a great communicator when you listen and ask questions. Be in less of a hurry to make your point and more patient understanding others.

Some other life truths—(1) Be honest. Never compromise about being truthful, even when it seems like evading it would be better; (2) Admit mistakes, real time. You will learn more in life from the times you fall down and get back up. Don't be afraid to fail. Failing never means you are a failure, it means you are learning; (3) Take measured risks. Do your due diligence when contemplating important decisions, ask good questions, and place bets where the odds are in your favor; (4) Respect personal space. Every person you meet in life is different and has their unique needs and qualities. Be careful not to assume your love language is the same as everyone else's; (5) Build and maintain your network. Keep important relationships "warm" and never burn bridges with anyone. It's a small world; (6) Be your strongest advocate. Stand tall, stand strong, and be your own person. Don't absorb other people's problems. Focus on you, your needs, your goals, and fight the good fight when you need to; (7) Let go of things you cannot change, have the courage to change the things you can and the wisdom to know the difference; (8) Your health is job #1. Do the things you need to do, consistently, to build and strengthen your constitution, in spite of the challenges you face. Exercise, eat right, and take time during each day for you, to relax, soothe yourself, and get re-centered; (9) Be willing to compromise. As right as we all feel about things, sometimes it is not worth the fight and better to just let go. The process of letting go and knowing when to fight the good fight can be hard to discern, but practice, practice; (10) Never apologize for being you.

Love, Mom & Dad

. . .

Mother's Day
May 8, 2016

Dear Diane,

Happy Mother's Day!
It has been another monumental year on so many levels. How great is it to have both our children living so close by? Kevin and Viki less than a mile away and Alana less than five miles away. It is amazing to think that Kevin is now twenty-eight and Alana twenty-two. It still feels like yesterday when you brought both our beautiful children into the world. It is easy to go back to the moment when Kevin first met us and was cooing on your chest just after he was cleaned up by the nurses and wrapped in a blanket. It is easy to go back to the moment when Alana first made her entrance into the world and did the same, after the nurses prepared her to lay on your chest and feel the heartbeat that had kept her company for so many months.

Fast-forward to today. Our children are grown, young adults, and building their own lives. Kevin is now married to Viki and working together to build a business. Alana is now working as a vice president of marketing for a Seattle-based company. You have so much to be proud of, Diane, for the incredibly hard work you have dedicated to both our children. They have grown up so much, matured, and built important life skills. You have always been attentive to their needs and gone out of your way with great sacrifice to do what you thought was best for them. Most importantly you have loved them with all your heart, and that love is something they embody and will be able to share with their families.

I don't think there is a harder job than being a mother.

A mother is the foundation of family, and values, and serving. You give a lot. You do have a heart for others. Think about what you did for Wint and her family when they first moved from Burma. You helped them get situated, supported them through their difficult family situation, found her financial support so she could pursue her dreams, and now look at her. She is a doctor! It's that serving others part of you that makes you such an amazing mother. Think about all the things you've done to support all of us. You've gone to great lengths to support Alana in so many ways. You've been to Palo Alto twice in the past year when she has needed surgery. You were there to support her when she had that terrible anaphylactic reaction. You've gone to great lengths to support Kevin. You found the unit they are living in now and convinced me to come look at it. You were the wise one who decided to move up furnishings from AZ so they could easily be moved into the new unit, which made it possible for Kevin and Viki to make the transition from China.

There are so many stories in the past year that continue to demonstrate the kind of mother you are. You support, love, care, give, and sacrifice for all of us, and none of what you do is lost on any of us. I hope you will remember today and every day that you are appreciated and loved. None of us could return the love you give to us, and we are grateful. My wish for you this year is that you find something that fulfills you in new ways you could never have imagined. You deserve purpose, recognition, joy, fulfillment, and love. Spread your wings and explore, experiment and find that something or somethings that will motivate and inspire you in new ways. You deserve it.

Love, Me

. . .

I have appointments periodically with Dr. Diane or other annual check-ups with my new SCI physiatrist, Dr. Rena Reyes (Dr. Barry shifted full-time to the VA to support our veterans with SCI), Dr. Edwin Rhim for dermatology, or Dr. Michael Soung for internal medicine. I don't see Dr. Jens on a regular basis, unless I become symptomatic, which fortunately hasn't been the case for several years.

Television, if I watch at all, is reserved for after dinner, usually to watch the news, or one of a few favorite Netflix shows like *House of Cards*, *Bloodline*, or dramas like *The Blacklist*. Often I am back on the computer after dinner or reading. I have several books that I am reading now, and usually several open and in progress at any one time—*Thrive* by Arianna Huffington, *All the Light We Cannot See* by Anthony Doerr, *Born to Run* by Christopher McDougall, *Big Magic* by Elizabeth Gilbert, and *Journeys Out of the Body* by Robert Monroe.

Before bed I do some stretching, which I also do intermittently during the day if I am perched in front of the computer. I don't spend a lot of time on the phone; most of my communication is through text and email. I'm not active on social media, although I am on Facebook and LinkedIn. Occasionally I'll post on Facebook, but that is infrequent. I haven't connected through Twitter yet.

Because morning exercise consumes a lot of "matches," my energy tank is sapped enough that I don't go out a lot during the day to run errands or do other kinds of activities because I know it's going to hurt. If given the choice between suffering or not, I'll choose the latter. When it comes to pain, I make a distinction in my mind about productive versus unproductive pain. Exercising, taking measured risks, and pursuing goals are productive. Doing these things gives me hope. It is when I feel most alive, and that matters to me. It helps me feel good about myself, and I get a strong sense of accomplishment, even though it hurts. I suffer, but strangely I'm suffering to gain benefit.

Unproductive pain is the pain of sitting in a chair right now as I write.

My back hurts. My hands hurt. My legs hurt. My buttocks hurt. My ankles and some of my toes hurt. I don't gain anything from this pain, other than energy depletion. Unproductive pain is standing in place while I am courteously talking with someone, and I can feel spasticity envelop my waist and my legs and feet like they are being squeezed in a vise.

When I'm done talking or listening, resuming movement is extraordinarily difficult. My balance is worse. It takes thirty to forty steps—careful, calculated, mindful steps—to break through this "spastic lock" and start walking again. This is why when people stop me after exercise and want to talk, I often have to interrupt and say, "I gotta keep moving."

I'm more willing to put up with suffering when there is some benefit—physical, mental, social, or relational. It's more difficult when it involves doing a house chore, washing dishes, making beds, vacuuming, doing laundry, cooking, running errands, or grocery shopping. Hygiene is important, and I make it a priority every day, but again, I always pay a price. Before I go to bed at night I'll brush and floss my teeth, which takes about fifteen minutes. As I stand in place for that time, I am constantly moving my legs and stretching my torso to combat muscles seizing in my back and legs.

If I had the choice, would I opt to put myself through the suffering? No. In most of these cases, like hygiene, I don't give myself an option; it has to be done, pain and all. I help out with some house chores as I did prior to being injured. I do appreciate times when I am fatigued and could use an assist from Diane or Alana with laundry, bed making, dishes, vacuuming, or other house chores.

Of course, I have my social time with friends for dinner or have a few cocktail socials. By midday the medicines I took in the early morning have worn off and pain and spasticity make their comeback. To intercede, I take my afternoon medications at different times. This usually gives me decent coverage until I go to bed between 9 and 10 p.m. Depending on how I'm feeling, particularly on exercise days, I may sprinkle in a nap, but as mentioned, I never feel good after a nap.

My day ends with me lying in bed, watching the final news report on my phone, taking a moment to commend myself for doing the day, and taking my evening medicines. As I turn off the lights and lie in the darkness, today, I remember that I wrote my loving wife a Happy Mother's Day letter and spent time having a special brunch with all my family. I reflect on the tears that came to my eyes as Diane read the letter aloud at the table. As she cried, so did I. So did the children. It was heartfelt. It reminded me how great it is to be alive and to celebrate such an important day, feeling alive. I fall asleep, knowing that more joy is yet to come.

CHAPTER 22

I Thought Nobody Was Watching

Sometimes I think the word "disabled" is a misnomer. The most able people I know are considered disabled by our society. We don't know why these things happen. We only know that as a result of our catastrophic injuries, we have delved deeper into ourselves for a strength we never knew existed and that we may have otherwise never known.

Possibly we are the vanguard of a special group chosen to motivate others by setting an example of how to cope with catastrophic events— giving hope to others that they can still function successfully in the land-scape of life. I see disabled people all the time. I used to feel sorry for them and was thankful it wasn't me. But my outlook has changed after hearing so many uplifting stories.

I was recently connected to a website for a very famous Paralympian, Kevin Saunders (KevinSaunders.com.). He was catastrophically injured while working for the USDA. There was an explosion in a grain elevator that hurled him three hundred feet onto a concrete slab. As a result he is a paraplegic and confined to a wheelchair. In spite of his "disability," he has done some amazing things with his life and is a highly sought-after motivational speaker. He travels all over the world. I can see why.

He has overcome so many obstacles, and in doing so has impacted countless lives. He was the first person with a disability appointed to the President's Council on Physical Fitness and Sports, and he has com-peted in hundreds of races, won hundreds of gold medals, written several books, pushed his wheelchair 2,500 miles across the country, and worked alongside famous actors and other celebrities.

When I read stories like Kevin's, I feel empowered. His story is beyond incredible, and the work he has done and continues to do is what gives me hope and inspiration. I, too, want to leave the world, in some way, a better place. Kevin has no idea who I am and no idea that his story brings me hope and inspiration. I am sure many others just like me have drawn courage, inspiration, and motivation from his story.

I have a young niece, Cassandra, who had severe seizures after she was born a healthy girl and was diagnosed with cerebral palsy several months later. Fast-forward twenty-five years later and, after graduating from the Clark Honors College at the University of Oregon, she is now in graduate school at the Wagner School of Public Service at NYU. During her junior year of high school, in an article written about her in the school newspaper, Cassandra noted, "People have always looked at it like it's a struggle for me. But I've never struggled with it. I don't know a life without cerebral palsy."

I was at the hospital when Cassandra was in the neonatal ICU and things were dicey. She may not know it, but I have been watching her amazing progress and determination since the hours just after her birth, and I can say she has empowered me in the same way to persist and achieve through the challenges of SCI.

Being around like-minded athletic types at the gym is a source of great inspiration for me. When I notice someone doing a challenging exercise that I haven't seen or done before, it gets my competitive juices going. It's like when I was first in the ICU, and nurse Carrie handed me that breathing machine to see what I could do. This is how it is in the gym. I'm not interested in competing with anyone else. I'm interested in challenging myself.

For example, I observed someone doing pull-ups on a new device and this individual cranked out ten full-arm suspended pull-ups. I was inspired and said to myself, "I'm going to try that." I was able to do five. My goal this year, as previously mentioned, is to get to ten.

I've watched a group of very strong athletes doing exercises using hanging rings, the same kind of rings you might see in a gymnastics competition. One day I will work with a trainer who can show me proper technique, so I can see what kind of things I can do. I am always on the lookout for challenges, and the gym inspires me to go after them.

One of the unexpected perks of going to the gym is when people are kind enough to share encouraging remarks with me. I often hear comments from people I know, and from those I don't, about how I inspire them, especially after they hear my story. This is always heartwarming and helps me keep going.

Last year I met a nice lady who introduced herself as we were leaving the gym. She could see I was having difficulty walking, and she was keenly interested in my story. She was amazed when I told her I was quadriplegic and wanted to know how that could be when I wasn't confined to a wheelchair.

I told her about my approach to recovery, my credo, and everything that I put into trying to maximize each day. She said she admired my tenacity and found my story compelling and inspirational. Several months later, she told me that she was working hard to develop her own business and that my story had nudged her to take some measured risks. These paid off in helping launch her business. I thanked her for sharing that story, because it lifted me up and reminded me about the power of purpose and intent, themes that are foundational to my own credo.

Another lady at the gym, named Karen, introduced herself to me a few months ago. She said how inspiring I was to her, because she was new to the gym and rededicating herself to better health. She said she could see how hard I worked in my walking movements, yet I persisted with my exercise program. She said she was also inspired by my consistency and the length of time I spent doing a workout session, as well as the types of exercises I was doing. I told her she had just made my day and wished her continued success in pursuit of better health.

Sam introduced me to Spencer shortly after we started working out together in 2010. Spencer used the weight room at the gym but often said he was not a particular fan of it. He primarily used the gym to play squash, a sport at which he excelled.

Many times, just the two of us worked out together, and at other times, we were part of a larger group with Sam and Samantha. Spencer suffered chronic pain like I did but would always be quick to point out, even expressing a little guilt, that his pain was really nothing to complain about when comparing it to my condition.

I told him his suffering was no less severe or important than mine. It's all relative. He commented at times that I was an inspiration to him, and one of the reasons why he made the effort to come into the weight room at all. Over the couple of years we did workouts together, his strength and conditioning improved dramatically, as did mine. I enjoyed our time together. He was fun, gregarious, and conversational, and it was enjoyable to challenge each other.

I have a former work colleague that I stay in touch with periodically. She has a heart of gold. We get together for cocktails and catch up on a variety of topics. She knows my story well and often refers to me as a source of strength and inspiration. She has shared comments like, "I miss leaders like you who had something to offer in terms of mentorship, integrity, and smarts." and "You continue to inspire me in ways you cannot imagine."

Comments like these stoke my fire and motivate me to push on. It is gratifying to know that my efforts are noticed and have an impact on the lives of other people.

Over a year ago, I was having an annual checkup with my rehab practitioner. I brought in my iPad, because I wanted to share some of the cool physical things I had achieved. She said she was impressed and inspired by my accomplishments and that my progress was going to motivate her to pursue more consistent exercise. I saw her again for my annual checkup a few months ago, and she remarked that she often shares my story, leaving out my name of course, with other SCI patients. Some found my story remarkable, and some were in disbelief that such milestones were even possible for people with SCI. She said she shares my story in the hopes that others might draw strength, inspiration, and hope from it.

A few years ago, I was on a walk in my neighborhood when something special happened. I was about fifteen minutes into my walk, lost in thought, and a FedEx truck pulled up and parked on the other side of the road. A middle-aged man got out and started walking toward me. My body is hypersensitive to anxiety, and I immediately started to tighten up. I stopped walking, feeling wary.

The man extended his hand and introduced himself as Mike. He said he had seen me walking around the neighborhood for the past couple of years and had wanted to stop several times to say how much he admired my persistence and determination. He had seen me walking in sun, rain, and wind (not snow or ice!) but was continually pressed for time with his route and unable to stop. That day he did. He also commented on the improvement he had noticed during the weeks and months I had been walking. I thanked him for taking time to stop, for thinking of me, and lifting my spirits. He thanked me. I told my counselor this story and said how moved I was by this event. She said, "You gave him something—hope. Watching you walking all those times on his route gave him hope. There could be something going on his life, or with someone he knows, and seeing you on your walk lifted his spirits, just in the same way his stopping lifted yours."

One day in the fall of 2010 at the SAC during an afternoon workout, I was doing my usual warm-up routine on the elliptical. The warm-up typically lasted twenty minutes. While in motion on the machine, I had a conversation with one of the personal trainers, Jake. I knew Jake from just being around the weight room, and he knew me from previous chats about my accident story, injury, and symptoms. I think he found my story a curious one, in part because I don't think he had seen someone with such impairments be so active in the weight room. I think he admired my determination, effort, and consistency.

I never had a training session with Jake, but having overlapped with him and his clients in the weight room, I learned many exercises just by observing them. He is clearly a fit, skilled, and popular trainer.

During our conversation, Jake mentioned he had recently been working with one of his clients who had been having difficulty getting motivated to do his workout sessions. Jake said they had walked by me one day while I was working out—struggling, sweating, shaking, grunting—and the client, aware of my story, said, "If that guy can push through his challenges to work out, well, then so can I."

Jake told me how I had inspired his client, not only to work out, but also to work out as aggressively as he had ever seen. He shared this with me, and then went on to say how many people in the club were watching and rooting for me, people who knew my story but didn't know me. I was having an impact on their lives, and they were inspired by me. "You wouldn't believe how many people are watching and rooting for you."

My eyes got teary as he talked, and Jake asked what was going on. I told him how much his words meant to me. This was 2010; over three years post injury. I suppose I had been working too hard to even notice the reactions of others. I said being immersed in this injury, being so close and integral, I often forget I am not alone. I told him how I get lost in my own world, struggling to do the day, willing myself to overcome and do things—all things—including coming to the gym because I know if I don't I am going to suffer and it is going to hurt.

Consumed in my own world, I don't always realize that other people are watching. Maybe we know others people's stories, maybe we don't. We can sense with our own eyes and ears, by observing very carefully, what people might be going through and the progress they are making. But they may never notice us watching them. This is what Jake was sharing with me. "People are paying attention to you," he said, "even when you don't know or want attention."

Since rejoining in 2010, I have had numerous conversations with people who have commented on my progress. They say, "You are walking faster, keep up the great work." "You work out harder than anyone at this gym." "Seeing you here every day inspires me to want to work harder." "Jamie, you've got game." "Your progress is just incredible, it is truly inspiring." People have hugged me, people I barely know, sharing their hearts with me. In many ways, these encounters are the wind under my sails. Being around all of them lifts me up and inspires me to work harder. Healing is often a two-way street.

You may be impacting someone's life in a positive way and not even know it. I told Jake how great this made me feel—that I could in some small way inspire someone else. It felt good to know that this was possible, and it reminded me that there is indeed a larger purpose.

Sometimes in my darker moments—and I have plenty of them, with frustration, fear, anger, lethargy, sadness, depression, pain—I forget that it is not just about me. I do get selfish. So many people lift me up, give me hope, and keep me going. These encounters with Mike and Jake reminded me that I'm giving something back—to the FedEx man; to my gym community at the SAC; to neighbors, family, and friends; to people I have yet to meet. It makes me feel good to know that just by continuing to choose to win, I can be impacting someone else's life—and not even know it.

CHAPTER 23

Measured Risks

I am generally risk averse. I take a conservative approach in almost everything I do, from recreational activities to managing finances. I have been this way my entire life. I have opted for less-risky choices in life, especially when it comes to adventurous activities.

Diane, Kevin, and Alana went skydiving several years prior to my injury and begged me to go. I said it just wasn't for me; I don't like heights and am extremely uncomfortable with the idea of putting my life on the line with a parachute.

Another time my wife and kids went bungee jumping in Whistler during the summer. Although I wasn't on that trip, I would never consider doing something like that for the same reason I avoided skydiving. I am not an adrenaline junkie and feel just fine staying fastened to the ground with gravity.

Some might say helicopter skiing is risky behavior. Having survived being buried in an avalanche, I would agree. At the time, I didn't think it was risky at all, given that we were skiing with professional guides, had been trained, carried beacons, and practiced every morning how we would use them to locate people if they were buried.

Choosing low-risk situations even extends into how I manage our home finances. I am fiscally conservative, analyze situations carefully, and pay high attention to detail. I stay away from risky investments, and when I do invest, I have a financial advisor to help me stick with very diversified portfolios and conservative returns.

I mention my non-risk personality traits as examples of how difficult it has been to change my mind-set to tackle the consequences of a spinal cord injury. Being paralyzed is a life game-changer. Defining my terms in recovering from my injury has involved cautious, measured risk taking. I had to stretch some boundaries.

The best example of measured risk taking is walking without trekking poles. Every time I am in a closed environment—gym, home, doctor's office, restaurants, movie theatres, etc.—I leave my poles in the car. I only use the poles when I am in an unfamiliar location, walking longer distances outside, or in early morning hours when my legs are acting overly spastic (which happens about ten percent of the time). I do this to challenge myself, challenge my neurological system, with the intent of continuing to teach my body new skills through practice, practice, and more practice.

I believe in my brain's plasticity and in its ability to adapt, reorganize, and create new circuits. While it would be much easier to use a walking aid, it goes back to my rather maniacal desire to "get independent." The only way that is going to happen is if I assume a little measured risk, push myself out of my comfort zone, and see if I can take my recovery to another level. My recovery has been a little unorthodox, but my methods have yielded some accomplishments in recent years of which I am extremely proud, all because I was willing to challenge myself by pushing boundaries.

To be able to take measured risks after my accident, I had to get comfortable with the possibility of unintended consequences. It wouldn't seem to be risky simply to walk across a room, but with SCI it most certainly can be, especially if I'm not using a walking aid.

Walking without an aid means I can fall at any time. Even using an aid doesn't guarantee I won't fall; in fact, the first fall I ever had happened while I was using a cane. Falls hurt, a lot. I had a pretty scary one coming out of the SAC one day. I had crossed the street and was walking downstairs to the parking garage. I was close to the rail and had my right hand hovering just above, not gripping it. I wanted to challenge myself to take steps without holding on to the railing.

Everything was going fine until I stubbed my left foot on a step and started to fall forward. I attempted to grab the railing with my right hand, missed, and my right arm slid between the railing and the wall, up to my armpit. The rest of my body twisted clockwise, and I ended up on my back, with the back of my head grazing the edge of a step and my head below my feet as I lay sprawled on the cement stairs.

Nobody was around. I quickly checked myself to confirm there were no breaks, sprains, or abrasions. After being momentarily dazed, I managed to get back on my feet with the hope no one would see me in this moment of embarrassment. I felt the back of my head checking for any blood and fortunately found none.

I made it to my car and drove home, unnerved and very worried that I might have traumatized my spine in some way. Once there, I immediately started my icing program along with ibuprofen, to try to get ahead of a possible inflammation response. I didn't have to seek medical intervention, but I was very sore for the next several days.

I had another fall at home, while walking from the living room to the bathroom. I was in a bit of a rush trying to get there before having an accident. I didn't have a bladder accident, but I did have an accident of a different kind. I was leaning slightly against the wall in the hallway for balance (a full bladder always intensifies spasticity), but I was positioned too far forward. This caused me to catch a toe on the floor, trip, and fall forward, landing on my chest. I was able to hold my chin up enough that it only nicked slightly on the hardwood floor; however, the slight force caused my jaw to clench, hard, and I could feel the pressure in my upper teeth, which is partially an artificial bridge.

I wasn't sure if I had cracked my bridge. I couldn't sense whether I had or not. I managed to get back up, embarrassed once again. Because the fall was a hard one, I did get my mouth checked out by my dentist, Dr. Rebecca, and X-rays revealed no bridge fracture. This was a huge relief given the time and considerable expense to replace it.

My workouts at SAC also involve elements of risk. At times I walk on the treadmill, which has front and side railings that I can use for balance support, and using them could be considered a low-risk activity. However, once I was walking on the treadmill at a moderate pace of two miles per hour, which I had done very successfully many times before without even using the railings. On this day, I was even using the railings for support. Suddenly my left toe stubbed the treadmill's rotating mat, and I went down—hard.

I quickly grabbed the railings, but the revolving surface quickly pulled me down and off the treadmill. I had the emergency stop strap attached to me; however, there was too much slack, which is why the treadmill didn't stop rotating right away. I had significant abrasions on my shins, as well as some bleeding, which I quickly patched up with a nearby first-aid kit. This was embarrassing, but the fall didn't stop me from using the treadmill, which I continue to use to this day.

One day I was practicing lunges to strengthen my very weak gluteus muscles and hamstrings. Maintaining a tight core is important for balance. A tight core means your abdominal, gluteus, hamstring, and interior thigh muscles are engaged and flexed. I envision my core as a corset—something wrapped tightly around my lower abdomen, waist, and upper thighs. I consider my "core" as a unit.

Your core is central to almost all your body movements, and many injuries—particularly back injuries—can be directly linked to core weakness. During my lunge training, to assist with balance, I was holding two lightweight PVC poles, each about five feet in length. I was exercising in a seldom-used hallway at the back of the club.

In the process of doing lunges, I lost my balance and was unable to arrest the fall with the poles. I fell down backwards, hit the floor, and then the cement wall, slamming the back of my head. It didn't knock me out, and I wasn't able to detect any blood by touching the back of my head. I was a bit dazed, which quickly passed. Frustrated at falling, I got back up, put the poles away, and decided to continue my exercise program emphasizing arms rather than legs. I was glad no one was around to see my fall. I hate the idea of showcasing my impairments as a consequence of a fall.

I have kept track of about two dozen falls since the crash and about a dozen more I haven't recorded. I have fallen at work, home, gym, and outside. So why take the risk when I could really hurt myself? After all, I've had some close calls.

Deep down I believe that any opportunity to teach my body, within reason, is an opportunity worth taking. Seeking dependence feels like a slippery slope. The more dependent I become, the more dependent I will become. I find this very unsettling, even given the risks that come with walking without trekking poles. Would it be better to use them? Yes, I suppose it might diminish the risk to some extent, but it wouldn't necessarily remove it.

There are many walking aids that would be helpful, including canes, forearm crutches, and walkers—and using one would be substantially less risky than walking unaided. The offset is that if I use one of these aids, my body learns nothing about how to regain function. Instead, I become dependent on the device, and my quality of life options, as well as freedom of movement, become considerably more restricted.

At this time in my life, I'm not ready to go there. There may be a time in the future when those devices become necessary, but I choose not to think that far ahead. My goal now is to teach and retrain my body, and the best way to do that, with managed risk, is to do as much independently as possible to promote more independence.

If I wanted to conduct my life without any risk, I would never get behind the steering wheel of a car. There is always a risk of being rear-ended in an auto accident, which could significantly retraumatize the site of my neck injury that rendered me quadriplegic. I have learned to be more conscious when driving now. When traffic slows abruptly, I am vigilant in watching the car in back of me via the rearview or side mirrors.

I also drive using an approach I call spacing. I leave about a car length of open space for every ten to twenty miles per hour that I am traveling between my car and the one in front. This gives me more time to react if I have to abruptly stop, and it lessens the risk of rear-ending someone, or vice versa. I also am conscious of "bail-out" options, keeping a mindful watch for possible places on the road—medians, emergency lanes, gaps in adjacent traffic—to bail out if I have no other way to avoid hitting something. These driving tactics have helped me avoid accidents in the past and are my methods of managing risk.

Of course, if I wanted to avoid all risk, I'd stay at home, be confined to a wheelchair, never venture out, be on an entitlement program, and count the days until my time was up. But that would be an extreme choice and is certainly not who I am. Life is constantly filled with risk. The balancing act is in choosing how much risk I am comfortable assuming to have a quality of life that works for me.

. . .

These efforts and so many others of managed risk taking had a single goal in mind—to build new circuits inside my spinal cord around the damaged area to regain fine and gross motor function. There were, of course, other significant benefits of improving strength, stamina, coordination, balance, confidence, and trust in myself.

The work I did in the weight room at the SAC, mentored by my two friends Sam and Samantha, helped set a foundation upon which I could reach and achieve even larger goals. I can't overstate the influence my two gym mentors had on my recovery and ability to reach new heights. Yes, I did the work, but they challenged me in a way I had never experienced before. It was extraordinarily hard work, and that's probably an understatement. In the process, I discovered that I was capable, especially when I stopped making excuses because I didn't want to attempt a certain exercise.

They treated me like I was anyone else working out in the gym. I didn't feel like a patient when I was with them. I didn't feel impaired. They didn't make excuses for me and wouldn't allow me to make excuses for myself. I've said many times how grateful I am for what they did in helping me regain so many aspects of my life.

CHAPTER 24

Make Your Own "Movies"

In 2014, as previously mentioned, I was living in Arizona while my daughter Alana was going to school at Arizona State University. At the same local LA Fitness club where I met Paul, I had the privilege to meet others who were working to overcome health problems, and at times, I would share my story.

One day, I was walking toward the stairs to make my way up to the second level, where the cardio machines were located. An elderly lady named Roberta sat near the base of the stairs on a rowing machine, resting for a moment. We introduced ourselves.

She could tell my walking was stiff and labored and inquired whether I was recovering from an injury to my hip. I said I was recovering from an injury, but it was much more involved. I explained to her some of the details of spinal cord injury. She asked where I was headed, and I said upstairs to the cardio room. She indicated there were cardio machines just around the corner on the first floor and that it might be easier to use those rather than walking upstairs.

I thanked her and mentioned that the challenge of walking upstairs was important to me. Roberta asked why. I told her that it would be easier not to do it, but that it would go against the grain of my entire mind-set for recovery. She asked what that mind-set was, and I answered, "Because those are my terms."

She seemed intrigued by that and wanted to know more. So I took a few minutes to explain that I had embraced a life credo since my injury, one that had led me to choose to win on my terms, not anyone else's. If there was a challenge in front of me to tackle, I was determined to do it.

I explained that I had set myself a challenge to be able to walk up those stairs without holding the railings and to do the same thing walking back down, unaided. I said I wasn't there yet but was committed to being able to do it no matter how long it took. She said, "Bravo, keep up the great work . . . I find your perseverance very inspiring." I asked how she was doing.

She told me she was dealing with severe osteoarthritis and was starting to use the rowing machine to force range of motion for her very stiff and painful joints. It looked almost as if her bones were protruding through her skin, yet there she was on the rowing machine. She told me how much medication she was taking, including methadone four times a day.

I shared that I had been there and done that, with terrible side effects. She said the medication worked well and allowed her to be active and come to the gym on a regular basis and row for about ten minutes. She didn't have the motivation or stamina to do more. I applauded her efforts to make it to the gym, and she said how much she admired my efforts and wished me continuing progress in my recovery.

Roberta and I ran to each other again several months later. She was on the rowing machine, moving back and forth on the slide with surprising aggression and effort. She didn't see me because I was observing from a distance. She had a good sweat going. I didn't want to interrupt her, so I walked up the stairs to do my cardio routine.

After I got upstairs, I was very curious and for another five minutes looked over the railing to watch her continue rowing with amazing tenacity. She came to a stop, and I walked back downstairs. She was breathing hard and wiping sweat off her brow. I walked over to her, and we greeted each other.

I told her how impressed I was watching her row. As a rowing "alum," I have a good sense for the effort it takes to do an "ergometer session" on a rowing machine. Roberta told me she had increased her rowing time from ten to thirty minutes since I had last seen her. She told me that my story about defining my terms, with regard to walking up and down the stairs with no handrail assistance, had inspired her to set her own goal of increasing her rowing time without stopping.

For months before we talked, she said she had just been going through the motions, with the single-minded goal of getting to the gym and rowing for ten minutes. After that day we'd talked, she had realized she could do more, and she had set a personal marker to increase her rowing time from ten to thirty minutes, and to do it all without stopping.

I thanked her and expressed my admiration for her ability to push new boundaries. I told her I was inspired by her accomplishment and humbled by her kind words. As I walked away from this lady, I was reminded of my good friend, John. I had worked with him for almost two decades.

As long as I have known John, he has had progressive problems with one of his ankles after sustaining a trauma while living in Colorado. Over the years, his ankle has been subjected to numerous surgeries and implants, none of which proved successful. John had constant pain and was on serious painkillers like Oxycontin for years.

He used to tell me about the pain, how debilitating and exhausting it was. All those years, John continued to work, and as time went on, he worked more often from home. At best, he slept only a few hours each night, and as a consequence was usually the first one into the office during the early morning hours.

I know he contemplated his options, which included amputation of his foot and ankle. He told me he just couldn't bring himself to do it, in part because of the experience of his relative, who had gone through an amputation but still experienced the pain. Sometimes after an amputation, patients will have a "phantom pain" that remains, which is no less debilitating than the pain they had prior to surgery.

He also told me that he often dreamt of riding a bicycle again and taking his beautiful little girls out to the slopes for some ski runs. John held out hope that medicine would someday come up with a breakthrough treatment. Most of his friends, including me, encouraged him to go the amputation route.

Credit John for not listening to us and doing things on his terms. His route to winning was hope—hope that medicine would come up with a new answer. He faced a lot of pushback from various sources—including friends and family. In the meantime, he continually suffered from a worsening and swelling ankle, which made it increasingly difficult for him to move around. Things were getting to the point where John was once again considering surgical intervention.

John consulted the top ankle surgeon in Seattle. At the doctor's office, he discovered a new procedure that would involve removing his ankle and replacing it with a matching cadaver ankle. He would keep his toes, which would be attached to the human prosthesis that would be attached to the leg bones in his calf above the ankle.

This procedure had only been tried on a handful of patients. It was a risk, but for John, it fit his visual of what he wanted, which was to avoid amputation and, hopefully, have his pain relieved. John was placing his trust in the hope that the medical field would someday find an answer.

His patience paid off. John had the surgery several years ago, and it was by all accounts an amazing success. Even his toes were successfully attached to the cadaver prosthesis, and he regained not only feeling in his toes but also function as well. Most importantly, he experienced total pain relief, and for the first time in many years was able to get restful, pain-free sleep.

John's story speaks directly to my credo of defining your terms, taking a stand, and choosing to win. He lived on his own terms, not on terms dictated by his friends, family, or even practitioners. John put up with continual suffering for years, all with the belief and hope that some day medicine would advance enough to fix his ankle and save his leg. I don't know many people who would endure that kind of suffering, but it resonates very personally with me and is a reminder of why this credo is so important. It can—and has—changed lives.

Two great success stories.

At other times, I have encountered people who continue to struggle. In the same gym where I met Roberta, I got acquainted with a man I will call Joe. Joe was in a wheelchair, and he was moving around the weight room when I met him. I came over to introduce myself. He met me with a big smile. I had seen Joe for several weeks but had not taken the initiative to introduce myself.

I told him about my spinal cord injury, how it happened, and how I had approached recovery. He seemed intrigued, especially when I told him that my practitioners had said recovery from a spinal cord injury typically tapers off after one to two years, although at the time in 2014, I was seven years out from injury and was continuing to make progress, in fact very significant progress, in many areas of the gym.

Just as I had with Roberta, I shared with him how my recovery was based on my terms, not on what science, or population studies, or anyone else had to say about it. I said I wanted to progress on my terms and was working off my own script. He said he thought that was really cool. I asked him if he wouldn't mind sharing a little of his story, mindful that I didn't want to probe into his personal life if he wasn't comfortable.

Joe told me he had been injured in an auto accident and suffered a spinal cord injury similar to mine, in his lower thoracic region, rendering him paraplegic. He was an incomplete like myself, had full upper body function, and was extremely well built from the waist up. He had suffered the injury about ten years earlier.

I asked what kind of residual deficits he was suffering from and what was confining him to a wheelchair. Joe indicated that he was suffering from severe tone or muscle spasticity that made standing extremely difficult. I asked if he had tried any medications to control the spasticity so that he might be able to walk more.

Joe said he had tried baclofen, a medication that I have taken four times a day for the past nine years. He said it had made him too drowsy, so he stopped taking it. I asked if he had tried anything else and he said no.

When I think of Joe, now, the word resignation comes to mind. I could be wrong, but he seemed resigned to his condition. "It's just the way it is and there is nothing more that I can do"—that is the thought bubble that I see when I think of others that I know, and countless more that I don't, who are dealing with some kind of illness, disease, or difficult life event.

Any affliction, infirmity, or difficult life situation can be overwhelming, so much so that you just want to throw up your arms and say, "Screw it, why bother." I know I've felt that way. The mental statement goes a little like this: "It's too difficult. I just want to be taken care of. I deserve entitlements, and I am going to use them. I'll just find a way to live with what I've got and the heck with investing effort in trying to find ways to get better and improve my quality of life. I'm just going to surrender."

I say no.

Don't surrender. Don't give in. We all have faculties, capabilities, and healing mechanisms that can be leveraged, just as we all have obstacles we want to overcome and goals we want to meet.

Perhaps your challenge is to make peace with a loved one or to reconcile a strained marriage. Perhaps it is finding ways to cope with chronic pain. Maybe it's dealing with the worst six-letter word any of us could ever hear from a medical practitioner—"I'm sorry to say, but you've got *cancer*."

Perhaps you are dealing with a chronic medical condition like diabetes or the loss of a loved one. Maybe you're learning to live with the loss of limbs from the battlefield, or PTSD. The possibilities are virtually limitless. Life has no cap on the number of challenges it can present to any one of us.

This is why Roberta's and John's stories are so inspiring to me. Both were dealing with difficult afflictions that presented them with terrible challenges in daily living. They had in common what I believe is most important in tackling any life challenge—the determination to make a hard choice. Once that choice is made, you are on your way to living life on your terms and accomplishing the things you want to do, regardless of headwinds, setbacks, or falls.

When you're struggling with living life on your own terms, it's important to take a look at your situation, at this part of your life journey, and realize it is a fork in the road. That's when you can see clearly which direction you have chosen to go—or have you chosen at all?

Sometimes not making a choice is easier than making one. It is easier to just stall and go through the motions, drift, and let life take you wherever it decides to take you. If you are at that "idling" point, what is keeping you from making a choice? This whole process of turning the corner and moving in a positive direction begins with a willingness and desire to choose to win.

If you are feeling down, defeated, and lost, like everything has turned against you and life feels like it's no longer worth living, then that makes it even harder to choose to win. I know. It can be tough to muster up enough interest to even *think* about making a choice when you are feeling down, sad, or depressed. I've been there, and it is a horrible place to be.

When you are in that darkness, it is very difficult to find the light. Love and support from others, along with seeking help from a good mental health professional, can help make the choice to win a little easier.

Perhaps you have decided to give in, feeling resigned to the unfairness that life has thrown at you. You may feel defeated and hopeless. Maybe the interventions you've sought haven't worked, and maybe you're afraid to try them again. Or at all. You may still be standing at that fork in the road, stalled, idling, not sure which way to go, not motivated to even consider the choices in front of you. The thought of getting better or of things improving might seem completely hopeless right now. Believing change is possible? Impossible.

Henry Ford once spoke these wise and famous words: "Whether you believe you can do a thing or not, you are right."[4]

Making the choice to win begins with overcoming the inevitable inertia to *start*. Pressing that start button, saying go, and moving forward is extremely difficult. It is new and requires persistence. Maybe it requires a leap of faith, because you don't know for sure whether the investment of effort is going to pay off. This is where your belief system comes into play.

Sometimes it takes belief before you can see results. Once the engine gets rolling and momentum builds the process of moving forward, it gets a little easier, because you have forces, tailwinds, pushing you along. Success begets more success. But it has to begin with belief.

Belief can be transformational depending on how think about it. If

....

4   The Reader's Digest Association [Filler item], *The Reader's Digest*, September 1947, vol. 51, 54.

you think about it in a positive way, like I believe I can, chances are very good that your belief will be realized. I've applied my belief system throughout my recovery journey with an "I can" mind-set.

I don't profess to understand all the science behind the power of the unconscious mind, but I believe that the messages you provide it—positive messages, affirmation messages, and belief messages—ultimately can come true. The unconscious mind is a powerful force and heavily influenced by these messages. Your body's behavior and actions are a manifestation of what your unconscious mind knows, and what it knows links directly to what you believe.

My encouragement to anyone facing hardship or adversity of any kind, is to take a deep breath, close your eyes, and try to visualize a different you, a better you, a healed you, a motivated you, a happy you. Visualize something you want to be or do.

When I was hospitalized in inpatient rehab, I did this for the first time. I pictured being able to transfer my paralyzed body from the hospital bed to a wheelchair. I thought about everything this would entail. I would need an assistant close by to ensure I didn't fall. The wheelchair would face the bed. I would need a transfer board about four feet in length that would allow me to slide from the bed to the wheelchair. I pictured lifting my body into an upright sitting position on the bed and breathing deeply so I wouldn't pass out from dizziness.

I thought about how I would use my hands to lift both legs and rotate them to the side of the bed and how the assistant would take the transfer board and, place one end under my rear and the other end on the wheelchair seat. I further scripted the scene, using my hands and arms to shimmy along the transfer board until I reached the wheelchair. I imagined mustering all the strength I could to clutch the arm rails of the wheelchair and lift myself off the board and onto the wheelchair seat.

When the time came two days later, the scene played out just the way I had pictured. The assistant commended me for my effort, remarking he had never seen anyone with a spinal cord injury do a bed to wheelchair transfer the first time on his or her own. I was elated. What a victory!

Later, after I was discharged from HMC, I visualized myself back on a bike again. I envisioned where I was—on my driveway—standing upright, holding a road bike by my side, with Diane standing close by. The day was sunny, with a deep blue sky above; flowers were blooming; it was springtime, which is my favorite time of year. I thought about how I would swing my right leg over the seat of the bike so I would be standing over it, with the top tube of the frame between my legs.

In detail, I went on to picture lifting my right leg and placing it on the foot pedal while balancing on my left leg. I pushed forward on the pavement with my left leg, sat down on the bike seat, brought my left leg onto the foot pedal, and started pedaling. My body was comfortable balancing the bike as I held the handlebars. I was leaning slightly forward as I slowly pedaled and moved out onto the street. I could feel amazing sensations, muscles contracting; I was breathing gently and felt relaxed and proud. I pedaled a very short distance, perhaps a half block each way on flat terrain, with my wife Diane and friend Bob O. jogging slowly on either side of me.

I've used this technique numerous times over the years. It's what I do. I'm a moviemaker. I imagine a scene and then break it down into great detail. I visualize every step, motion, sensation, feeling, and nuance, and make everything as multifaceted as I possibly can. I repeat the scene over and over in my head, completely immersed, oblivious to anything going on around me.

It's a second life, an alternate reality . . . until the time when it becomes a true reality.

Nine months after my accident, in the spring of 2008, I took my first ride on a road bicycle. It was a brief ride down our neighborhood block and back. The movie played out just the way I had scripted it in my mind.

. . .

Imagine a scene that you want to create. After you have that picture in mind, stay with it for a few minutes. Imagine writing a script, a script depicting the rest of your life and how you want to live it. Perhaps the script would show your physical infirmity healed or a relationship reconciled. Maybe it would include living out a dream, living a life free of pain, being told you are cancer free, or some other chronic medical condition being resolved.

Imagine whatever you feel is important in your life, what would bring you happiness. By visualizing that script, you've turned it into a short movie, with all the actors, location, movements, or environment included. Play that movie over and over in your head, picturing every detail, every nuance, refining and editing where necessary, until you can play the movie from start to finish without any conscious thought.

As you write your script, consider what actions you might take in the movie. You are the author. You are the scriptwriter. You are the editor, producer, director, and actor. It is all about you. Be a little selfish and embed the movie in your soul. I'd suggest starting your movie with baby steps: simple pedestrian steps that are achievable. Creating "movies" in your mind and taking action will help produce small victories, which will ultimately multiply and produce progressively bigger triumphs.

. . .

Once you choose to fight your particular battle, you are also choosing to never give up, regardless of how daunting it might seem or how difficult it gets. It's going to take effort—consistent, daily effort—and an unwavering commitment to the choice you've made. It requires a specific mindset, one of determination. You are choosing to believe that success will come, and the more success you have, the more you will crave it. Exercise and the release of endorphins was the elixir that produced my healthy exercise addiction, and I couldn't live life now without it.

For me, I believe I will always continue to get better. I believe I will continue to build strength, stamina, and capability. I believe I will continue to be a better person. I believe I will sleep better and chronic pain will eventually dissipate. A good example of my belief system in action was my decision to "get independent." I always believed I would.

I believed I would walk again, drive again, work again, exercise again, feed myself again, travel again, and so much more.

I believed from the time I made that decision in the hospital that I would accomplish these things and much more. I'm proud to say today that I have achieved what I envisioned, through hard work, determination, grit, and unwavering belief. This recovery process has no end. It is ongoing. It is a journey. I believe with every fiber of my being that the best is yet to come.

Without choice there is no way forward. And without moving forward, you are simply sitting on a merry-go-round or bounding along on a circular treadmill . . . going nowhere. For me, choice was the vector, the beacon, the roadmap that came to guide my recovery.

It is possible to "come back" and regain life the way you want it to be, infirmities and all. I'm not whole, in the sense that I don't have one hundred percent of my faculties intact, and neither do a lot of us for that matter. My decision to win started with a choice, and once I made that decision, it was about living life on my terms, setting goals, building on victories, forcing myself through the headwinds and setbacks, and prevailing.

This is all possible for you, too, but first, you must choose.

CHAPTER 25

Dreams Are Made True

We have owned a "week 52" timeshare in Whistler, British Columbia, Canada, since 1993. For many years, we used it often, and it was our family base for skiing. Since my injury in 2007 we hadn't been back. But a few days prior to Christmas 2012, I said to my wife and daughter, "I think I want to make the trip to Whistler for a few days and see what I can do." They were so excited! I don't think they expected to hear those words come out of my mouth.

Skiing had always been our staple family sport, and Whistler was where we had taught our children to ski. I had talked about wanting to ski sometime in the future, but had even said as recently as a few months before when winter was just getting started that I didn't think I would be ready to try skiing in the upcoming season. What changed? Timing.

I had always pictured what the conditions would be like—weather, temperature, snow pack. After checking the Whistler Blackcomb website, it looked like conditions were perfect. Further, I had been ungraciously separated from my former employer two weeks before and decided it was just time to get away, regardless of the price I was likely to pay. We were all feeling the "sting" of the separation and thought, what better way to refocus than to visit a place that had brought our family so much joy in the past? The decision was made.

On Christmas Eve, Diane, Alana, and I traveled to Whistler. We left our home on Mercer Island about 11 a.m. I wasn't planning to ski, but I left the door open when I said to Diane, "Let's pack my ski gear just in case my body feels right and everything falls into place to give it a go." I made no promises, other than to see if I could handle a four-and-a-half-hour car ride. I hadn't traveled outside of my Seattle bubble by car since 2007, and this multihour trip was going to be my first.

With a few stops and a short wait at the border crossing, we managed to make the trip without incident. It wasn't a pain-free ride, but I had taken some pain meds. As we passed through the town of Squamish, British Columbia, and started the gradual ascent to Whistler, I could see a fair amount of new snow on the side of the road. The snowbanks grew progressively higher as we reached the village. When we arrived at Whistler, it was cold, in the twenties, with relatively clear roads and a solid coating of new, dry snow.

We stayed at our timeshare condominium, a two bedroom, two bathroom, 1,100-square-foot unit at a building called Ironwood, which is located about one kilometer outside of the main village of Whistler. It is situated on a slightly elevated plateau overlooking Blackcomb and Whistler mountains on Blueberry Hill. It was a fixed-week timeshare, and our slot was always week fifty-two on the calendar. This is the week usually after Christmas that overlaps New Year's—a seven-night stay from Sunday to Sunday. As an extra bonus because of the timeshare calendar, week 52 owners get the benefit of a second follow-on week every sixth year. We also chose this fixed week because for the children it would always fall during holiday break and not interfere with school schedules.

On Christmas Day 2012, Tuesday, I woke up and said to the ladies, "I have a Christmas present for you. I want to try to ski today." They were elated, almost tearful.

Since I was first hospitalized I had visualized this day. I had played this movie in my head countless times—what the day would be like; putting on my ski gear; buckling my boots; the just right sub-thirty-two-degree weather; the quality of the snow, dry and powdery; how my body would feel; taking extra medicine in the morning before leaving and having some extra if needed; wind conditions; crowd conditions; ensuring a graduated process of starting on the bunny hill; side stepping up from ski base enough to try to make a few turns, ensuring I could stop; visualizing my weight transfer as I made turns; and so much more. It was all choreographed in my mind. And now it was going to happen, body willing.

On the way to Whistler, I had been concerned about the cold temperature and how it would affect me. Although it was in the high twenties those two days, with no wind and partly cloudy skies, I had to be careful not to allow my body core to get cold. One of the issues SCI patients face is an impaired internal thermostat. I have had difficulties, especially in my early post-injury years, regulating my body temperature in cold weather.

If my body core got cold, then my spasticity symptoms got markedly worse to the point that my lower half went rigid, which made movement next to impossible until I warmed up. A good indicator of a cold body core is having cold hands, and I could easily tell when I touched them to my face, which was usually warm, whether they were too cold. Fortunately, on this ski outing I had brought plenty of layers.

At first, it was awkward trudging around in ski boots, because my legs were not used to having any weight on them greater than lightweight Keen shoes. Having ski poles was helpful in terms of maintaining my balance.

We went to the base of Blackcomb Mountain, in the upper village where there is a beginner's slope that's roped off for the kiddie carpet. I started first by trying to step into my ski bindings. I quickly realized how uncoordinated my leg muscles were as I tried to do something I never had to think about before my injury. I managed after multiple attempts to clip in, and then I started to move forward, poles in hand, past the lift line to the slope itself.

It was exhilarating. My balance was wobbly at first, as I tried to get my bearings. After a few minutes, Diane and I marched alongside each other, reached the slope, and started a gradual process of sidestepping up the hill for one hundred feet or so. Once we'd made it, I looked down at Alana, waiting at the bottom, ready to memorialize this event on her mobile phone.

I could feel my body start to tense and then said to myself, "You know this movie, you've played it countless times, you've skied almost your entire life! This is your time—now go." And go I did.

My primary objective was to prove I could stop. My skiing was tentative, awkward, but I managed three stem Christie turns and, most importantly, was able to come to a stop—safely. No falls. Alana came up to me with tears in her eyes and said how proud she was.

It was a strange juxtaposition to be the one learning (relearning) how to ski on exactly the same run where I had taught both my children to ski years earlier.

I repeated the run again, and then we went inside the lodge. We sat down at a table, speechless, held hands, and cried. Sobbed. Convulsively. It didn't matter that everyone in the place was gawking, curious, and wondering what was going on. I felt like standing up and shouting, "I did it!!"

So many years. So much heartbreak. So much effort.

And here we were, at our favorite lodge, and I had just taken my first ski run, with no accommodation, using no assistive devices, with just my regular ski gear and my dear family. How I wished Kevin had been with us instead of in China, but I'm sure he was there in spirit. It is a moment I'll never forget.

This was only the beginning.

We called it a day, mission accomplished. Two days later, December 27, I woke up and said, "I think I want to try the Magic Chair lift today."

"No way, really?" Diane said.

"Yes way, let's go make it happen!"

We returned to the same location. This time I said I wanted to try the kiddie carpet, which I was able to navigate without falling, and it took me up a little bit farther than where I had sidestepped two days before. I took a few practice runs in this fenced-off area, and when I was satisfied that I was ready, I said to the ladies, "Let's go try the Magic Chair."

The Magic Chair is a beginner's run chairlift; it traveled a pretty good length and was not overly crowded. Alana recorded our conversation as I sat down on the chair and we were taken upward. I had already played the process of getting off the chairlift in my mind, how I would need to readjust my balance and come to a stop. It worked out fine.

We assembled together after we came off the chair. I looked down the slope, asked Alana if she was ready to film, closed my eyes, took a deep breath, played the movie one more time in my mind, and away we went.

It went just as I had pictured.

Alana skied by my side, at times well ahead of me, and sometimes even skiing backward as she filmed. Diane was perched behind me to guard against any wayward skiers/boarders who might be at risk of plowing into me. She was ready to block and tackle if necessary. The turns came naturally to me, not labored, the cold air caressed my face, and I had a smile as big as Seattle. I stopped about halfway down the run, and both of the ladies were so excited. I was elated.

My muscle memories from all the years of skiing were still intact. I never felt afraid of falling that day. My concern was making sure I was breathing and keeping my body from seizing or going spastic, which would have made it impossible to maneuver. Because I have limited sensation in my waist, legs, and feet, I had to rely on the movie reel in my head, muscle memory, and most importantly, visual cues. None of my body functions work automatically. It all requires mindfulness—purposeful thought.

We took several runs in the morning, had lunch at the same place we had visited on Christmas Day—crying again with happy tears—and then decided to try a few more runs in the afternoon. I took a total of eight runs on the Magic Chair that day. On the last run, I could feel the medications wearing off, my legs tightening, and the turns becoming more labored. I decided not to push it any further and called it a day.

What a day it was. I never fell. Not once.

I knew I would pay a price for this incredible experience on skis, and I did. For the next couple of days, my pain symptoms fluctuated between six and nine, with ten being the most intense. This was well beyond my usual daily pain levels, which live between three and five. I spent time in the hot tub, stretching, taking pain meds and the like, but with little benefit. I might as well have been eating candy. I sucked it up and did the best I could.

On Friday December 28, we packed the car and made the four-and-a-half-hour trip home. This was in 2012, over four years ago. It was an epic experience, but the price I paid afterward isn't something I was in a hurry to repeat. Until Christmas holiday of 2015.

In December 2015, Diane and I returned to Whistler Blackcomb. There was plenty of snow, and the temps in the valley were in the teens to twenties. The skies each day were deep blue without a cloud. Winds were calm. I skied two consecutive days for a couple of hours each day. Both days I did seven runs on the beginner's Magic Chair for a total of fourteen runs.

My body responded well on the slopes, and I was filled with excitement and emotion. I met up with one my of old squash buddies, Naveen, who graciously interrupted his ski day higher up on the more challenging runs to come down to the bottom and take a few runs with us. He also took video of one of our runs. Once again it was epic.

As expected, my body paid the price for the next couple of days, with pain levels at eight. I had difficulty moving around. It was, however, so worth it. This is not something I'll do on a regular basis, but it was good for the soul—beautiful surroundings, fresh mountain air, great company, and a chance to do my favorite outdoor activity. I felt so alive!

I also had a new, ambitious goal for this trip—to go to the top of Blackcomb and ski all the way to the bottom, all five thousand vertical feet. Not nonstop, but in sections with plenty of stops and rest points. I would stay near the lifts in the event I couldn't ski anymore and needed to download down the mountain on the ski lift. The route down was already mapped in my head, physical conditioning was good, and mentally I was ready to take on the next challenge.

Unfortunately, it was just a bit too cold to make the attempt. Once my body core gets cold all bets are off. That goal will just have to wait until our next trip north. Check off one goal and move on to the next.

. . .

Backing up a bit, in the spring of 2014, Diane, Alana, and I were living in Arizona. I had been practicing cycling on stationary bikes at the nearby LA Fitness club. As I grappled with the neurological disconnect between the upper and lower halves of my body, I was hoping I could improve the situation with stationary cycling.

The gym had a few flavors of stationary bikes, including upright, recumbent, and spin bikes. I practiced on the upright initially, trying to get my legs to move in a smooth cadence, not herky-jerky. I found the longer I rode on the bike—longer than fifteen minutes—the smoother my pedal stroke became. In addition, I could slowly amp up the revolutions per minute (rpm). I practiced every day, and I could see improvement. Soon I didn't have to consciously think about moving my legs and was able to push the rpms from sixty to short spurts at one hundred.

This was a big deal. Anything I do where my body is trying to move faster can quickly send me into the "zone" where spasticity gets severe and my body parts lock up and become so rigid I can't move. I easily reached the "zone" many times, and had to throttle back to be able to continue cycling. The cool thing was that over a period of months, the threshold for triggering the "zone" went from sixty to one hundred rpm. Over the ensuing year, I even had a brief moment when I spun it up to 130 rpm.

I took the next step and went to the spin bike. The spin bike has a closer configuration to an actual road cycle. I wasn't ready to try a spin class, but I practiced in the spin studio by myself when no classes were happening. There were mirrors all around, which I used to check my form, body positioning, and cycling mechanics. With practice, I was able to master different levels of resistance, as well as cycling out of the saddle, standing on the pedals as if I were doing a climb. When I did that and wasn't careful about leg extension on the down stroke, my hamstrings would immediately go spastic, rigid, tremble, and stop my forward leg movement.

As on the stationary bike, I learned that I could pedal on the spin bike but had to be careful not to aggravate my hamstrings with too much pressure. During these sessions, which initially lasted fifteen minutes, before I worked my way up to forty-five minutes, my mind would drift to rides I had done in France. While out of the saddle, I could picture myself in the French Alps, climbing one of the many-storied mountain passes. Le Mont Ventoux, located in the Provence region of southern France, was the mother of all climbs and one I enjoyed going back to in my mind. Lost in thought, I would picture other famous cycling venues, envisioning my entire body invested in the effort. The sweat would pour off of me, which felt great. For those brief moments, it was a relief to not feel impaired.

My next goal was to try to ride the spin bike with road cycling shoes that have cleats on the bottom and are used to clip into specially made foot pedals on the bike. This setup allows a cyclist to better transfer energy from their effort to the bike. The spin bike had a meter on it to track my rpms, speed, time, and most important, wattage. Wattage is the best measure of effort.

It took some time to relearn how to clip into the bike pedals, and I had to hold and guide my legs into the right position and then jiggle my foot the correct way to get clipped in. This did not come naturally and required considerable effort. I eventually figured it out and practiced many spin rides in the studio to get used to the shoes, cleats, and pedal stroke. I also taught myself how to clip out and release my feet from the pedals, which requires some technique to twist your foot slightly side to side. Because of the disconnect in my midsection caused by the SCI, these movements are not natural and take special focus and concentration.

This was a segue to the ultimate goal of riding my road bicycle outside, with cleats, around the neighborhood. I had ridden on a road bike for the first time in spring 2008, albeit just for a few hundred feet, and without cleats. I hadn't ridden again outside on a bike until this moment—spring 2014. I told my wife and daughter I was ready to give outside riding a go.

Diane wanted to ride with me, and Alana drove her car. To get on the bike took some doing, as I no longer had the leg flexion or balance to lift one leg over the bike seat and straddle the frame before clipping in. I opted to stand next to my car so I had something to balance against.

I tilted the bike down toward me, perhaps at sixty degrees, took one leg and stepped over the main triangle frame, and then pulled the bike up between my legs. It worked! Now I was ready for the big test. In this position and with one hand still touching the car for balance, I clipped in one foot, raised my body up so that my weight was supported on one pedal, and pushed off. I was able to balance on the bike as it moved, but while I still had forward speed I had to quickly get the other foot clipped in. After a few failed attempts, I succeeded. We were ready to go.

We rode about twelve miles at an average speed of about ten to twelve miles per hour, which was nothing like my easy pre-injury cruising speeds of twenty-plus miles per hour. It was awesome to be back on the bike again, although the position felt uncomfortable, especially where my upper body was in a fixed position. It is not a happy position, but the elation of riding, moving, and enjoying the scenery and my riding partner overrode all the pain sensors. During the ride we came to a small hill, perhaps a hundred yards high or so. I thought to myself, *This should be no problem; I've practiced that many times on the spin bike.*

I nearly went over.

As I started the short climb, I geared down to the easiest gear. I got out of the saddle to try to finish the climb, but I could feel my hamstrings locking up, impeding the pedal stroke, and nearly bringing any forward motion to a stop. My body sensed anxiety, and when it does, spasticity kicks in and short-circuits body movement—in this case my legs.

I was right on the edge of falling, but I put all my mental focus on breathing. *Don't stop breathing. Try to relax those muscles and keep pedaling.* It worked, and I made it to the top. It was dicey, and it freaked me out. Why were my muscles behaving this way outside, when I had successfully simulated this type of climb many times on the indoor spin bike?

I realized there were two reasons—first, my body wasn't warm enough yet and my muscles were too tight; second, I had to figure out a way to get control over my fear and anxiety. They were getting in the way. Breathing, breathing, breathing was the answer.

Medications can help reduce some of the muscle seizing, and so can breathing. We finished the ride in about an hour. My body, predictably, was killing me, but it didn't matter at the time. I was so excited about what I had accomplished. I believe I succeeded by using the same process I had in Whistler—writing, producing, and directing my own movie in my head, and rehearsing it over and over again before actually doing it. It worked.

In early 2015, I started attending an actual hour-long spin class. The first couple of times I could go twenty to thirty minutes at my own pace, enjoying the loud music, but unable to keep up with the instructions of the teacher. In spin class I could pretty much go at whatever cadence and resistance I wanted. After we returned to Seattle in May 2015, I became much more active in spin class, doing it two to three times a week. I can now go the full hour, and for the most part can follow all the instructions from the teacher.

I can't push the cadence or wattage as high as I would like, but as my cycling strength continues to improve, I have confidence it will return. Just in the past few months I have seen a marked increase in my average wattage output, which is the best test of overall strength. I do spin class twice a week in the morning, usually with a 6 a.m. start on Friday and 9 a.m. start on Sunday. This checks off another box on the goals I have set for myself.

My next goal in spin? Increase my average wattage and total calories burned over a sixty-minute period. I'm not interested in burned calories per se, just tracking the number itself in terms of absolute value, and then trying to improve upon it.

I don't need anyone to compete with other than myself; I am always trying to raise the bar. I always pay a price for these efforts. Once my body cools down after my shower, I am barely able to walk. Muscle seizing returns.

It's as if the switch that allowed me to perform the exercise quickly turns off, and I am back to feeling very impaired. I live for those moments when my body is warm and fluid—like on the road cycle, or spin bike, or ski slopes—where for a brief time I don't feel impaired. I feel like my old self.

. . .

Trail hiking for longer time and distance is another goal I have had on my list. I tried once before in 2011 when Ronge, a foreign exchange student, was with us. That effort was quite limited, perhaps just a few hundred yards. I tried again earlier this spring at another entry point on Tiger Mountain. This time I was by myself. There was some risk associated with doing this on my own, especially if I had a fall.

I had gone for a drive one Saturday afternoon (the family was away). I had both trekking poles with me. I found a trail, but it turned out to be a shared trail for hikers and mountain bikers. I carefully started on an undulating trail, watching my steps carefully, and mindful of any noises of bikes coming my way. The trail was marked with a sign indicating about one-half mile before I'd arrive at an intersection of another trail. I managed to make it there and back, a total of one mile.

This was significantly longer than the time I tried hiking in 2011. It took a little less than hour, which is long time to be on my feet. I also was a bit on edge the whole time, especially wary of mountain bikers coming around a corner and not having time to get out of their way. The trail was pretty narrow, and any time one passed me, I had to stop and step to the side of the trail. My body warmed up, even to a small sweat, although it was fairly cool with temperatures in the low fifties.

I felt good when I finished, satisfied with my accomplishment, endorphins doing their magic in alleviating pain and providing feelings of well-being. On the forty-minute drive home, I could feel pain come back and muscles start to stiffen. It was expected but didn't take away the happy feeling I had from being in the outdoors, smelling deciduous aromas, and listening to the audible chatter of wildlife. It was good for the soul.

Like other experiences, I had visualized this in great detail. I imagined the trail and its undulations, standing among tall trees, fresh mountain air, wildlife sounds, roots on the trail, flexing my ankles before any ascending slope (going uphill), small streams gurgling, taking intermittent stops, overcoming the inevitable discomfort of being on my feet for a long time, and mindful of anything on the trail that could turn my ankle. Mostly, I had scripted being alone, at one with my surroundings.

Everything played out as I had envisioned, with one exception. I hadn't expected to be around mountain bikers, which raised my alertness antennae to ensure I wouldn't get broadsided. It didn't detract from the experience though, and I am anxious to do it again for a longer distance, perhaps a mile in and a mile out.

I didn't tell Diane or the children about it, because I was concerned their reaction might be concern and worry, something to the effect of "don't venture out on your own without one of us." I could appreciate their feelings but would reassure them that the trail was heavily traveled and there would be plenty of people around should something have happened. It might not have allayed their worries, but that was my reason for not sharing the experience.

. . .

In fall 2014, Diane and I planned a trip to Shanghai to visit Kevin and Viki. I had contemplated making this trip for a couple of years, once in the previous year even going so far as to get visas and make complete travel arrangements. Unfortunately I had to cancel due to my health issue with a blood infection, which subsequently was resolved.

This trip was going to be quite a stretch for me, because I had only traveled domestically since my injury. But it was a long-standing goal of mine, ever since Kevin had moved there in 2010. I had played the movie many times in my head. I scripted the airplane ride, medications I would take, periodic movements during the flight to keep circulation going,

going through Chinese customs, traveling ninety minutes from Shanghai airport to Kevin's apartment, how I would handle a squeaky bladder, what items I would need with me, where we would stay, what we would do, where I would go if I needed medical intervention.

Mostly, I pictured experiencing Kevin's life in China, seeing Viki, meeting her parents, traveling to the farm where he was working, seeing the big city sights of Shanghai, walking the Bund, experiencing authentic Chinese cuisine like "hot pot."

With one significant exception, the ten-day trip played out just as I had envisioned. On our flight leg from Seattle to Tokyo's Narita airport, halfway across the Pacific, I started urinating blood.

I had no prior symptoms; this came without warning and was quite painful. When we arrived at Narita, we had a four-hour layover before catching a connection to Shanghai. I urinated again, and the blood was clumpy and even more prevalent. Diane and I were both freaking out.

With the language barrier, we struggled to find medical help at the airport, but eventually we did. I received a strong prescription, made our flight connection, and the next day in Shanghai went to a hospital with English-speaking doctors who properly diagnosed the problem. Within a few days the issue had resolved, and the remainder of the ten-day epic journey went off without a hitch.

The culmination of the trip was the final night, when Kevin proposed to Viki with Diane and me present, and with Viki's parents who had traveled eight hours by bus from their home to join us. We were so very happy for our son and his bride-to-be.

I felt an amazing satisfaction in making such a long journey, being out of country for a week and a half. It was a huge goal and a huge accomplishment. I was very proud of myself and had pushed a very big boundary that I had been very anxious to attempt.

. . .

On Father's Day 2015, I told my wife and daughter I wanted to go to the driving range. Like skiing, golf was one of my favorite pre-injury pastimes. I loved to golf, enjoyed the camaraderie, friendly competition, joking, and sparring. I was never a notable golfer, had an average handicap, but I just loved walking the green grass and being outside.

My dad taught me how to play golf in my teens, and I have played ever since, recreationally. I had worked hard to regain hand and finger function and was now able to grip a golf club. The question was this: Could I tolerate standing for a period of time, swing, make contact with the ball, and not fall over?

As with our skiing adventure, Alana brought her mobile phone to memorialize the event on video. After several practice swings and being reasonably confident I could maintain my balance, I took several swings with my short irons—pitching wedge and 9-iron. I topped a number of balls but wasn't falling over. Everything felt awkward. Suddenly all the mental techniques came back in terms of grip, posture, head position, feet, tempo, and rotation.

I have very stiff hip flexors, which restricted my backswing as well as my forward swing. Despite those limitations, by retapping the same muscle memory as I had for skiing, I began to make legit contact. I could get the golf ball airborne, straight, and about one-half to two-thirds the distance I would typically hit with those clubs. That was exciting!

I moved to an 8- and then 7-iron, followed by a driver. With each club, I experienced the same initial problem with making contact but quickly got the technique down and—lo and behold—was hitting the ball! I had to sit a few times to relieve the pressure buildup in my legs, waist, and back, but then I would resume hitting more golf balls.

After we were done, I said I wanted to try another "first." I took my golf bag, pulled the straps over my shoulders, and walked about twenty feet, gingerly, with no assistance, to show myself that I could do it. I had to be incredibly mindful about what I was doing to ensure each step was proper and my balance was maintained. It wasn't much more than a shuffle, but I did it, pretending like I was a real golfer. The power of visualization was at it again. I had choreographed this in my mind for years, picturing all the details in terms of location, swing, stance, ball contact, and the elation I would feel.

I loved being with family and experiencing the beautiful sunny day, great vistas, and calm winds. I especially loved how it felt to accomplish another huge goal that I had visualized and played in my head for so many years. Perhaps it was extra exciting because it happened when the US Open had just been held at Chambers Bay, just south of Seattle in Tacoma, one of the very few times a PGA "major" has come to the Pacific Northwest.

. . .

It seemed like I was on a roll in the spring of 2015. With my focus on a new goal, I took a trip back to my alma mater, Ithaca College in Ithaca, New York. I had rowed Division III crew for Ithaca from 1976 to 1979. I was a lightweight oarsman, meaning the average weight in the eight-man shell had to be 155 pounds with no oarsman weighing more than 159 pounds.

One of my crewmates, Dan, was in the same class of 1979 and we rowed together each of those years. Dan continued with the IC crew program after graduation and went on to become head coach, where he has been for the past thirty-six years. The crew program has thrived under Dan's leadership for men's crew and under his wife Becky's leadership for women's crew. Two years ago, Dan contacted me and said he wanted to organize a crew class reunion. He also said he wanted to dedicate a new eight-man crew shell in my name during the reunion.

We had a great turnout for the four-day event. One of many goals after my injury was to get in a real crew shell again and attempt to row. Since graduation in 1979, I hadn't done this. With my injury, just getting into a shell was going to be daunting, let alone gripping an oar and making a legit stroke without throwing the entire boat off-kilter. Like the other milestones of skiing, cycling, and golfing, I had visualized rowing in a shell for years.

At the SAC where I regularly exercised, I taught myself how to row again on a stationary rowing machine. I would sit there on the ergometer, feeling the slide, imitating the catch, driving my legs, finishing with my hands, and swinging my torso forward to begin the forward motion of the slide. Due to spasticity, I had to meter the cadence of my stroke, keeping it about twenty-two to twenty-five strokes per minute. A couple of times, I practiced trying to accelerate the cadence only to have my legs start to lock up and seize, at which point I would back it down.

It was awkward at first, rowing on the machine, especially with the lack of flexion in my waist and ankles, but I was determined to go to Ithaca, get in a real shell, be on the water again, and row with my old college crewmates—in a shell named after me, called the James Osborne '79, aka the "Oz." Having just read Daniel James Brown's book *The Boys in the Boat* about the University of Washington eight-man team crewing in the 1936 Olympics in Berlin, I was even more motivated.

On Saturday morning, June 6, 2015, with a slight breeze and clearing skies, my buddies lifted the shell off the racks in the new boathouse, walked it down to the dock, and set it carefully in the water. Diane helped me down the ramp to the dock, where I took off my sneakers and tried to figure out how I was going to get myself into the shell. I decided to sit down on the dock—quite a task in itself—grabbed the gunnels, and lifted myself with my legs in front into the #3 seat of the shell, starboard side.

I inserted my feet in the boat shoes, which are fastened inside the shell. A friend set my oar blade in the rig. What a feeling! I held the oar handle in my hand, looked down in the boat, and tried to keep my emotions in check. Another dream was about to come true. I wasn't nervous, maybe a bit excited, but mostly I was focused on the things I needed to do to properly execute stroke mechanics.

We were out on the water for about twenty minutes. I was able to do it, and for the most part maintained the same cadence with the rest of my crewmates. I wasn't able to take a full slide, more like half a slide, because my legs were stiff and spasticity active, but it was not enough to prevent me from rowing. It was exhilarating. Epic.

I didn't have any problems and avoided the dreaded "crab," which occurs when your oar blade gets caught in the water while the boat is moving. A momentary flaw in oar technique causes it, and it has happened to just about anyone who has ever rowed in a crew shell. Sometimes the rower can quickly recover, or it can be so forceful that it causes the rower to be ejected from the boat.

As we came into the dock, I yelped in excitement and high-fived my two friends—Pete, immediately in front of me, and Jon, immediately behind. This time the tears streamed down my face. I didn't hold back.

I had rehearsed this experience in my head for years. This is the power of visualization. Moments like these allow me to feel like "me," the old "me." Yes, impaired, trying to find a new normal, but feeling a great sense of who I had once been, and who I still am.

Recently I achieved another cool cycling milestone. I rode my road bicycle around Mercer Island, Washington, the town where I live. It is a thirteen-mile loop that I have ridden many times prior to 2007. I've trained on it and know every nook and cranny on the road surface, every undulation. My wife, daughter, son, and daughter-in-law trailed behind me in the car. Kevin filmed the entire hour-long ride on his cell phone, and Viki took numerous still pictures.

The day was picture-perfect, temperatures in the mid-seventies, little wind, and deep blue skies. There was very little traffic. As with these other events, I had made and refined this movie in my head for years, picturing the day, who would be with me, what direction I would go around the island (clockwise), how I would handle the few brief climbs, climbing out of the saddle, timing my medications, and how I would relax my muscles if they started to seize. Just the other week I rode it a second time, this time with a little more speed, and even had a chance to get competitive with another cyclist, which I love to do. I paid the usual price in terms of pain, a few hours after cooling down, and managed it with ibuprofen, ice, and arnica gel.

Up to nine years in the making, and these movies came true. These dreams came true. These dreams were made true. All these achievements were things I had visualized, scripted, and rehearsed in my head over and over again. The tremendous satisfaction of making these dreams come true are the moments when I have felt most alive, and it is an awesome feeling. Each time I was entirely in the moment and didn't worry about the inevitable aftereffects. I was happy, excited, hooting and hollering. There aren't many times since I was injured that I have felt that kind of elation. It is so good for my soul.

Sports and travel have always been my sanctuary. Relearning and readjusting to them post injury has been extremely difficult, but I've reaped a reward in the process of overcoming—overcoming the impairment, overcoming fear and doubt, overcoming setbacks. How I did it comes down to these words:

Define your terms. Take a stand. Choose to win.

About the Author

 Exercise and fitness were a central part of Jamie Osborne's life throughout his adult years, offering him a place of refuge, solace, camaraderie, and hard work. Jamie gave his all when running, skiing, cycling, rowing, or participating in various court sports. The workout and competition always brought him great joy and fulfillment . . . until June 2007.

Catastrophically, Jamie was in a cycling accident and sustained a spinal cord injury that rendered him permanently disabled. As a result, his life was turned upside down. His professional career as an information technology leader was significantly altered, and his time as a recreational enthusiast was brought to an abrupt halt. He and his family have struggled mightily and Jamie has fought daily with the residual deficits of this "unimaginable injury." He has been relentless in his recovery, harnessing all of his faculties to battle this condition. Remarkably, he has regained many aspects of the functions he lost while coming to grips with this new normal. Today, he lives independently, with minimal assistance. Although his life was turned upside down, his will to recover has allowed his physicality to completely reset because he has devoted countless hours to rebuilding himself and conquering enormous obstacles with grit, determination, positive thinking, and resilience.

Jamie has found life meaning again, and his healing message can help others. He has been invited to speak in person at several medical conferences and on the radio, sharing his unusual and rare story of recovery.

Jamie writes in a conversational tone that is real, authentic, deeply personal, and, in places, vulnerable. He is totally unfiltered and opens up about many things in his life that have been both tragic and triumphant.

His first book, *Will Your Way Back*, chronicles his remarkable story that will inspire and give hope to anyone facing life's adversity.

And he can now exercise again!